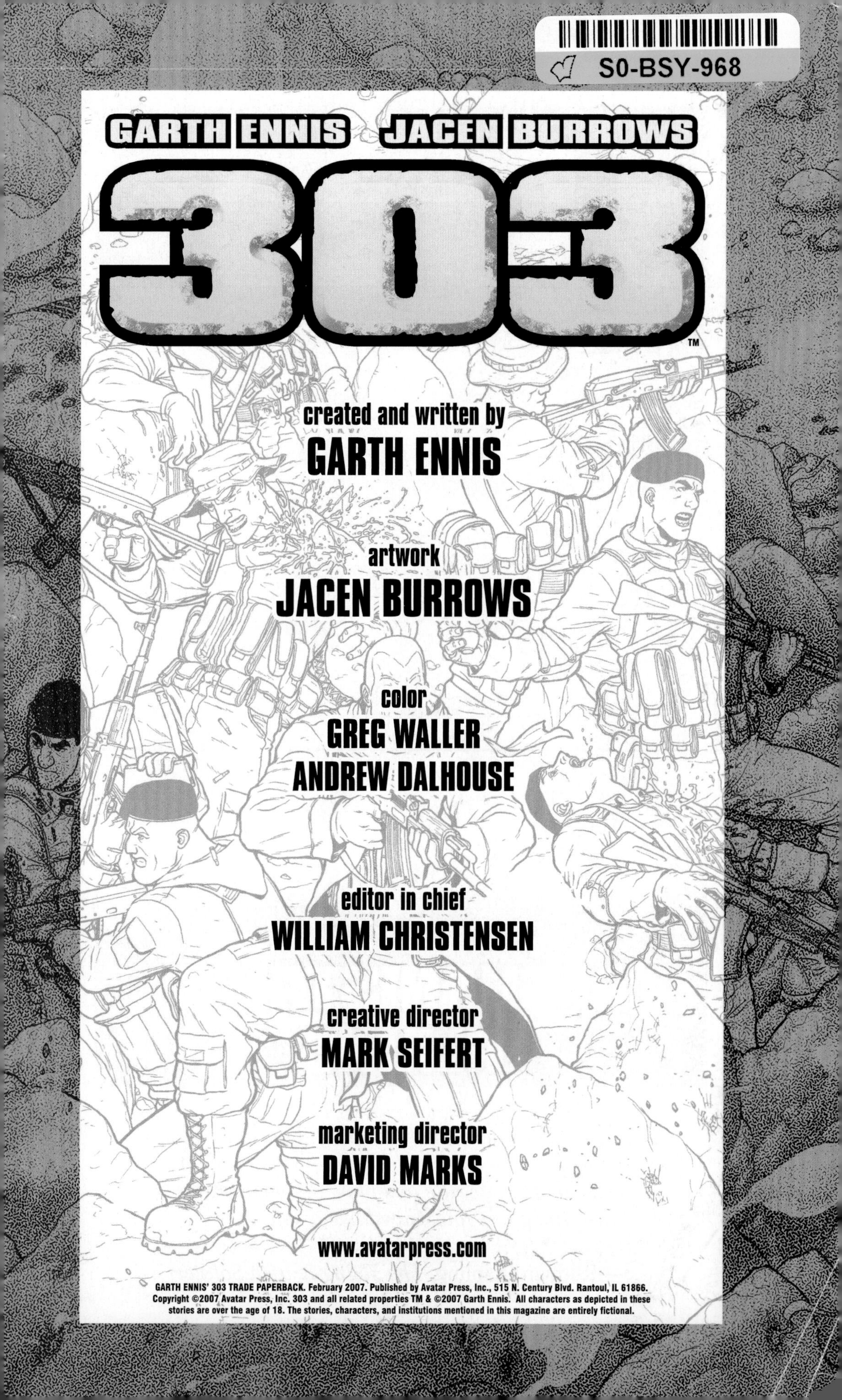

GARTH ENNIS JACEN BURROWS

303™

created and written by
GARTH ENNIS

artwork
JACEN BURROWS

color
GREG WALLER
ANDREW DALHOUSE

editor in chief
WILLIAM CHRISTENSEN

creative director
MARK SEIFERT

marketing director
DAVID MARKS

www.avatarpress.com

GARTH ENNIS' 303 TRADE PAPERBACK. February 2007. Published by Avatar Press, Inc., 515 N. Century Blvd. Rantoul, IL 61866.

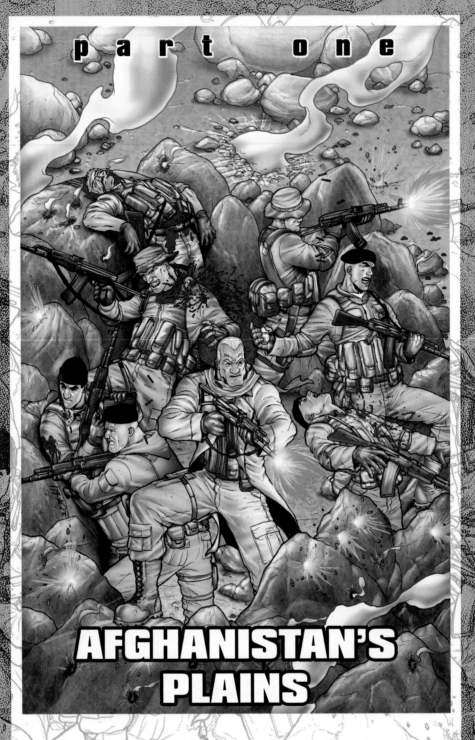

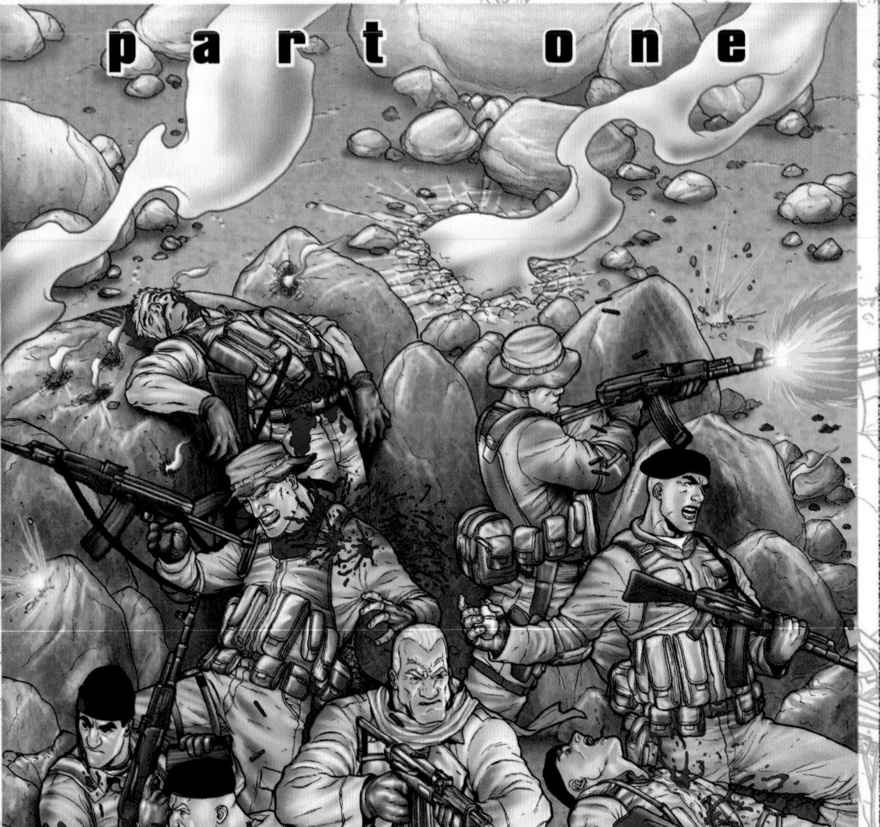
part one
AFGHANISTAN'S
PLAINS

When you're wounded and left on Afghanistan's plains,
And the women come out to cut up what remains,
Jest role to your rifle and blow out your brains
An' go to your Gawd like a soldier.

— Rudyard Kipling, *The Young British Soldier*

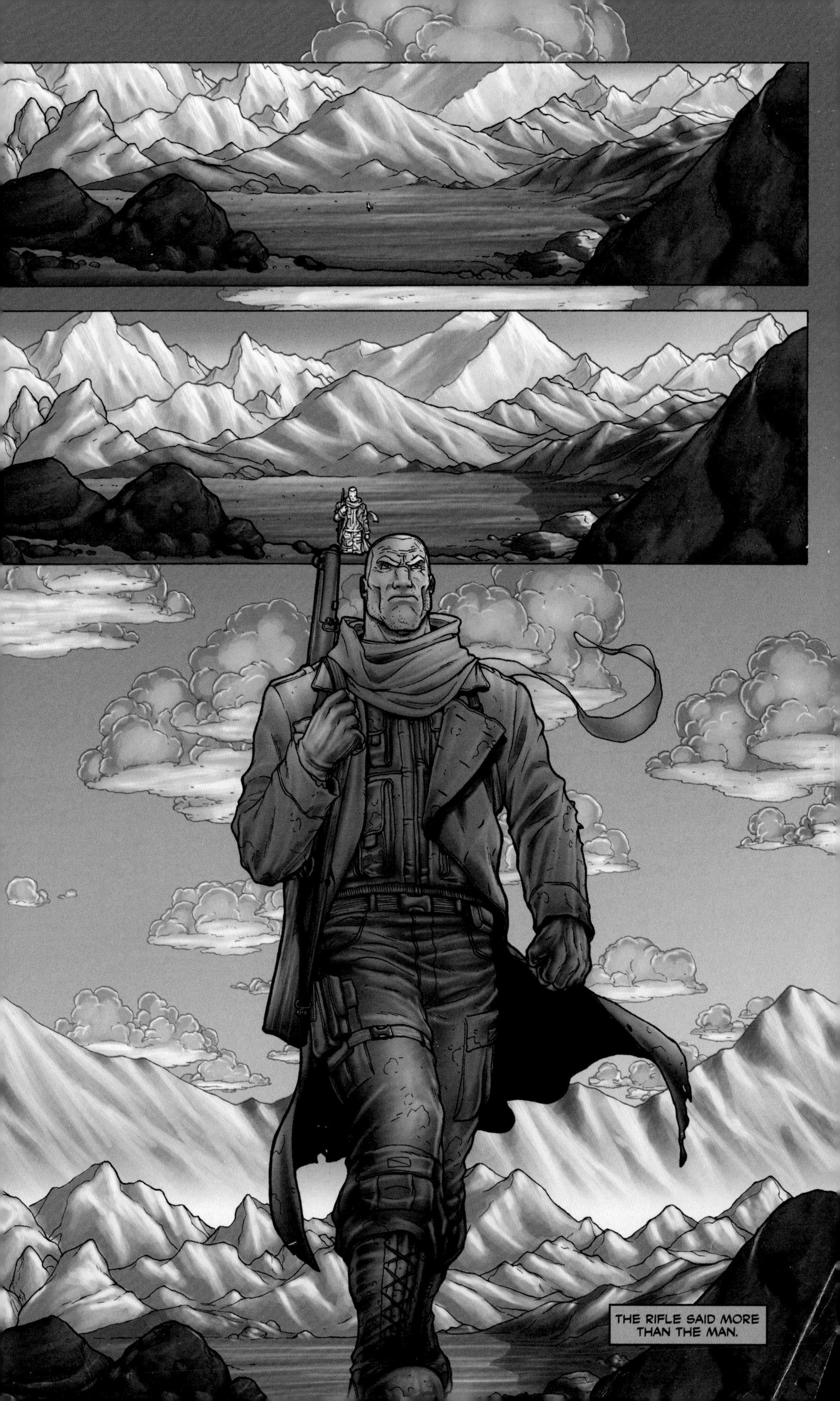
THE RIFLE SAID MORE THAN THE MAN.

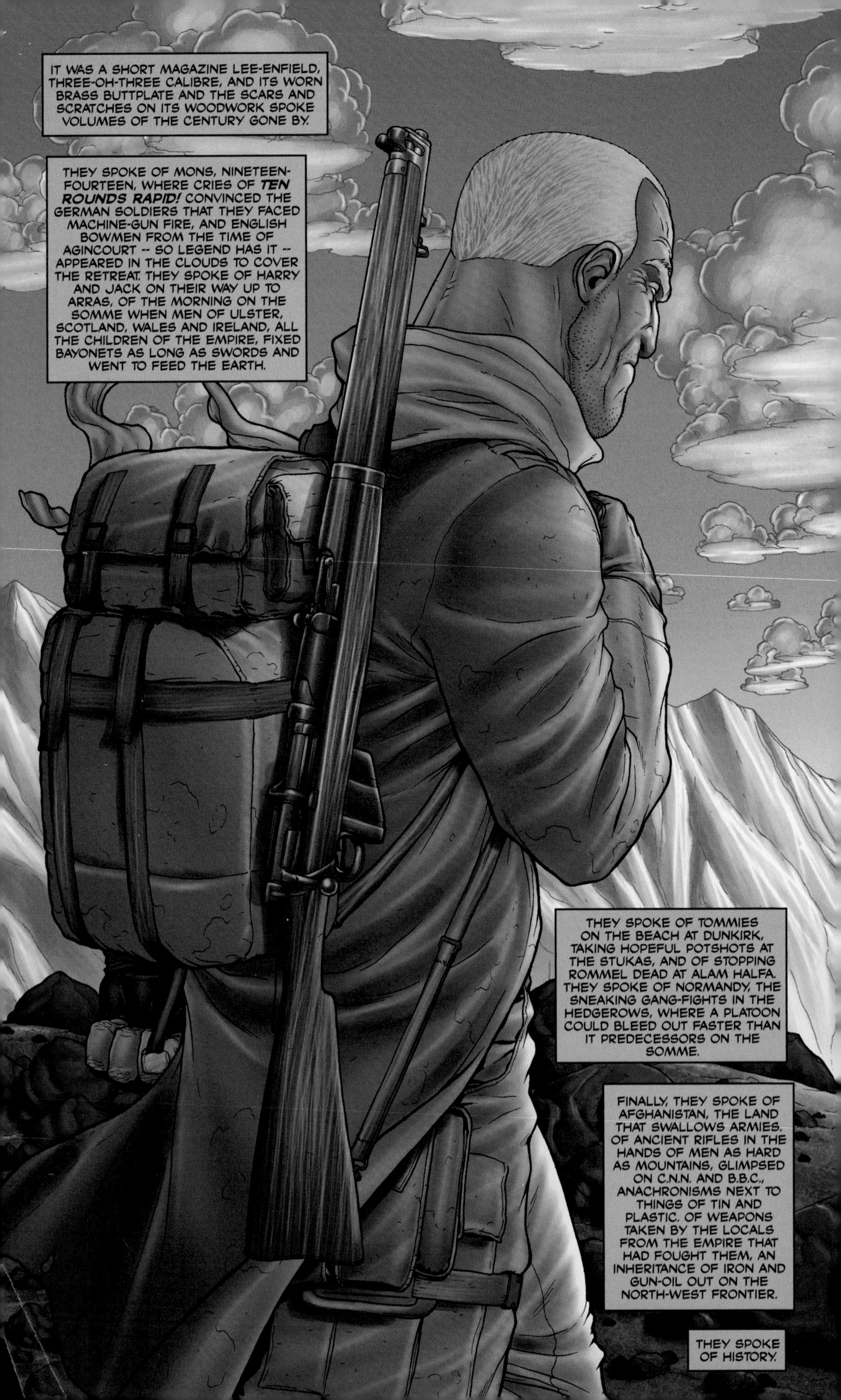
IT WAS A SHORT MAGAZINE LEE-ENFIELD, THREE-OH-THREE CALIBRE, AND ITS WORN BRASS BUTTPLATE AND THE SCARS AND SCRATCHES ON ITS WOODWORK SPOKE VOLUMES OF THE CENTURY GONE BY.
THEY SPOKE OF MONS, NINETEEN-FOURTEEN, WHERE CRIES OF ***TEN ROUNDS RAPID!*** CONVINCED THE GERMAN SOLDIERS THAT THEY FACED MACHINE-GUN FIRE, AND ENGLISH BOWMEN FROM THE TIME OF AGINCOURT -- SO LEGEND HAS IT -- APPEARED IN THE CLOUDS TO COVER THE RETREAT. THEY SPOKE OF HARRY AND JACK ON THEIR WAY UP TO ARRAS, OF THE MORNING ON THE SOMME WHEN MEN OF ULSTER, SCOTLAND, WALES AND IRELAND, ALL THE CHILDREN OF THE EMPIRE, FIXED BAYONETS AS LONG AS SWORDS AND WENT TO FEED THE EARTH.
THEY SPOKE OF TOMMIES ON THE BEACH AT DUNKIRK, TAKING HOPEFUL POTSHOTS AT THE STUKAS, AND OF STOPPING ROMMEL DEAD AT ALAM HALFA. THEY SPOKE OF NORMANDY, THE SNEAKING GANG-FIGHTS IN THE HEDGEROWS, WHERE A PLATOON COULD BLEED OUT FASTER THAN IT PREDECESSORS ON THE SOMME.
FINALLY, THEY SPOKE OF AFGHANISTAN, THE LAND THAT SWALLOWS ARMIES. OF ANCIENT RIFLES IN THE HANDS OF MEN AS HARD AS MOUNTAINS, GLIMPSED ON C.N.N. AND B.B.C., ANACHRONISMS NEXT TO THINGS OF TIN AND PLASTIC. OF WEAPONS TAKEN BY THE LOCALS FROM THE EMPIRE THAT HAD FOUGHT THEM, AN INHERITANCE OF IRON AND GUN-OIL OUT ON THE NORTH-WEST FRONTIER.
THEY SPOKE OF HISTORY.

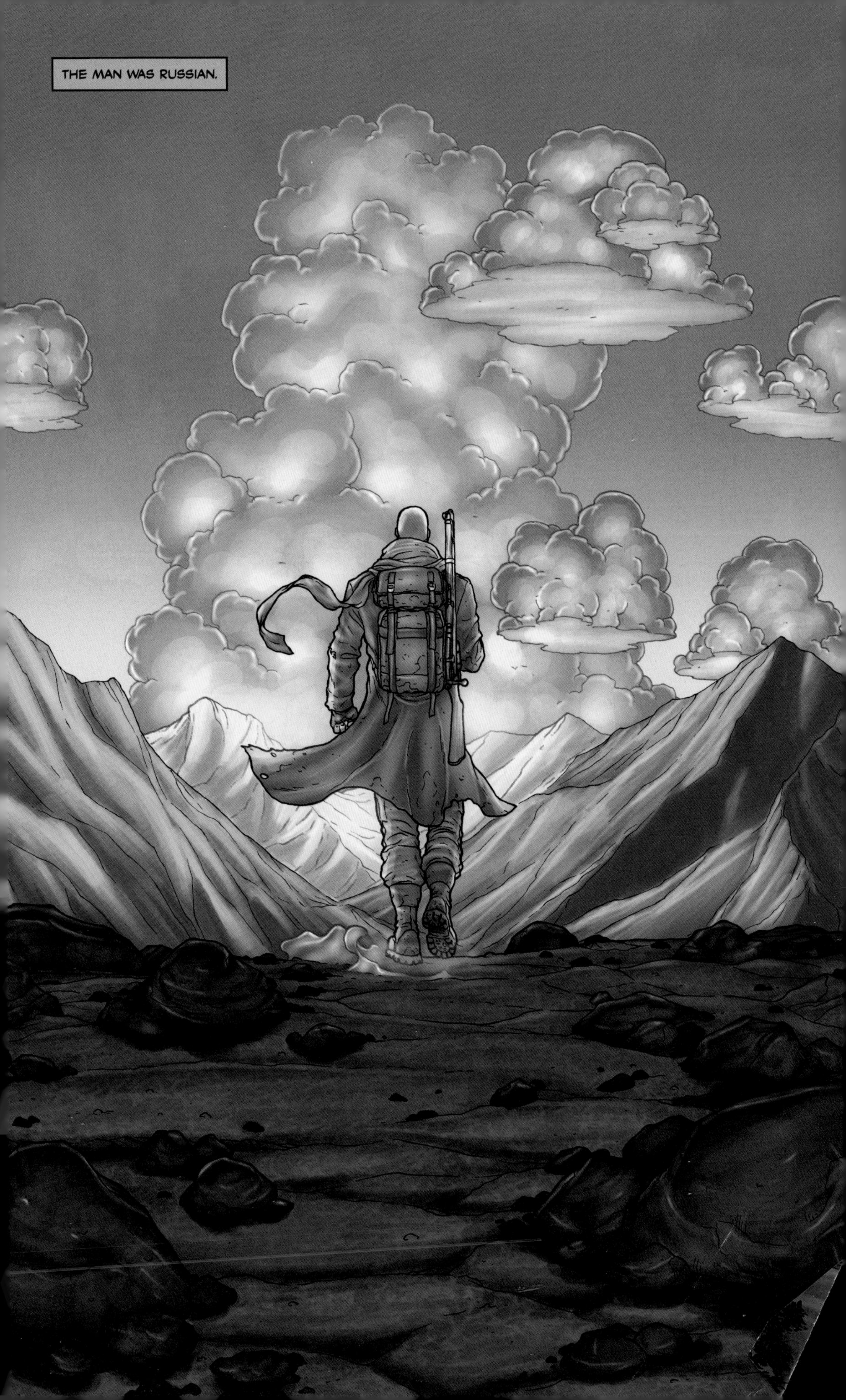
THE MAN WAS RUSSIAN.

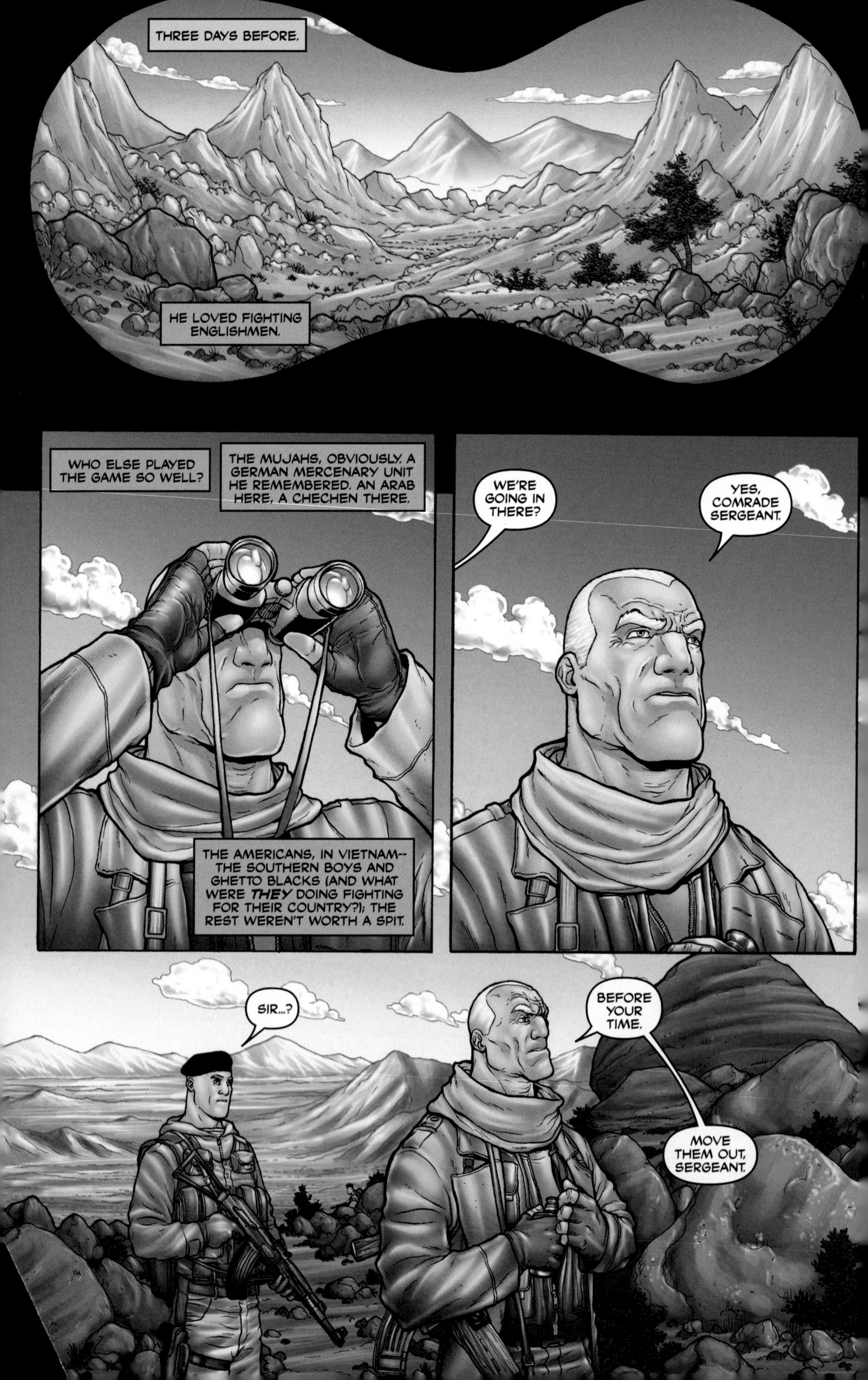
THREE DAYS BEFORE.
HE LOVED FIGHTING ENGLISHMEN.
WHO ELSE PLAYED THE GAME SO WELL?
THE MUJAHS, OBVIOUSLY. A GERMAN MERCENARY UNIT HE REMEMBERED. AN ARAB HERE, A CHECHEN THERE.
THE AMERICANS, IN VIETNAM-- THE SOUTHERN BOYS AND GHETTO BLACKS (AND WHAT WERE THEY DOING FIGHTING FOR THEIR COUNTRY?); THE REST WEREN'T WORTH A SPIT.
WE'RE GOING IN THERE?
YES, COMRADE SERGEANT.
SIR...?
BEFORE YOUR TIME.
MOVE THEM OUT, SERGEANT.

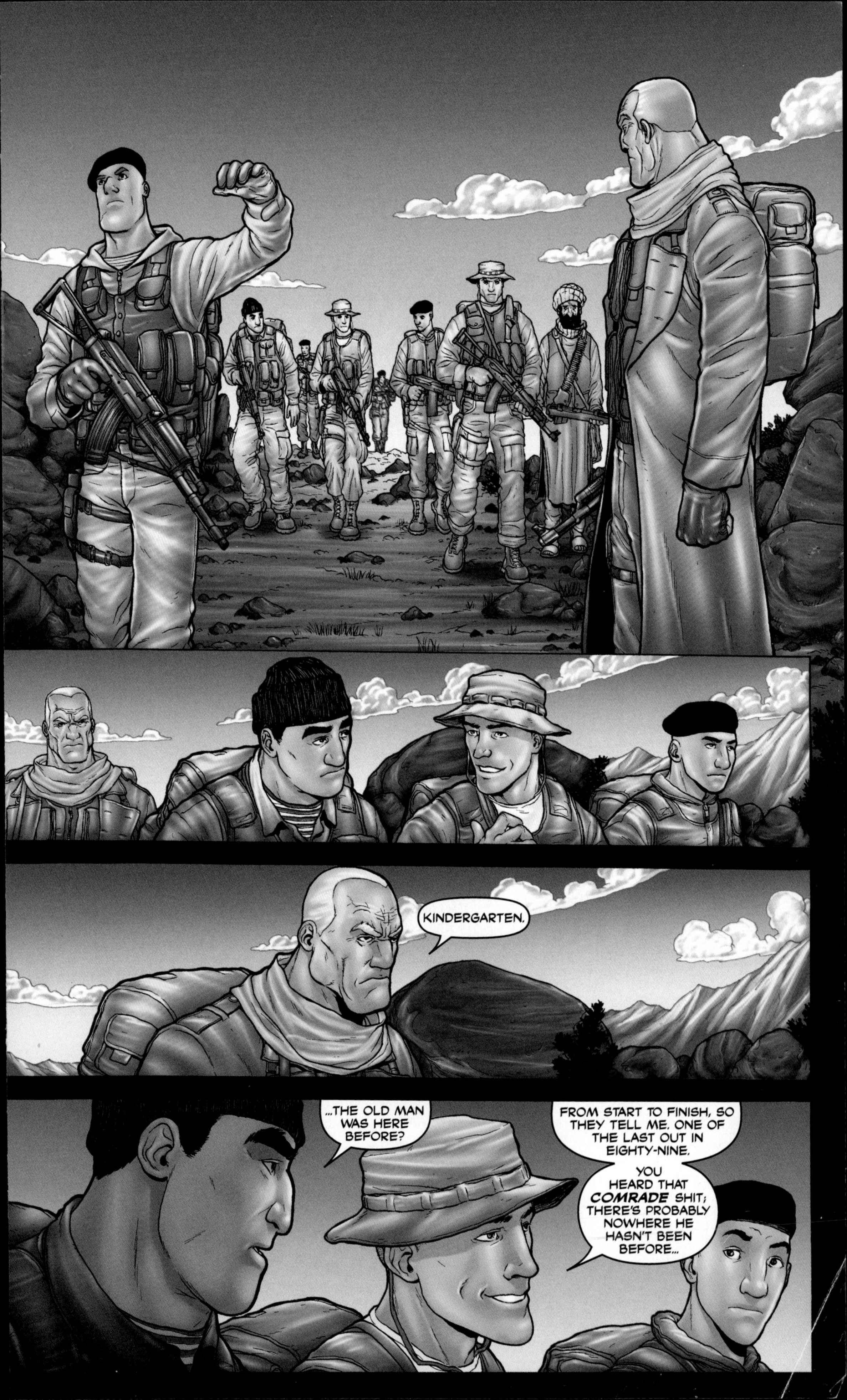
KINDERGARTEN.
...THE OLD MAN WAS HERE BEFORE?
FROM START TO FINISH, SO THEY TELL ME. ONE OF THE LAST OUT IN EIGHTY-NINE.
YOU HEARD THAT COMRADE SHIT; THERE'S PROBABLY NOWHERE HE HASN'T BEEN BEFORE...

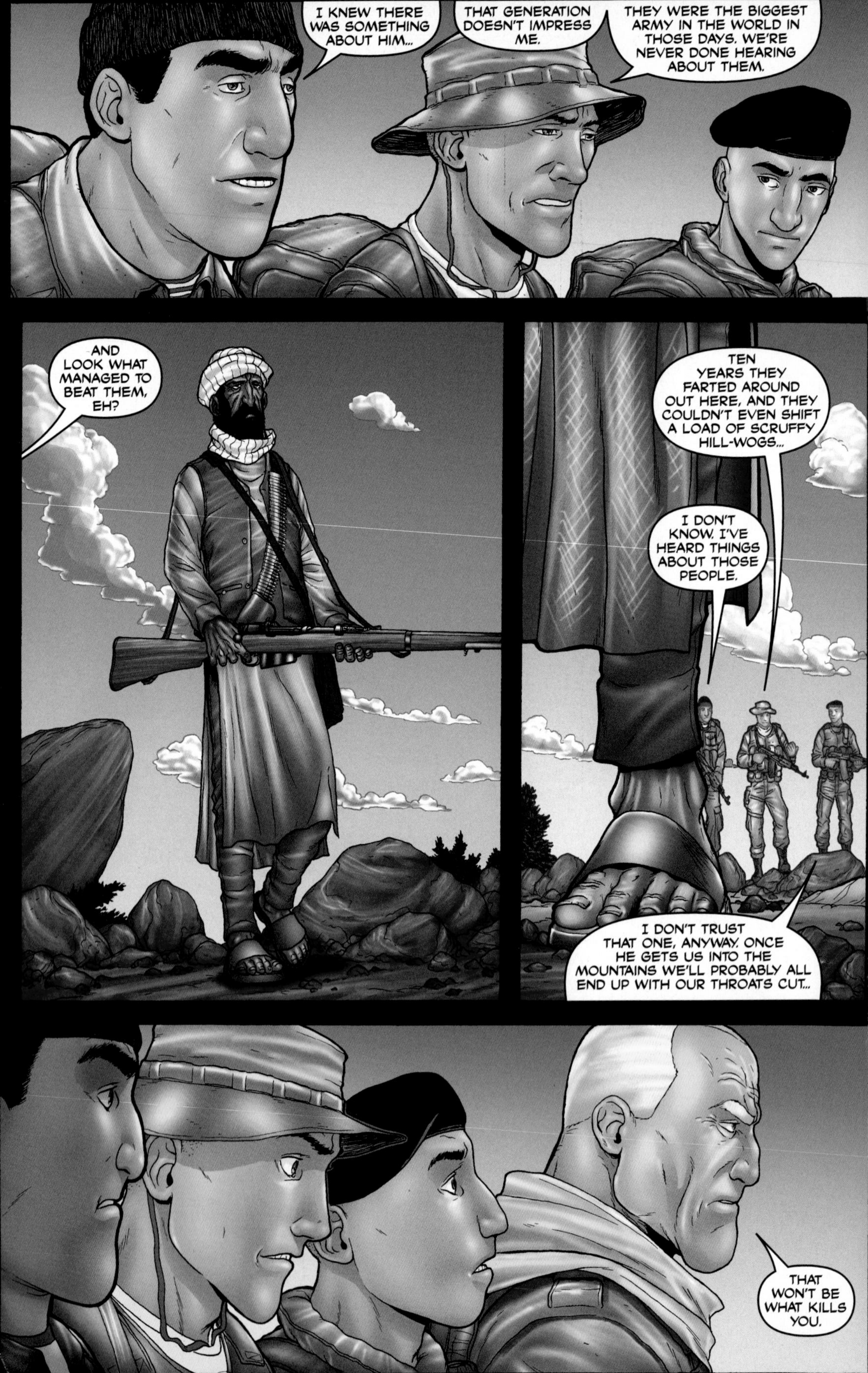
I KNEW THERE WAS SOMETHING ABOUT HIM...
THAT GENERATION DOESN'T IMPRESS ME.
THEY WERE THE BIGGEST ARMY IN THE WORLD IN THOSE DAYS. WE'RE NEVER DONE HEARING ABOUT THEM.
AND LOOK WHAT MANAGED TO BEAT THEM, EH?
TEN YEARS THEY FARTED AROUND OUT HERE, AND THEY COULDN'T EVEN SHIFT A LOAD OF SCRUFFY HILL-WOGS...
I DON'T KNOW. I'VE HEARD THINGS ABOUT THOSE PEOPLE.
I DON'T TRUST THAT ONE, ANYWAY. ONCE HE GETS US INTO THE MOUNTAINS WE'LL PROBABLY ALL END UP WITH OUR THROATS CUT...
THAT WON'T BE WHAT KILLS YOU.

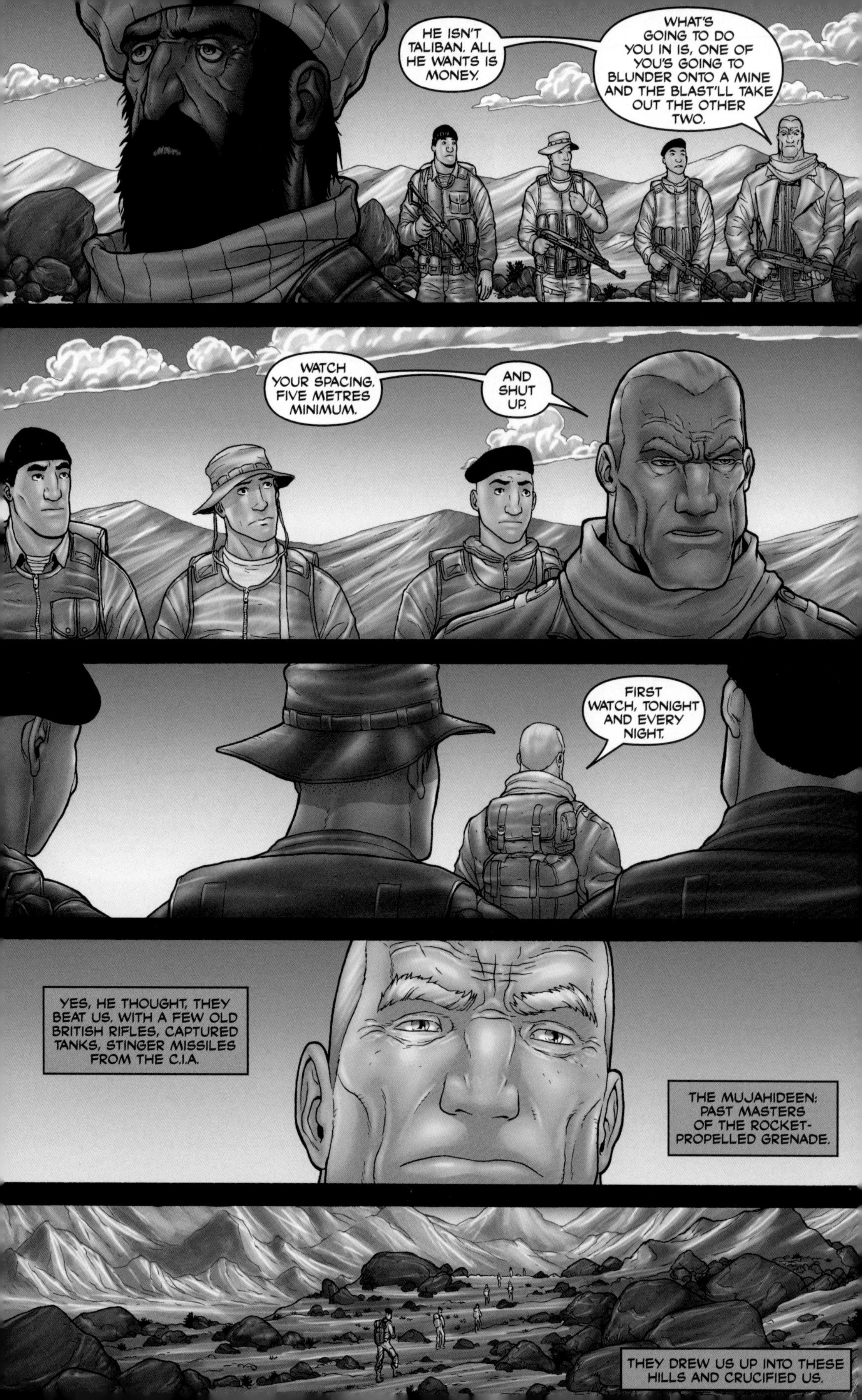
HE ISN'T TALIBAN. ALL HE WANTS IS MONEY.
WHAT'S GOING TO DO YOU IN IS, ONE OF YOU'S GOING TO BLUNDER ONTO A MINE AND THE BLAST'LL TAKE OUT THE OTHER TWO.
WATCH YOUR SPACING. FIVE METRES MINIMUM.
AND SHUT UP.
FIRST WATCH, TONIGHT AND EVERY NIGHT.
YES, HE THOUGHT, THEY BEAT US. WITH A FEW OLD BRITISH RIFLES, CAPTURED TANKS, STINGER MISSILES FROM THE C.I.A.
THE MUJAHIDEEN: PAST MASTERS OF THE ROCKET-PROPELLED GRENADE.
THEY DREW US UP INTO THESE HILLS AND CRUCIFIED US.

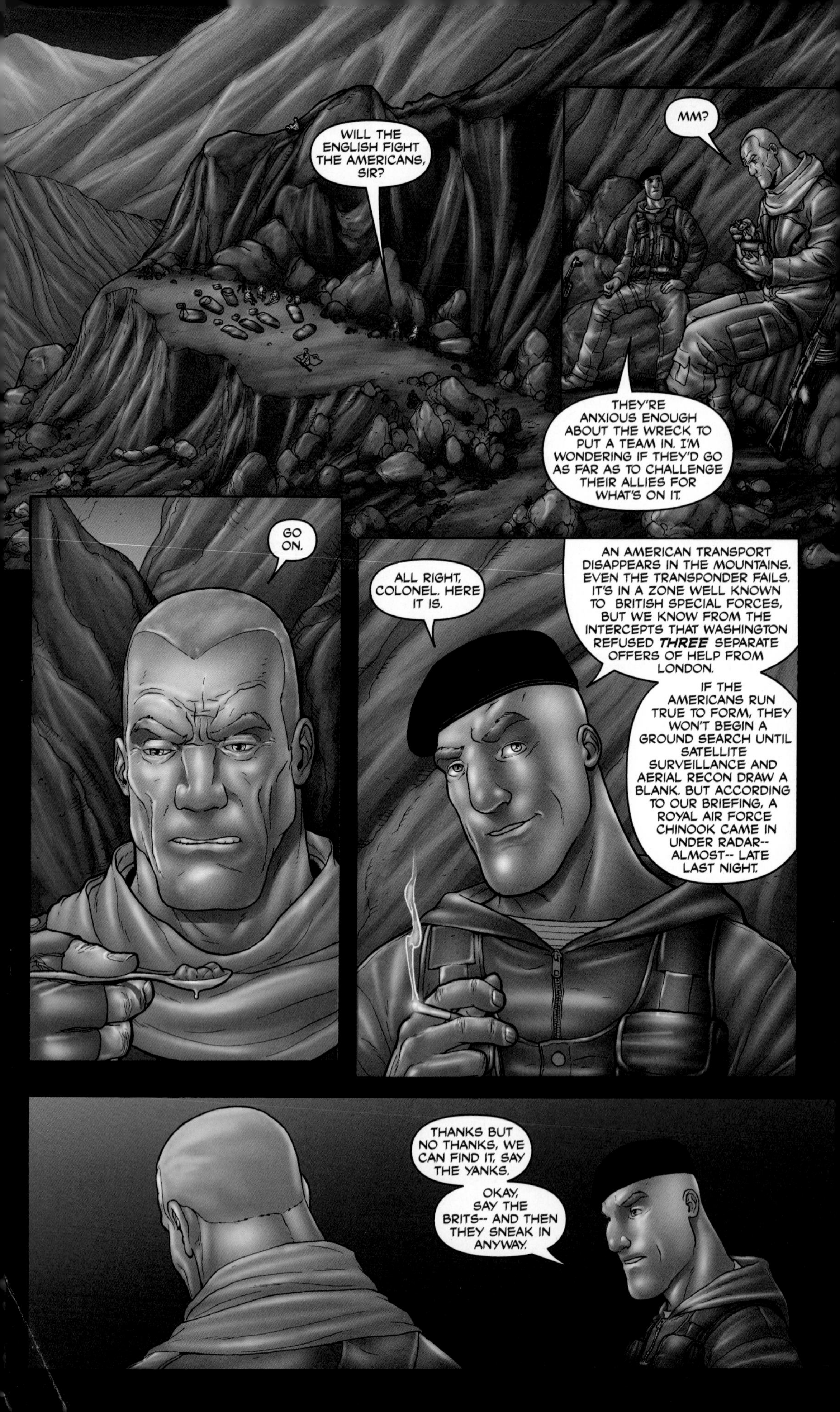
WILL THE ENGLISH FIGHT THE AMERICANS, SIR?
MM?
THEY'RE ANXIOUS ENOUGH ABOUT THE WRECK TO PUT A TEAM IN. I'M WONDERING IF THEY'D GO AS FAR AS TO CHALLENGE THEIR ALLIES FOR WHAT'S ON IT.
GO ON.
ALL RIGHT, COLONEL. HERE IT IS.
AN AMERICAN TRANSPORT DISAPPEARS IN THE MOUNTAINS. EVEN THE TRANSPONDER FAILS. IT'S IN A ZONE WELL KNOWN TO BRITISH SPECIAL FORCES, BUT WE KNOW FROM THE INTERCEPTS THAT WASHINGTON REFUSED *THREE* SEPARATE OFFERS OF HELP FROM LONDON.
IF THE AMERICANS RUN TRUE TO FORM, THEY WON'T BEGIN A GROUND SEARCH UNTIL SATELLITE SURVEILLANCE AND AERIAL RECON DRAW A BLANK. BUT ACCORDING TO OUR BRIEFING, A ROYAL AIR FORCE CHINOOK CAME IN UNDER RADAR-- ALMOST-- LATE LAST NIGHT.
THANKS BUT NO THANKS, WE CAN FIND IT, SAY THE YANKS.
OKAY, SAY THE BRITS-- AND THEN THEY SNEAK IN ANYWAY.

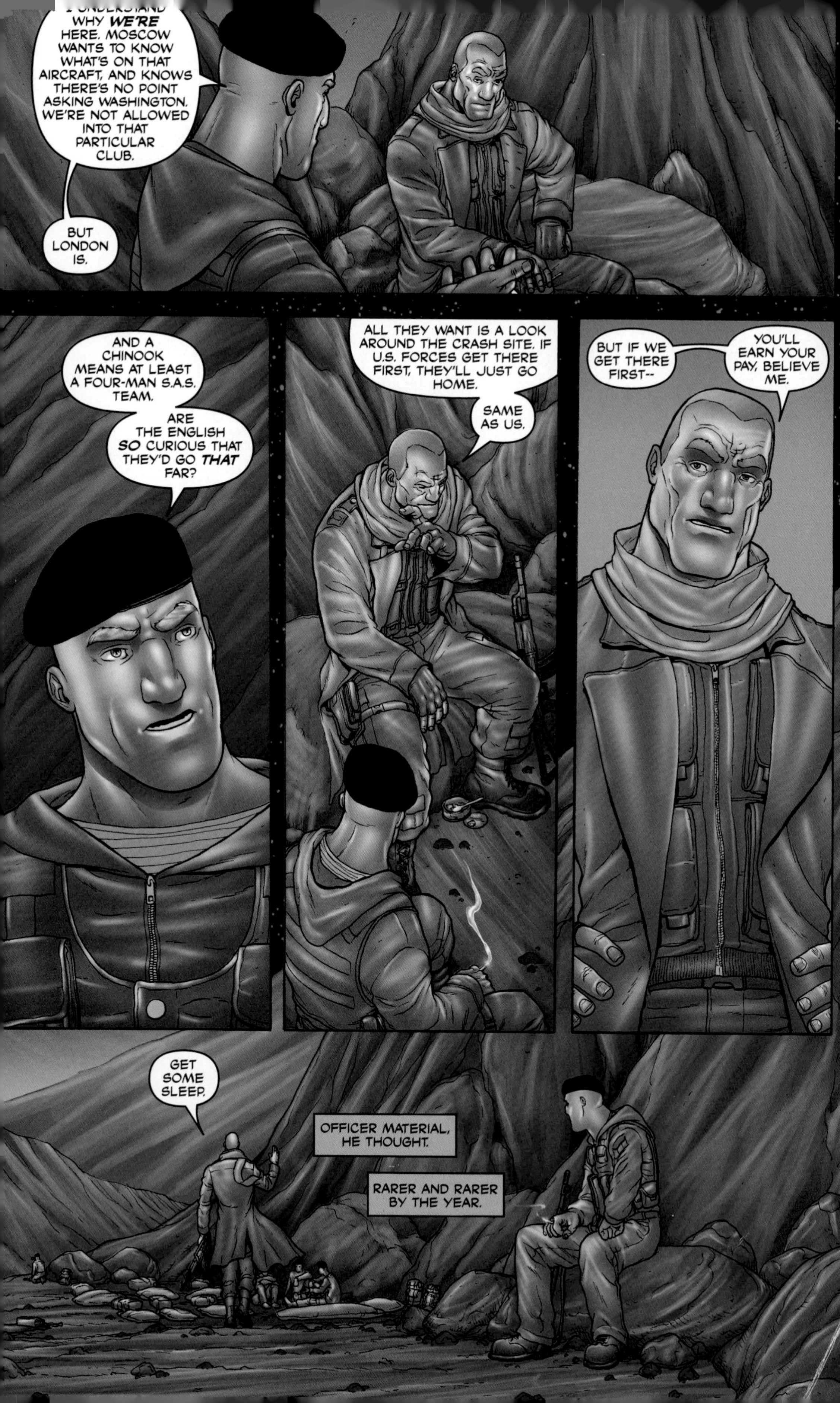
WHY WE'RE HERE. MOSCOW WANTS TO KNOW WHAT'S ON THAT AIRCRAFT, AND KNOWS THERE'S NO POINT ASKING WASHINGTON. WE'RE NOT ALLOWED INTO THAT PARTICULAR CLUB.
BUT LONDON IS.
AND A CHINOOK MEANS AT LEAST A FOUR-MAN S.A.S. TEAM.
ARE THE ENGLISH SO CURIOUS THAT THEY'D GO THAT FAR?
ALL THEY WANT IS A LOOK AROUND THE CRASH SITE. IF U.S. FORCES GET THERE FIRST, THEY'LL JUST GO HOME.
SAME AS US.
BUT IF WE GET THERE FIRST--
YOU'LL EARN YOUR PAY, BELIEVE ME.
GET SOME SLEEP.
OFFICER MATERIAL, HE THOUGHT.
RARER AND RARER BY THE YEAR.

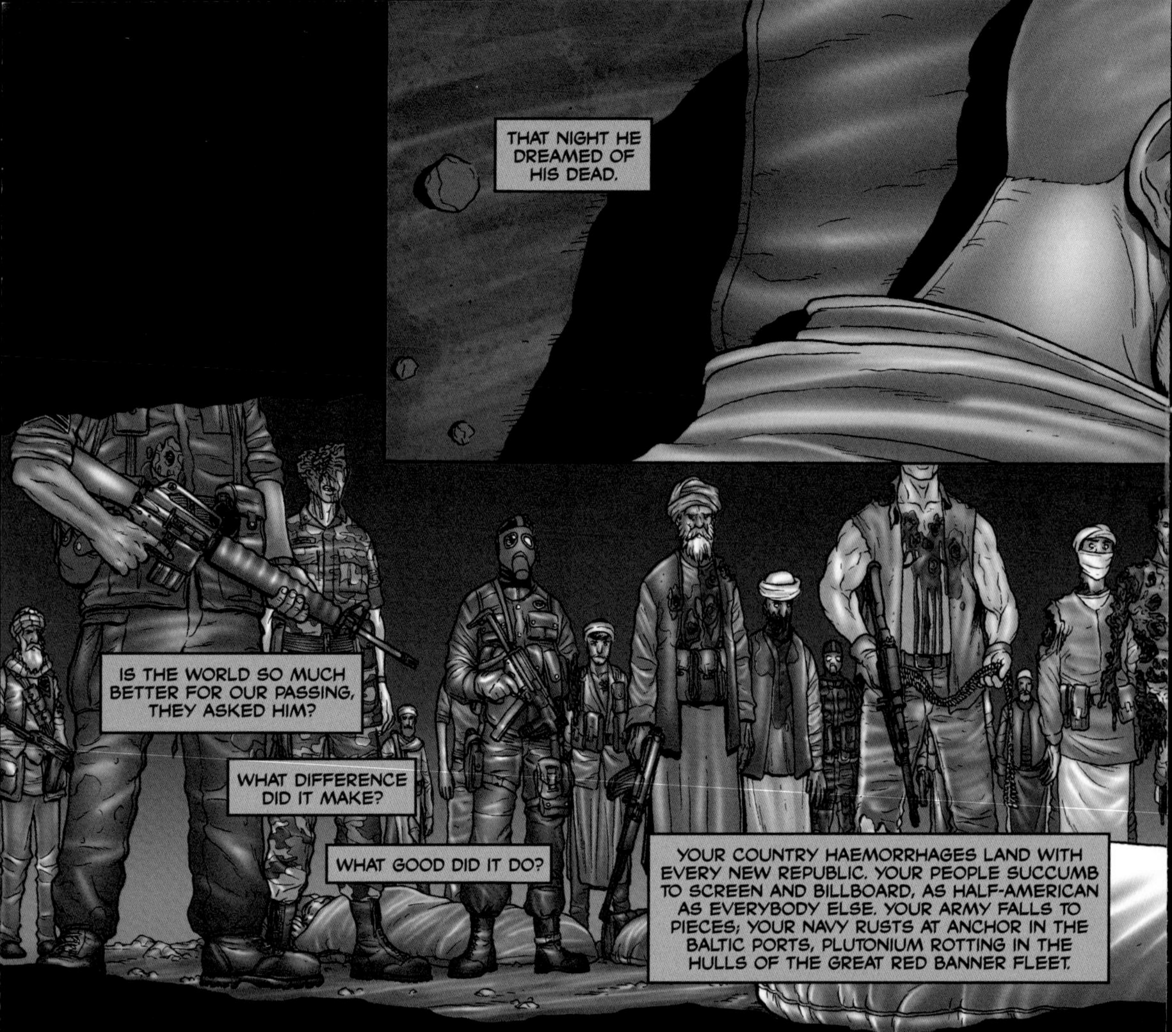
THAT NIGHT HE DREAMED OF HIS DEAD.
IS THE WORLD SO MUCH BETTER FOR OUR PASSING, THEY ASKED HIM?
WHAT DIFFERENCE DID IT MAKE?
WHAT GOOD DID IT DO?
YOUR COUNTRY HAEMORRHAGES LAND WITH EVERY NEW REPUBLIC. YOUR PEOPLE SUCCUMB TO SCREEN AND BILLBOARD, AS HALF-AMERICAN AS EVERYBODY ELSE. YOUR ARMY FALLS TO PIECES; YOUR NAVY RUSTS AT ANCHOR IN THE BALTIC PORTS, PLUTONIUM ROTTING IN THE HULLS OF THE GREAT RED BANNER FLEET.

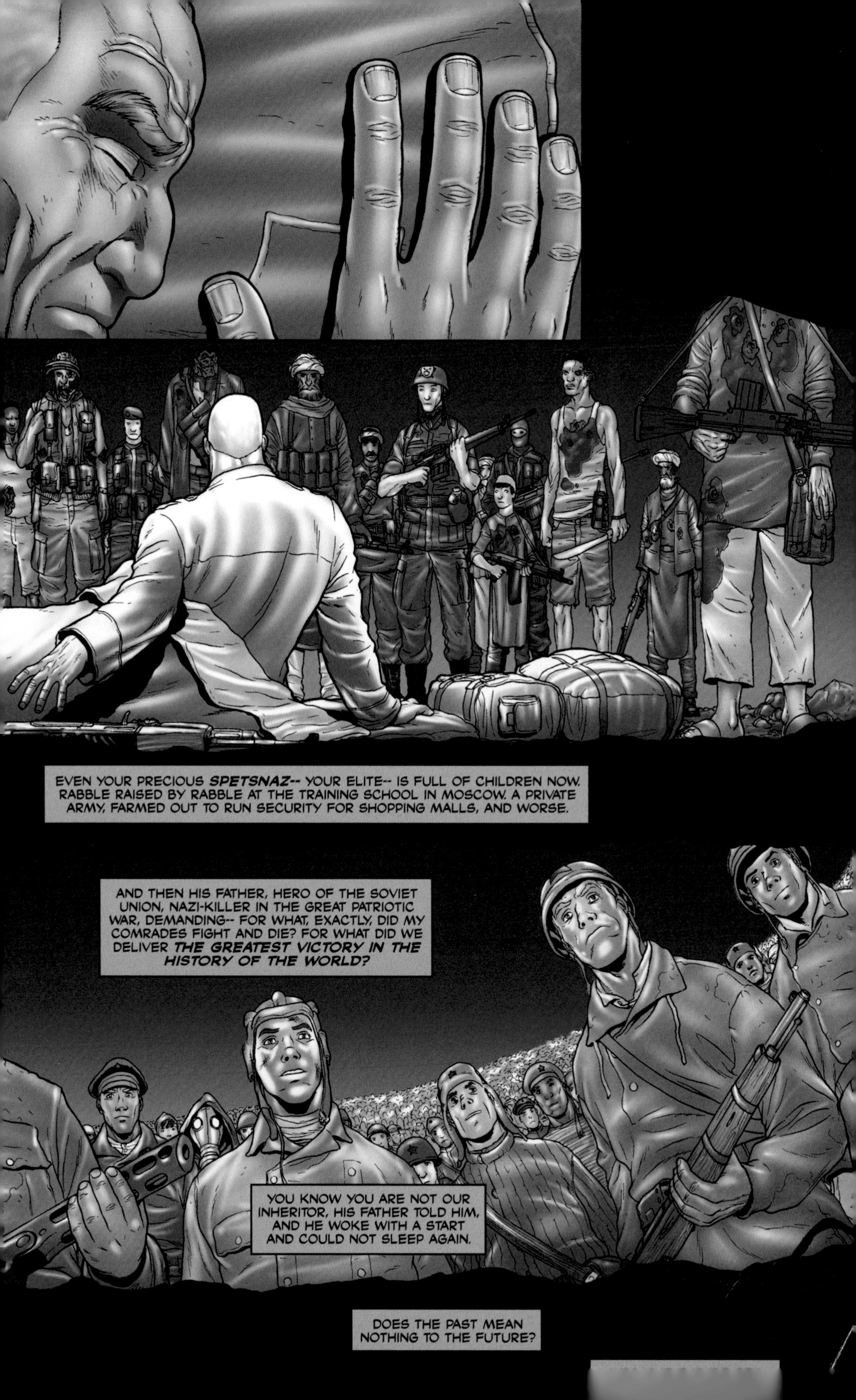
EVEN YOUR PRECIOUS SPETSNAZ-- YOUR ELITE-- IS FULL OF CHILDREN NOW. RABBLE RAISED BY RABBLE AT THE TRAINING SCHOOL IN MOSCOW. A PRIVATE ARMY, FARMED OUT TO RUN SECURITY FOR SHOPPING MALLS, AND WORSE.
AND THEN HIS FATHER, HERO OF THE SOVIET UNION, NAZI-KILLER IN THE GREAT PATRIOTIC WAR, DEMANDING-- FOR WHAT, EXACTLY, DID MY COMRADES FIGHT AND DIE? FOR WHAT DID WE DELIVER THE GREATEST VICTORY IN THE HISTORY OF THE WORLD?
YOU KNOW YOU ARE NOT OUR INHERITOR, HIS FATHER TOLD HIM, AND HE WOKE WITH A START AND COULD NOT SLEEP AGAIN.
DOES THE PAST MEAN NOTHING TO THE FUTURE?

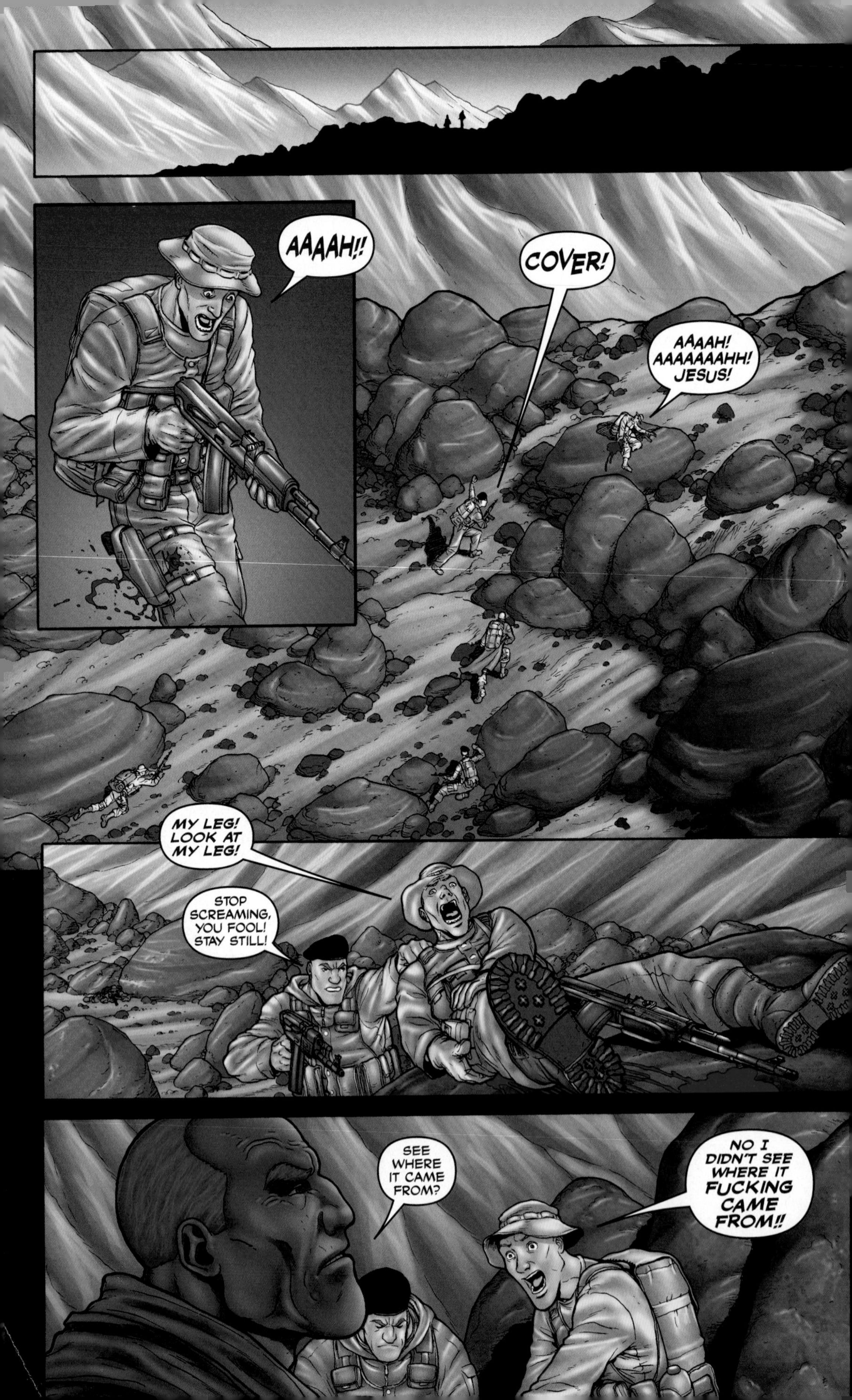
AAAAH!!
COVER!
AAAAH! AAAAAAAAHH! JESUS!
MY LEG! LOOK AT MY LEG!
STOP SCREAMING, YOU FOOL! STAY STILL!
SEE WHERE IT CAME FROM?
NO I DIDN'T SEE WHERE IT FUCKING CAME FROM!!

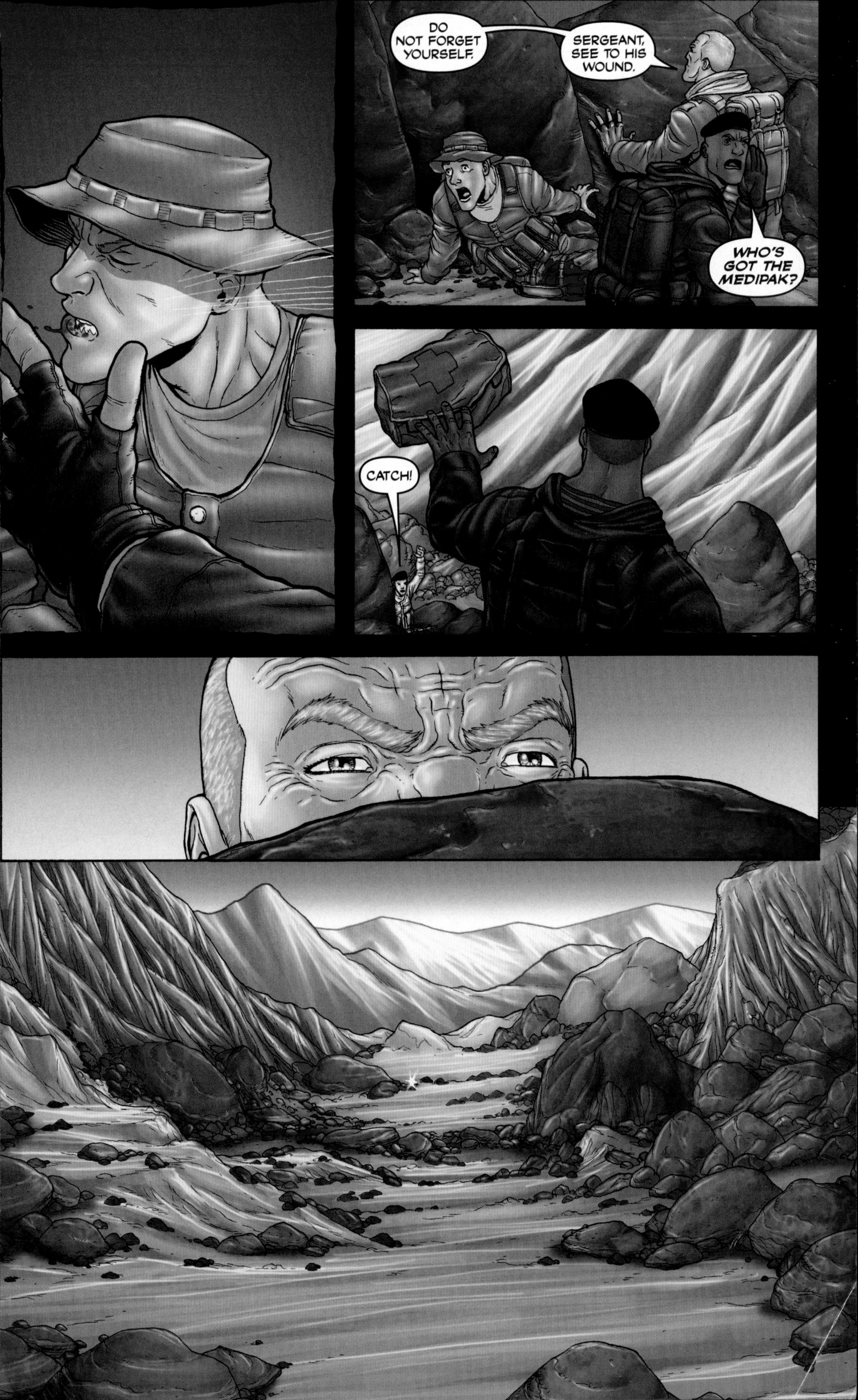
DO NOT FORGET YOURSELF.
SERGEANT, SEE TO HIS WOUND.
WHO'S GOT THE MEDIPAK?
CATCH!

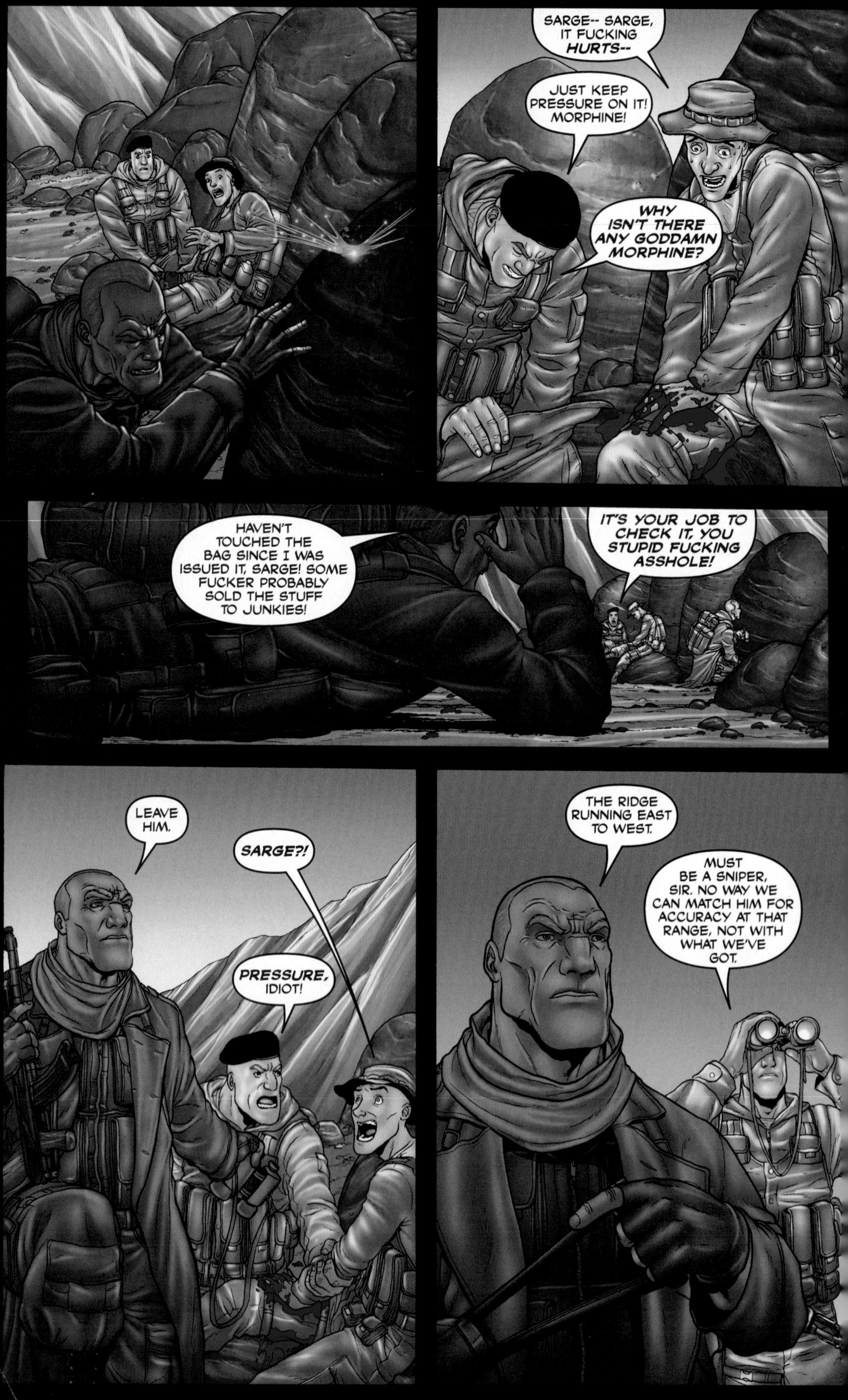
SARGE-- SARGE, IT FUCKING HURTS--
JUST KEEP PRESSURE ON IT! MORPHINE!
WHY ISN'T THERE ANY GODDAMN MORPHINE?
HAVEN'T TOUCHED THE BAG SINCE I WAS ISSUED IT, SARGE! SOME FUCKER PROBABLY SOLD THE STUFF TO JUNKIES!
IT'S YOUR JOB TO CHECK IT, YOU STUPID FUCKING ASSHOLE!
LEAVE HIM.
SARGE?!
PRESSURE, IDIOT!
THE RIDGE RUNNING EAST TO WEST.
MUST BE A SNIPER, SIR. NO WAY WE CAN MATCH HIM FOR ACCURACY AT THAT RANGE, NOT WITH WHAT WE'VE GOT.

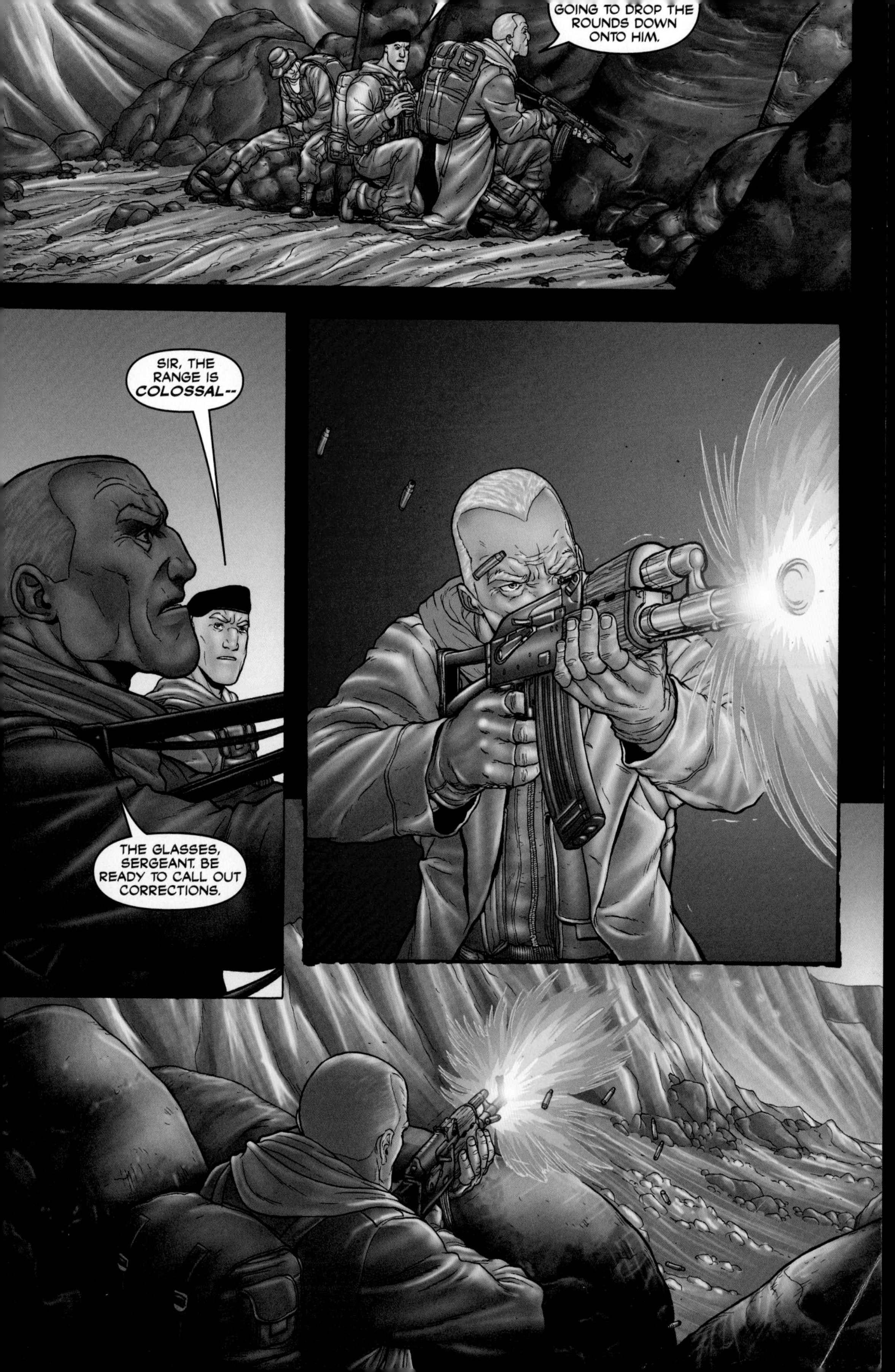
GOING TO DROP THE ROUNDS DOWN ONTO HIM.
SIR, THE RANGE IS COLOSSAL--
THE GLASSES, SERGEANT. BE READY TO CALL OUT CORRECTIONS.

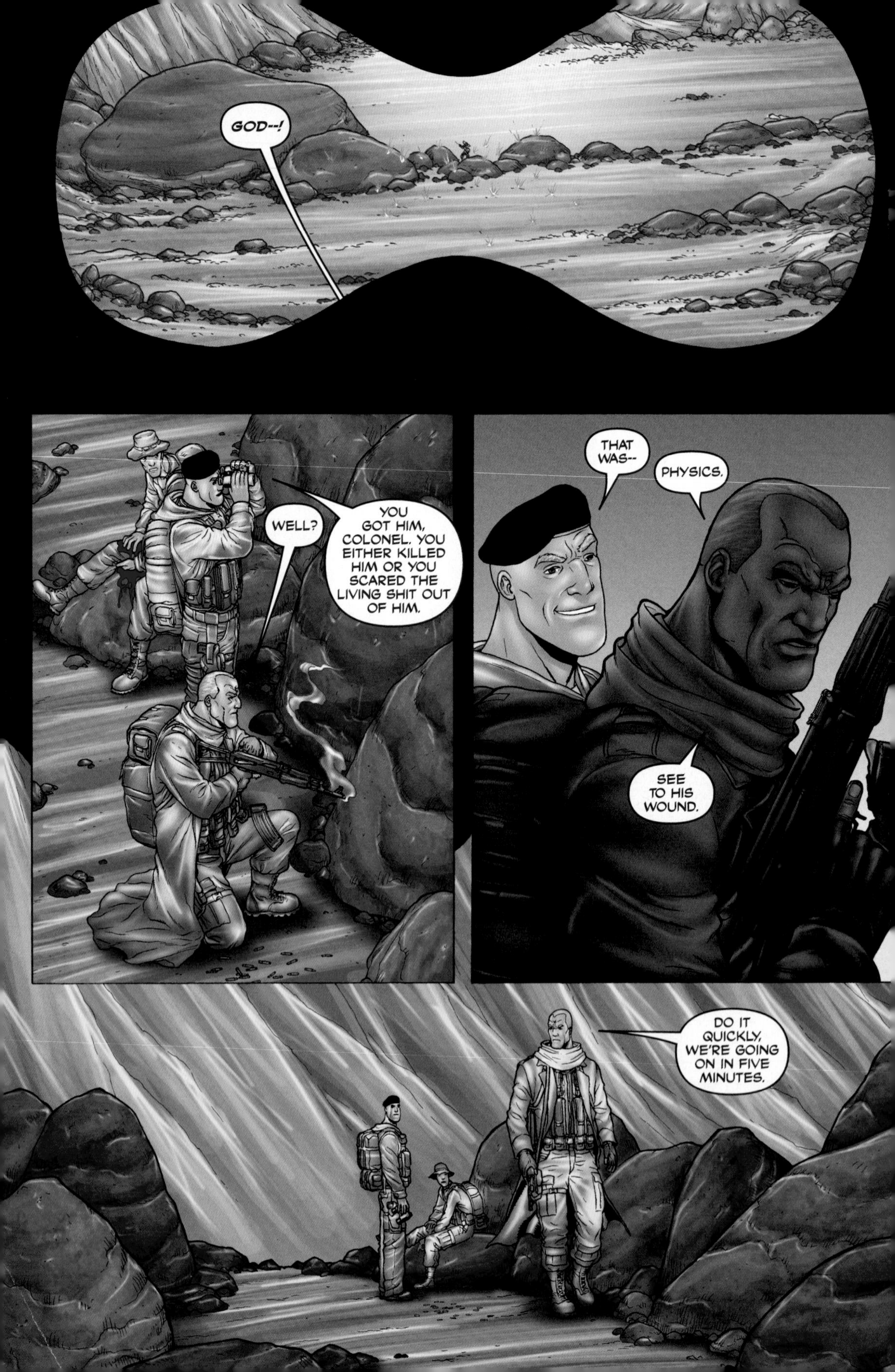
GOD--!
WELL?
YOU GOT HIM, COLONEL. YOU EITHER KILLED HIM OR YOU SCARED THE LIVING SHIT OUT OF HIM.
THAT WAS--
PHYSICS.
SEE TO HIS WOUND.
DO IT QUICKLY, WE'RE GOING ON IN FIVE MINUTES.

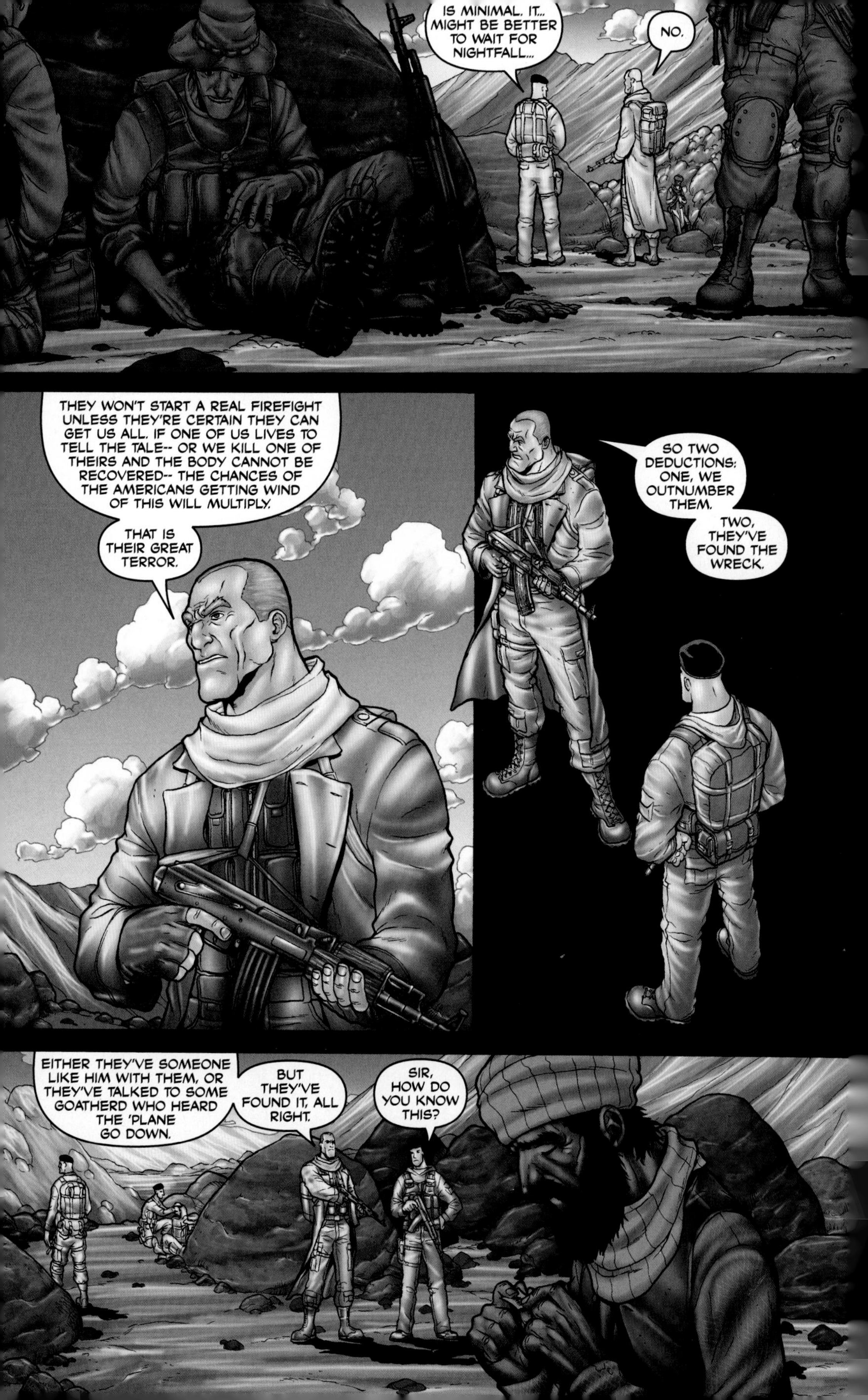
IS MINIMAL. IT... MIGHT BE BETTER TO WAIT FOR NIGHTFALL...
NO.
THEY WON'T START A REAL FIREFIGHT UNLESS THEY'RE CERTAIN THEY CAN GET US ALL. IF ONE OF US LIVES TO TELL THE TALE-- OR WE KILL ONE OF THEIRS AND THE BODY CANNOT BE RECOVERED-- THE CHANCES OF THE AMERICANS GETTING WIND OF THIS WILL MULTIPLY.
THAT IS THEIR GREAT TERROR.
SO TWO DEDUCTIONS: ONE, WE OUTNUMBER THEM.
TWO, THEY'VE FOUND THE WRECK.
EITHER THEY'VE SOMEONE LIKE HIM WITH THEM, OR THEY'VE TALKED TO SOME GOATHERD WHO HEARD THE 'PLANE GO DOWN.
BUT THEY'VE FOUND IT, ALL RIGHT.
SIR, HOW DO YOU KNOW THIS?

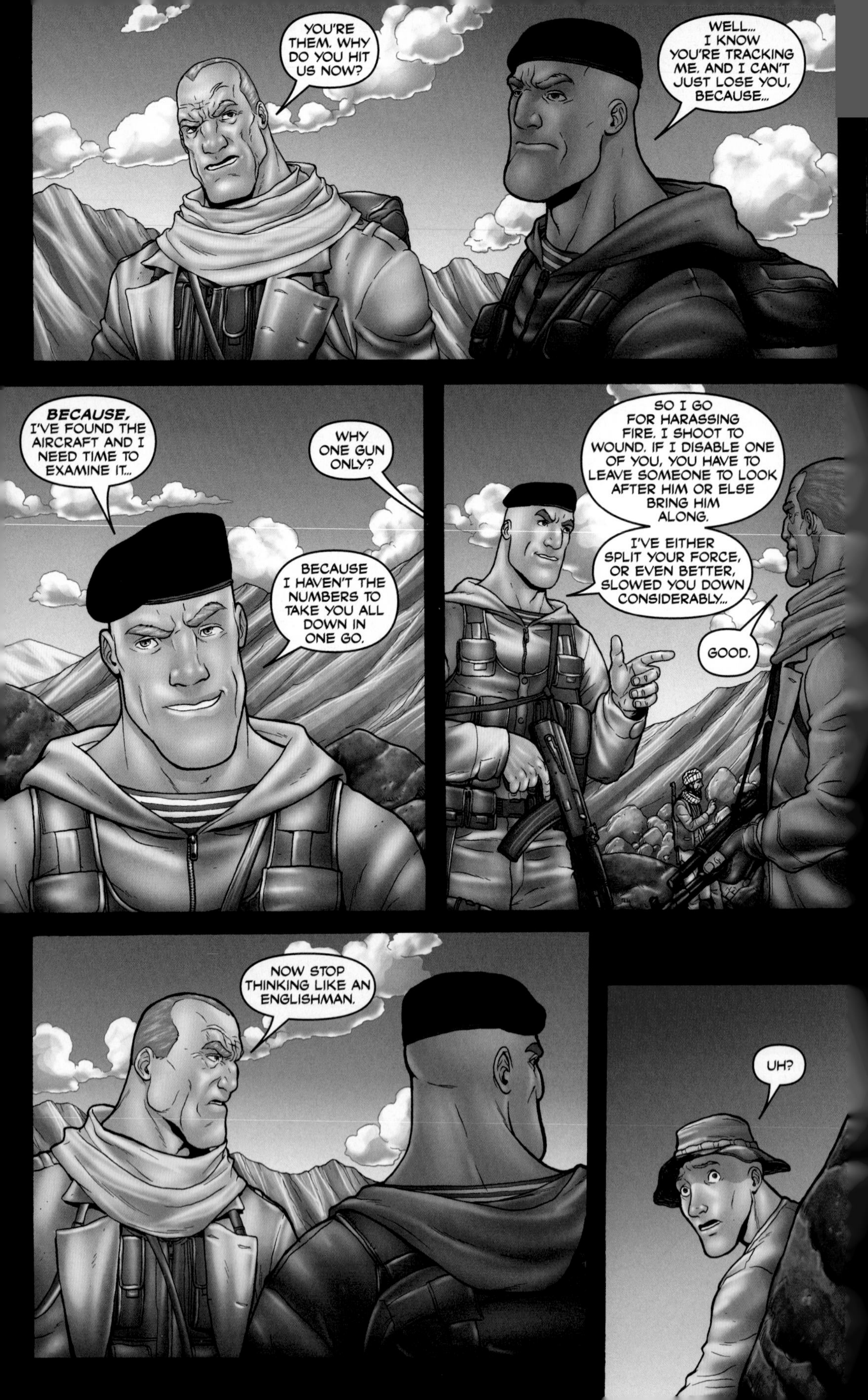
YOU'RE THEM. WHY DO YOU HIT US NOW?
WELL... I KNOW YOU'RE TRACKING ME. AND I CAN'T JUST LOSE YOU, BECAUSE...
BECAUSE, I'VE FOUND THE AIRCRAFT AND I NEED TIME TO EXAMINE IT...
WHY ONE GUN ONLY?
BECAUSE I HAVEN'T THE NUMBERS TO TAKE YOU ALL DOWN IN ONE GO.
SO I GO FOR HARASSING FIRE. I SHOOT TO WOUND. IF I DISABLE ONE OF YOU, YOU HAVE TO LEAVE SOMEONE TO LOOK AFTER HIM OR ELSE BRING HIM ALONG.
I'VE EITHER SPLIT YOUR FORCE, OR EVEN BETTER, SLOWED YOU DOWN CONSIDERABLY...
GOOD.
NOW STOP THINKING LIKE AN ENGLISHMAN.
UH?

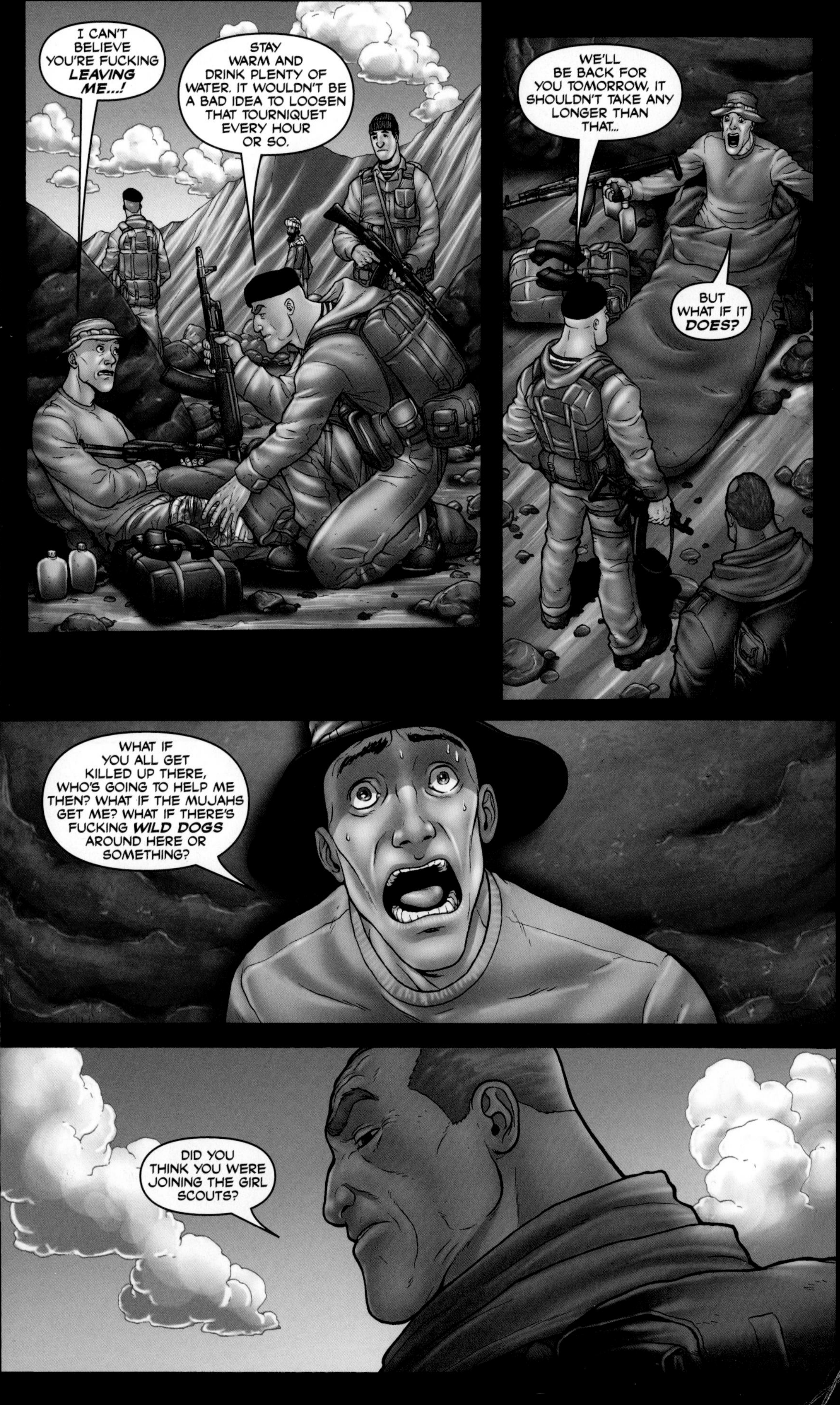
I CAN'T BELIEVE YOU'RE FUCKING LEAVING ME...!
STAY WARM AND DRINK PLENTY OF WATER. IT WOULDN'T BE A BAD IDEA TO LOOSEN THAT TOURNIQUET EVERY HOUR OR SO.
WE'LL BE BACK FOR YOU TOMORROW, IT SHOULDN'T TAKE ANY LONGER THAN THAT...
BUT WHAT IF IT DOES?
WHAT IF YOU ALL GET KILLED UP THERE, WHO'S GOING TO HELP ME THEN? WHAT IF THE MUJAHS GET ME? WHAT IF THERE'S FUCKING WILD DOGS AROUND HERE OR SOMETHING?
DID YOU THINK YOU WERE JOINING THE GIRL SCOUTS?

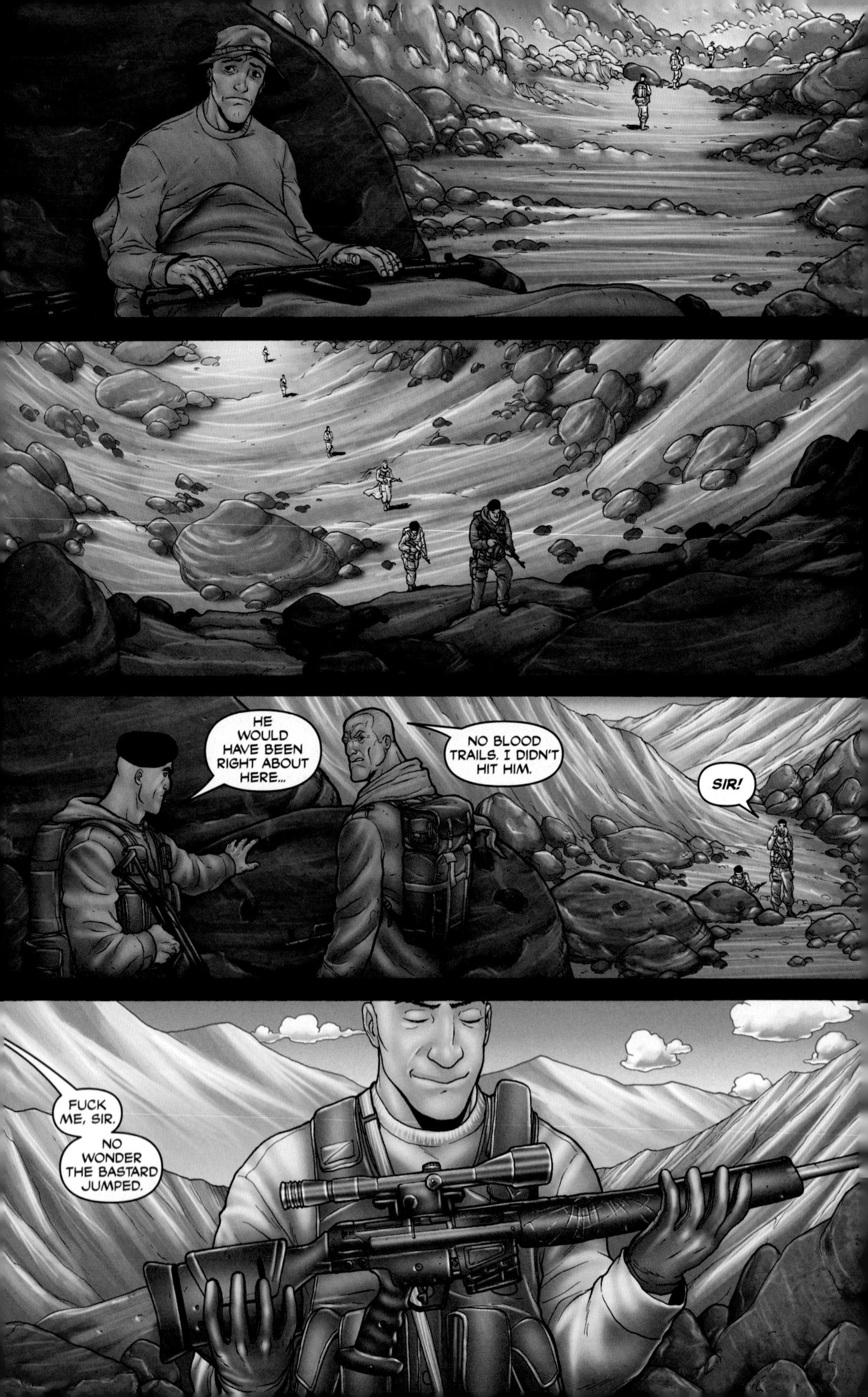
HE WOULD HAVE BEEN RIGHT ABOUT HERE...
NO BLOOD TRAILS. I DIDN'T HIT HIM.
SIR!
FUCK ME, SIR.
NO WONDER THE BASTARD JUMPED.

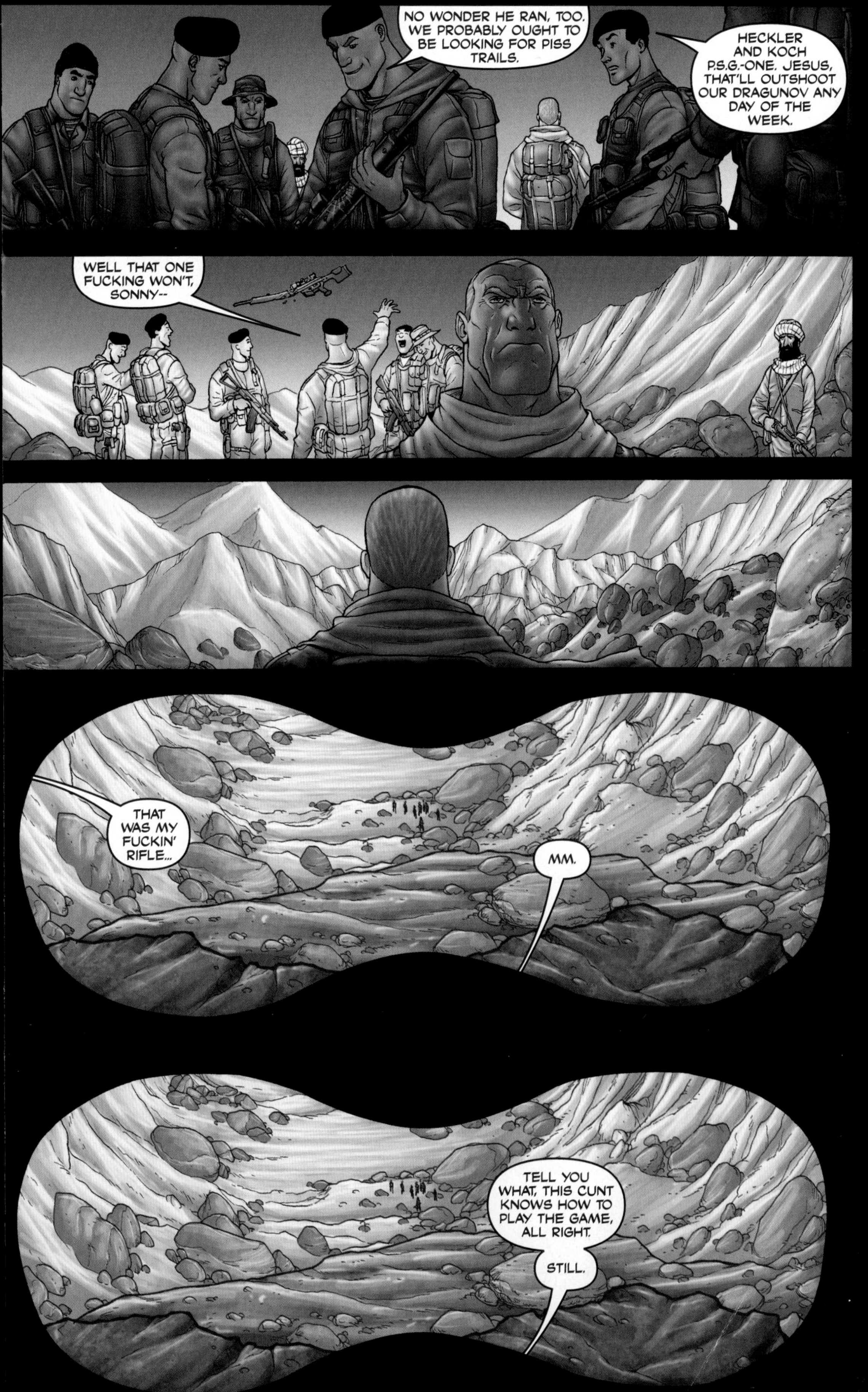
NO WONDER HE RAN, TOO. WE PROBABLY OUGHT TO BE LOOKING FOR PISS TRAILS.
HECKLER AND KOCH P.S.G.-ONE. JESUS, THAT'LL OUTSHOOT OUR DRAGUNOV ANY DAY OF THE WEEK.
WELL THAT ONE FUCKING WON'T, SONNY--
THAT WAS MY FUCKIN' RIFLE...
MM.
TELL YOU WHAT, THIS CUNT KNOWS HOW TO PLAY THE GAME, ALL RIGHT.
STILL.

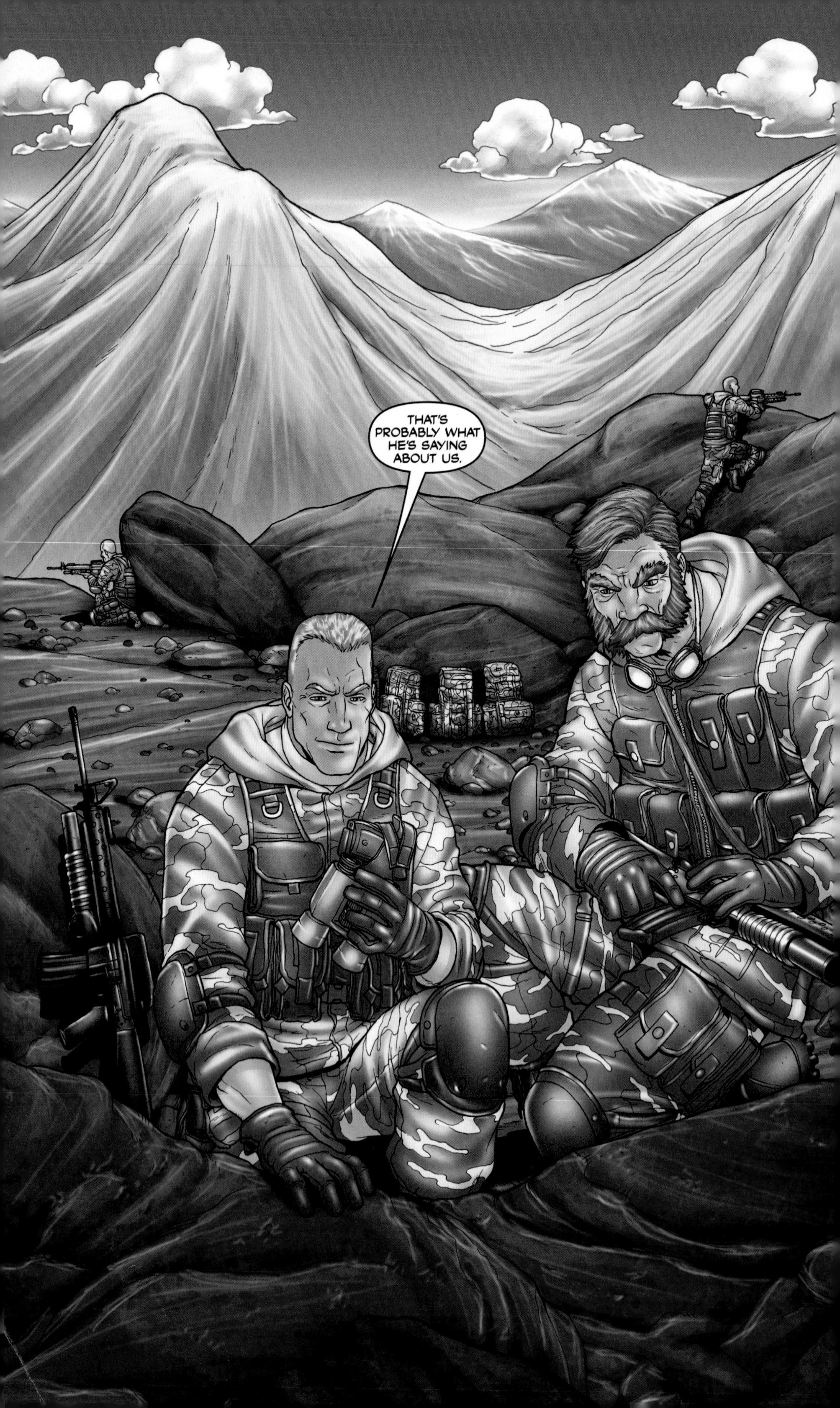
THAT'S PROBABLY WHAT HE'S SAYING ABOUT US.

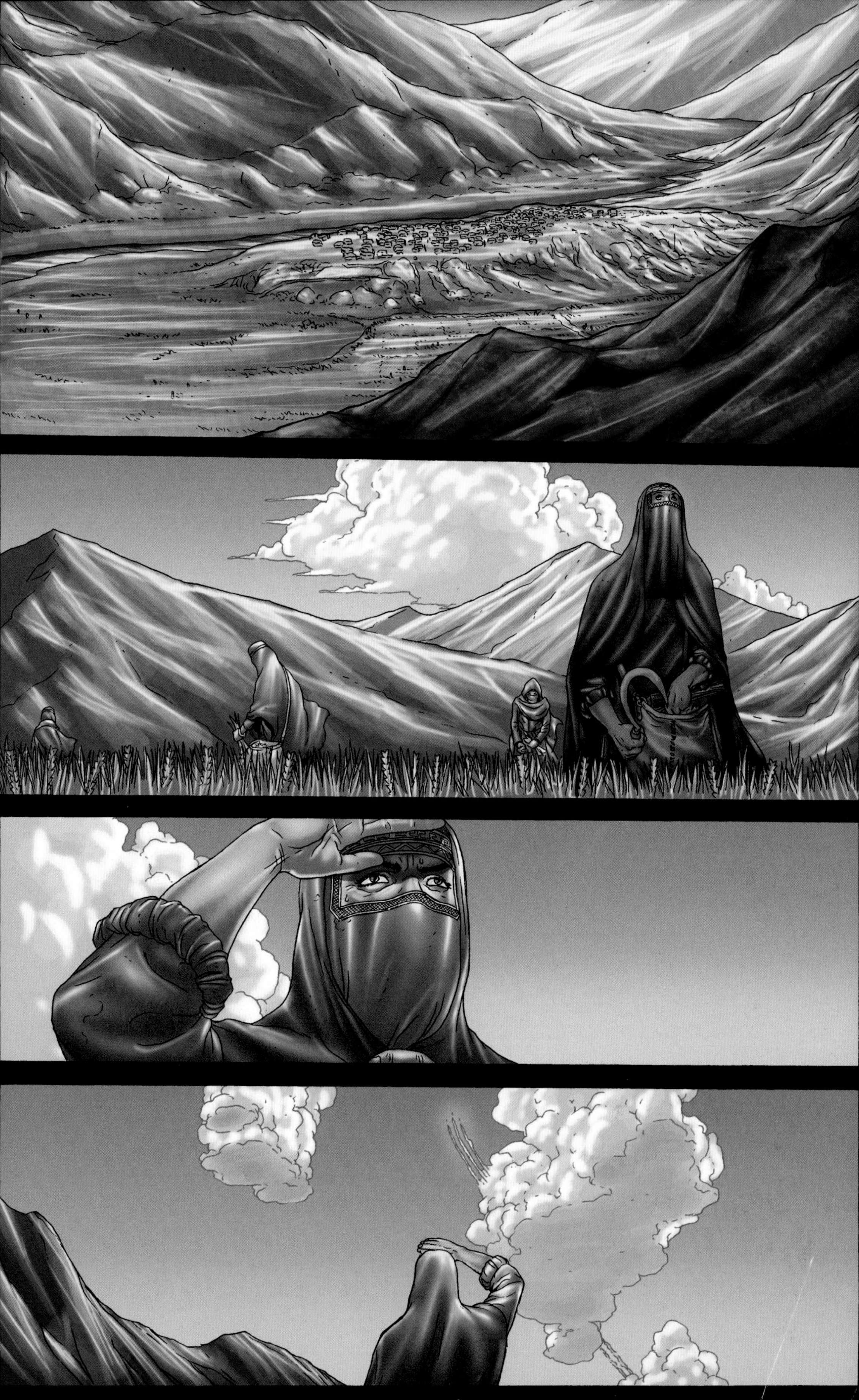

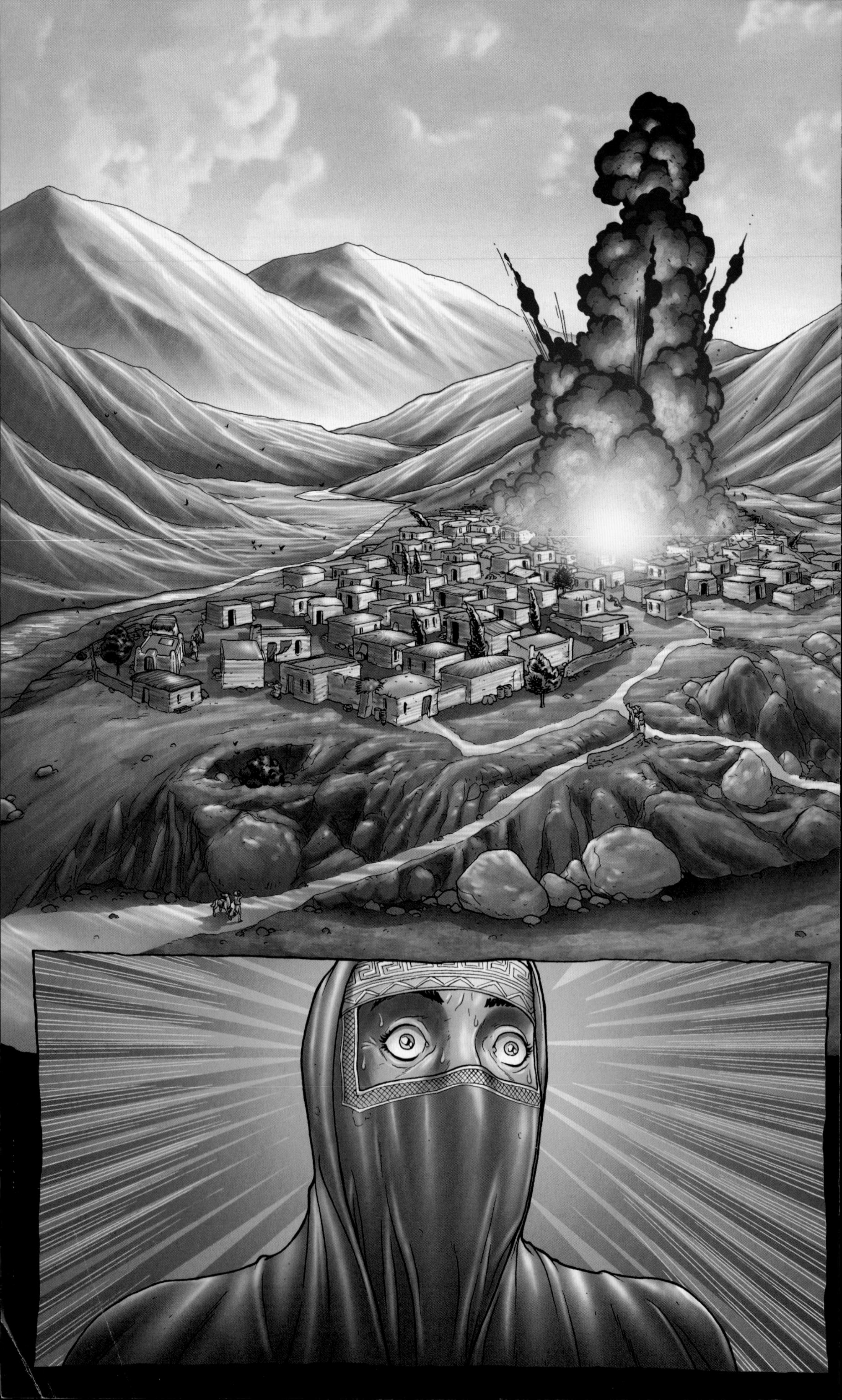

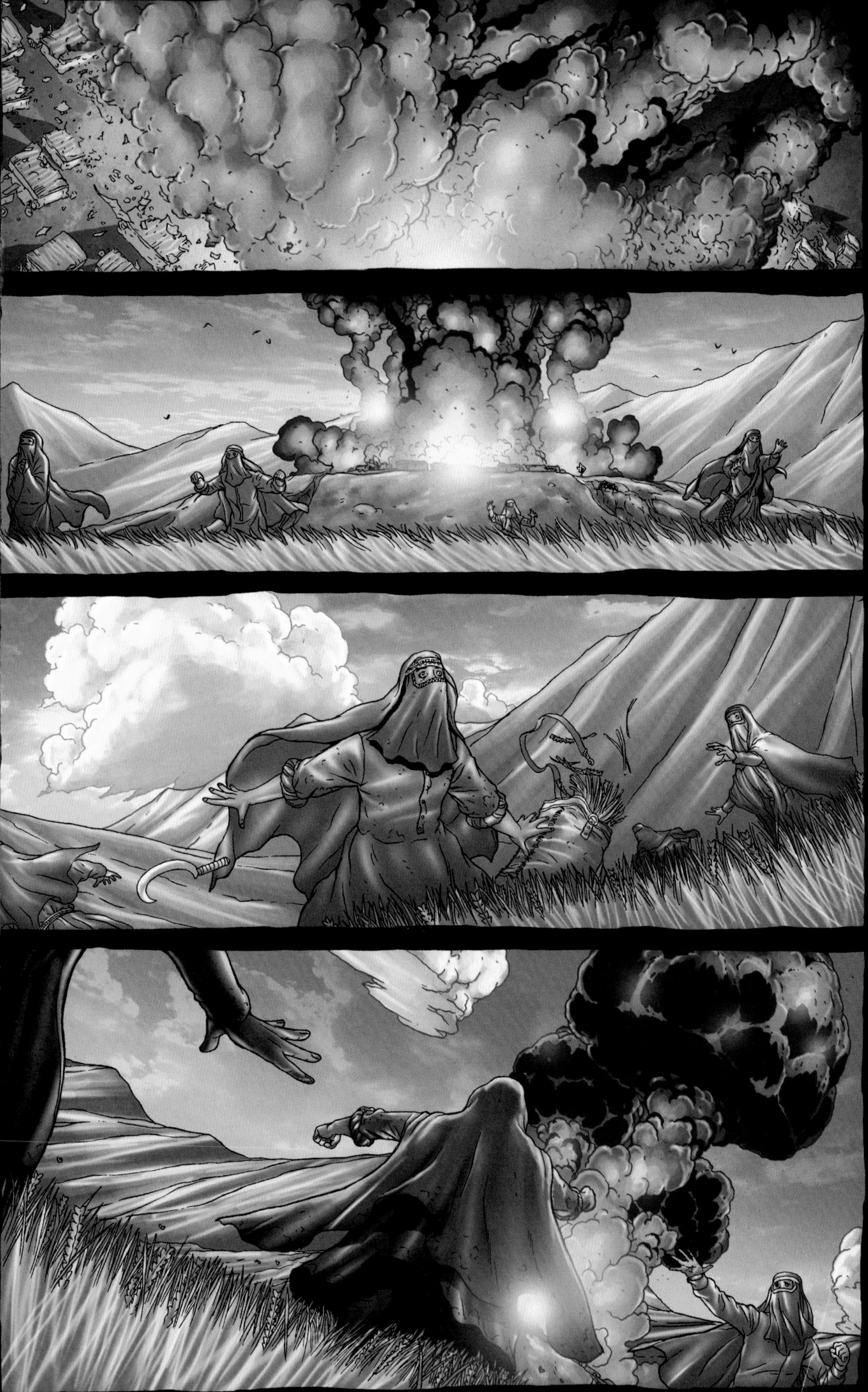

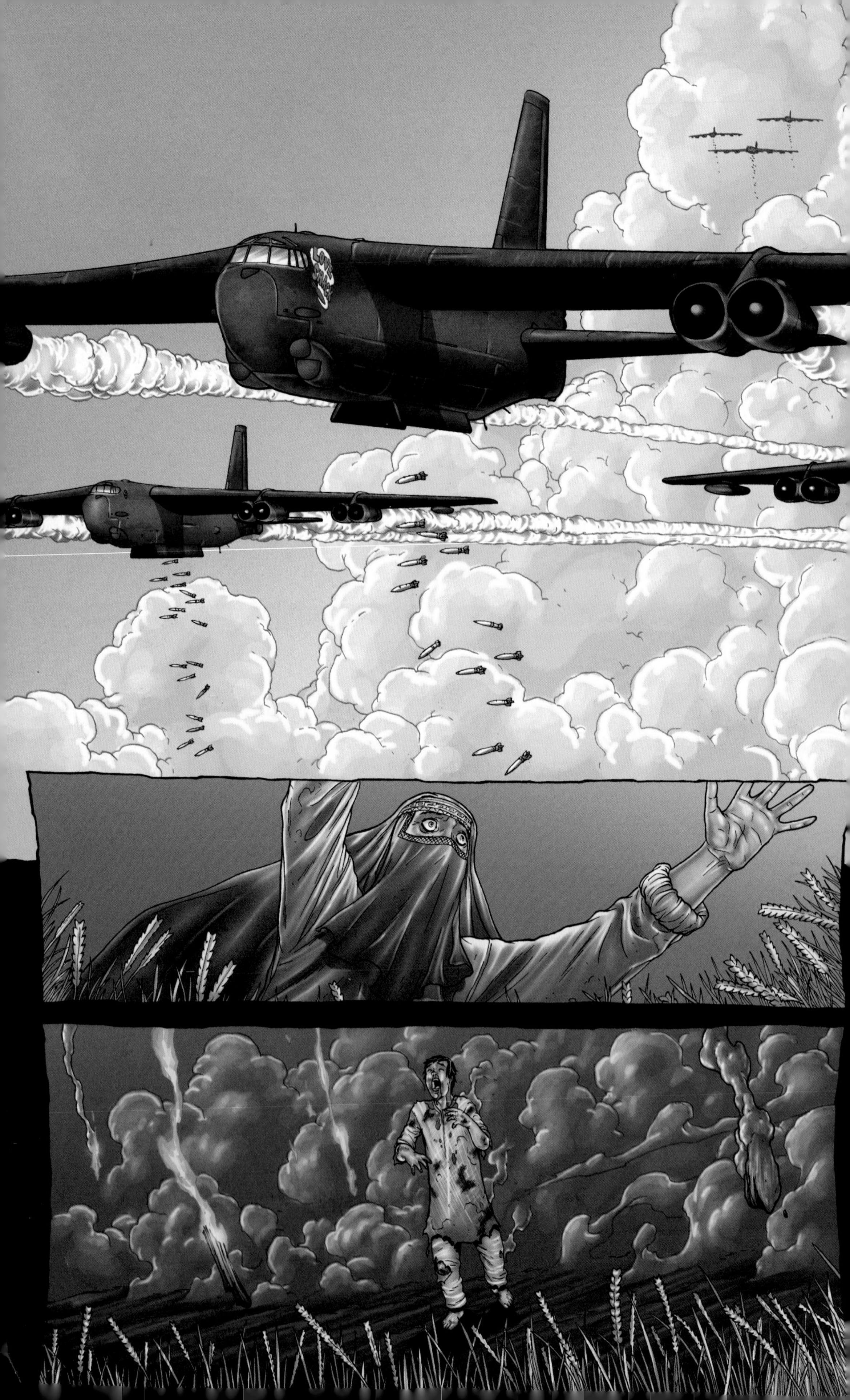
LOVE SHACK

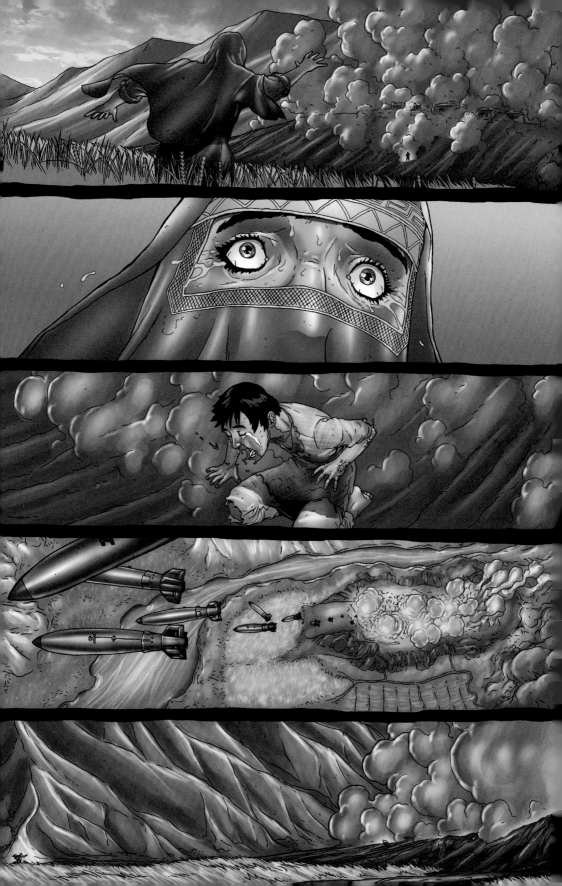

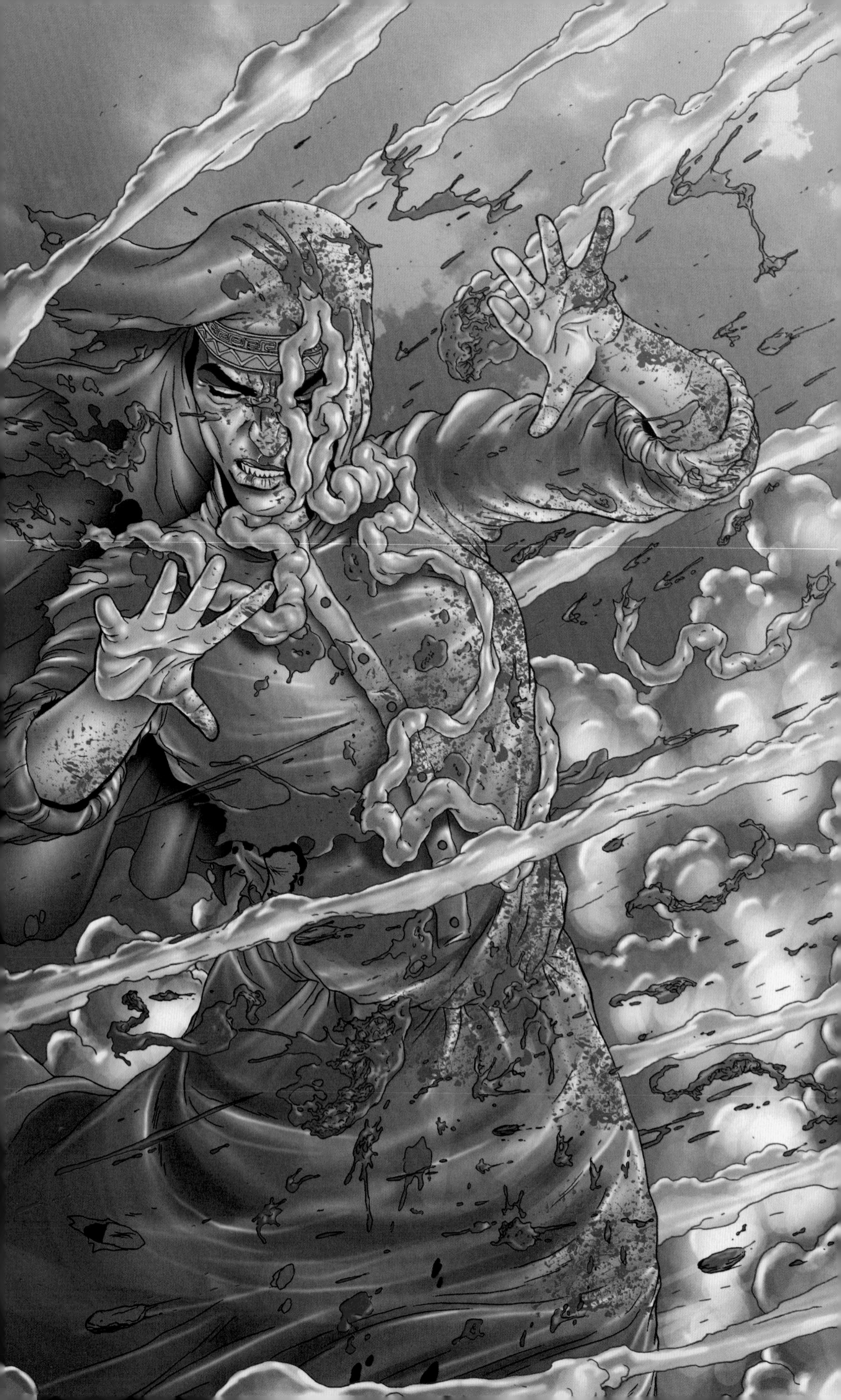

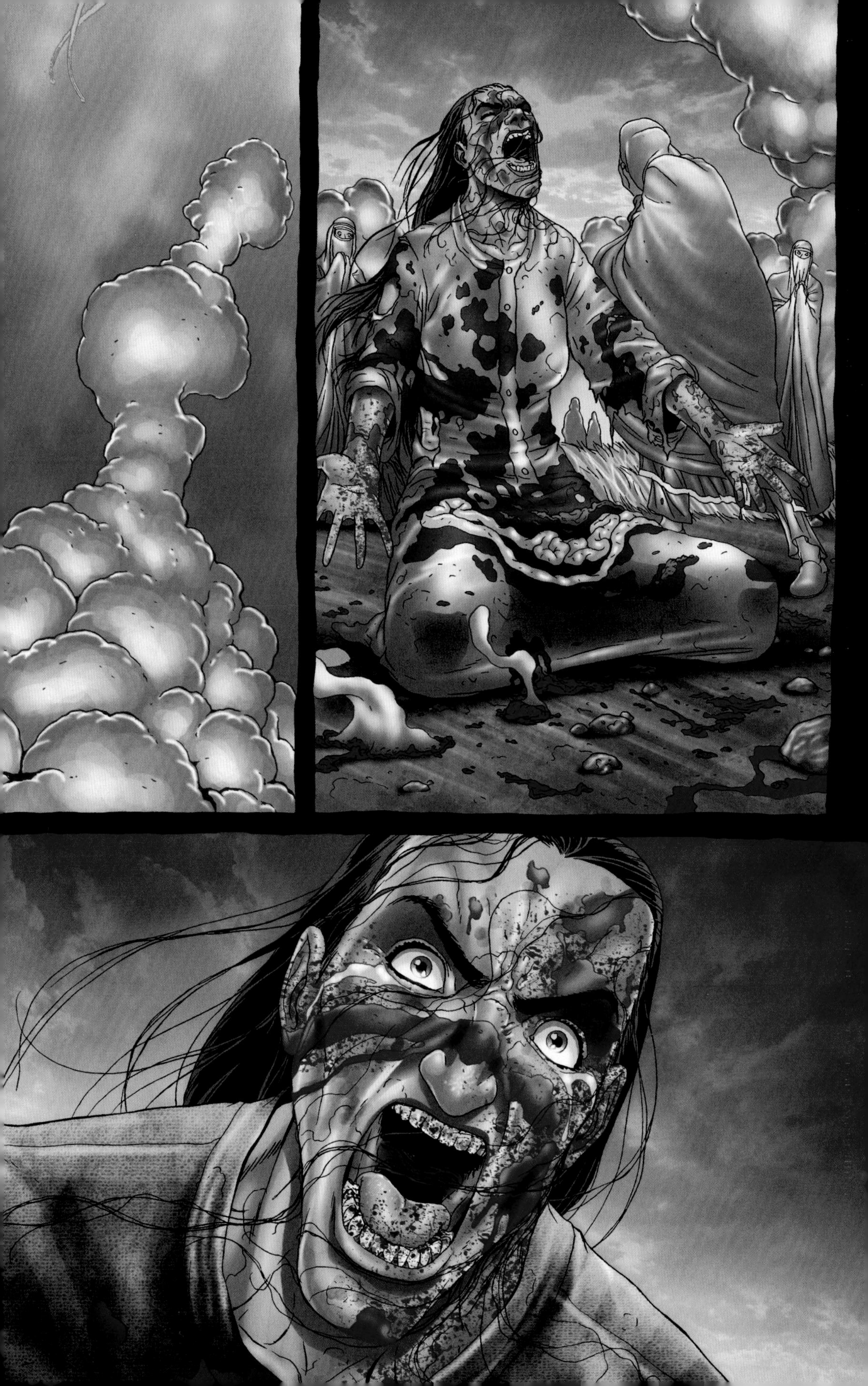

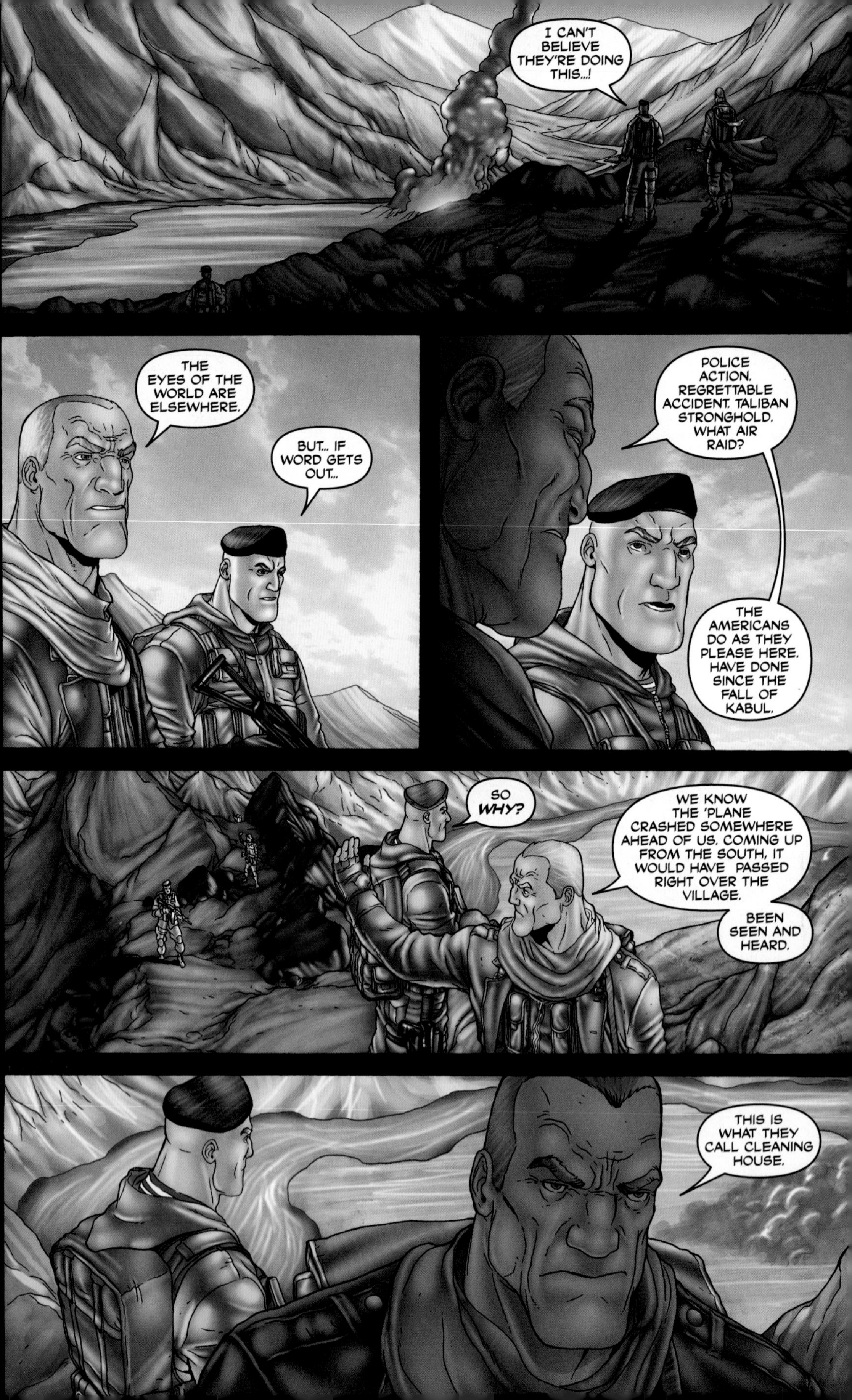
I CAN'T BELIEVE THEY'RE DOING THIS...!
THE EYES OF THE WORLD ARE ELSEWHERE.
BUT... IF WORD GETS OUT...
POLICE ACTION. REGRETTABLE ACCIDENT. TALIBAN STRONGHOLD. WHAT AIR RAID?
THE AMERICANS DO AS THEY PLEASE HERE. HAVE DONE SINCE THE FALL OF KABUL.
SO *WHY?*
WE KNOW THE 'PLANE CRASHED SOMEWHERE AHEAD OF US. COMING UP FROM THE SOUTH, IT WOULD HAVE PASSED RIGHT OVER THE VILLAGE.
BEEN SEEN AND HEARD.
THIS IS WHAT THEY CALL CLEANING HOUSE.

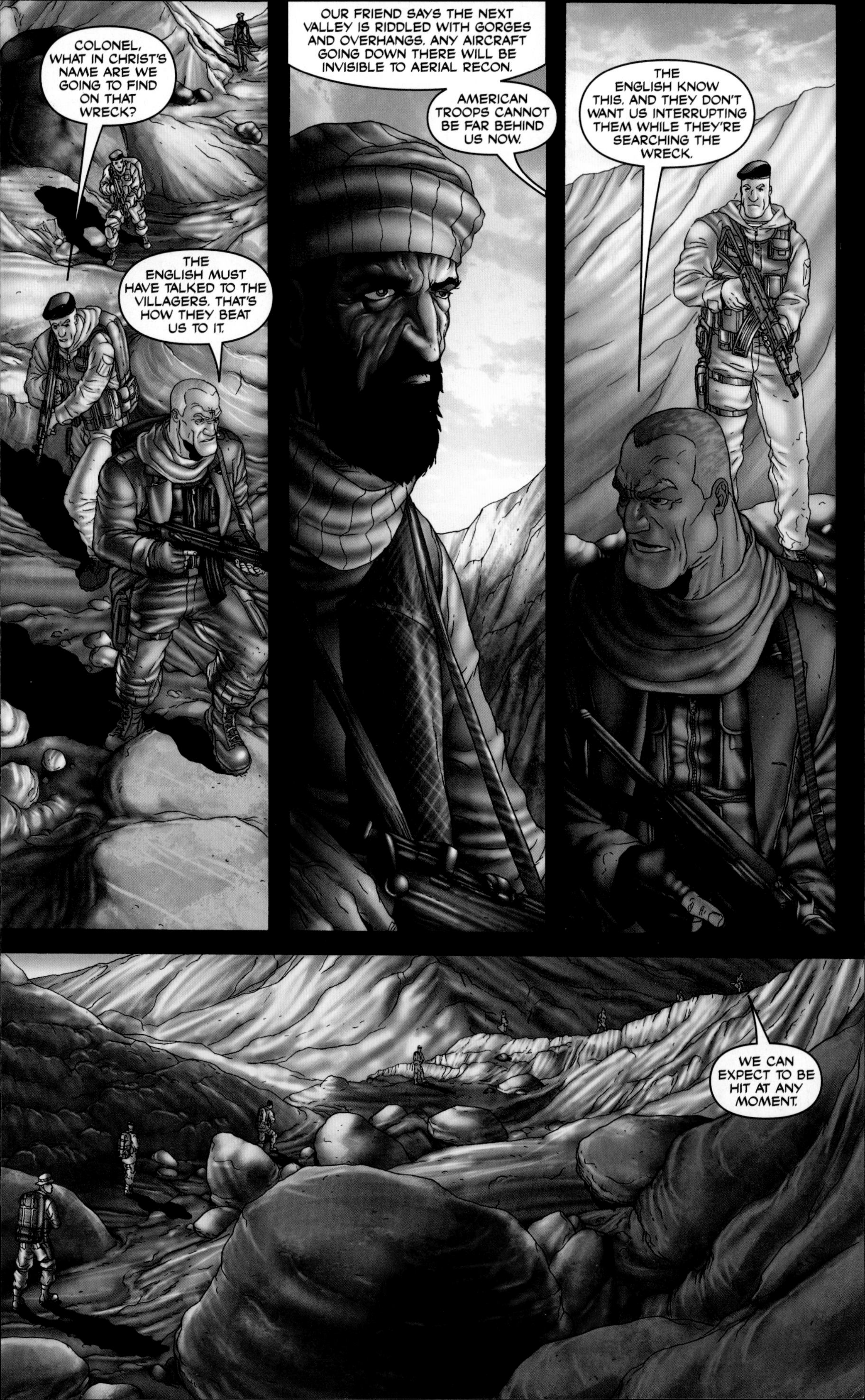
COLONEL, WHAT IN CHRIST'S NAME ARE WE GOING TO FIND ON THAT WRECK?
THE ENGLISH MUST HAVE TALKED TO THE VILLAGERS. THAT'S HOW THEY BEAT US TO IT.
OUR FRIEND SAYS THE NEXT VALLEY IS RIDDLED WITH GORGES AND OVERHANGS. ANY AIRCRAFT GOING DOWN THERE WILL BE INVISIBLE TO AERIAL RECON.
AMERICAN TROOPS CANNOT BE FAR BEHIND US NOW.
THE ENGLISH KNOW THIS, AND THEY DON'T WANT US INTERRUPTING THEM WHILE THEY'RE SEARCHING THE WRECK.
WE CAN EXPECT TO BE HIT AT ANY MOMENT.

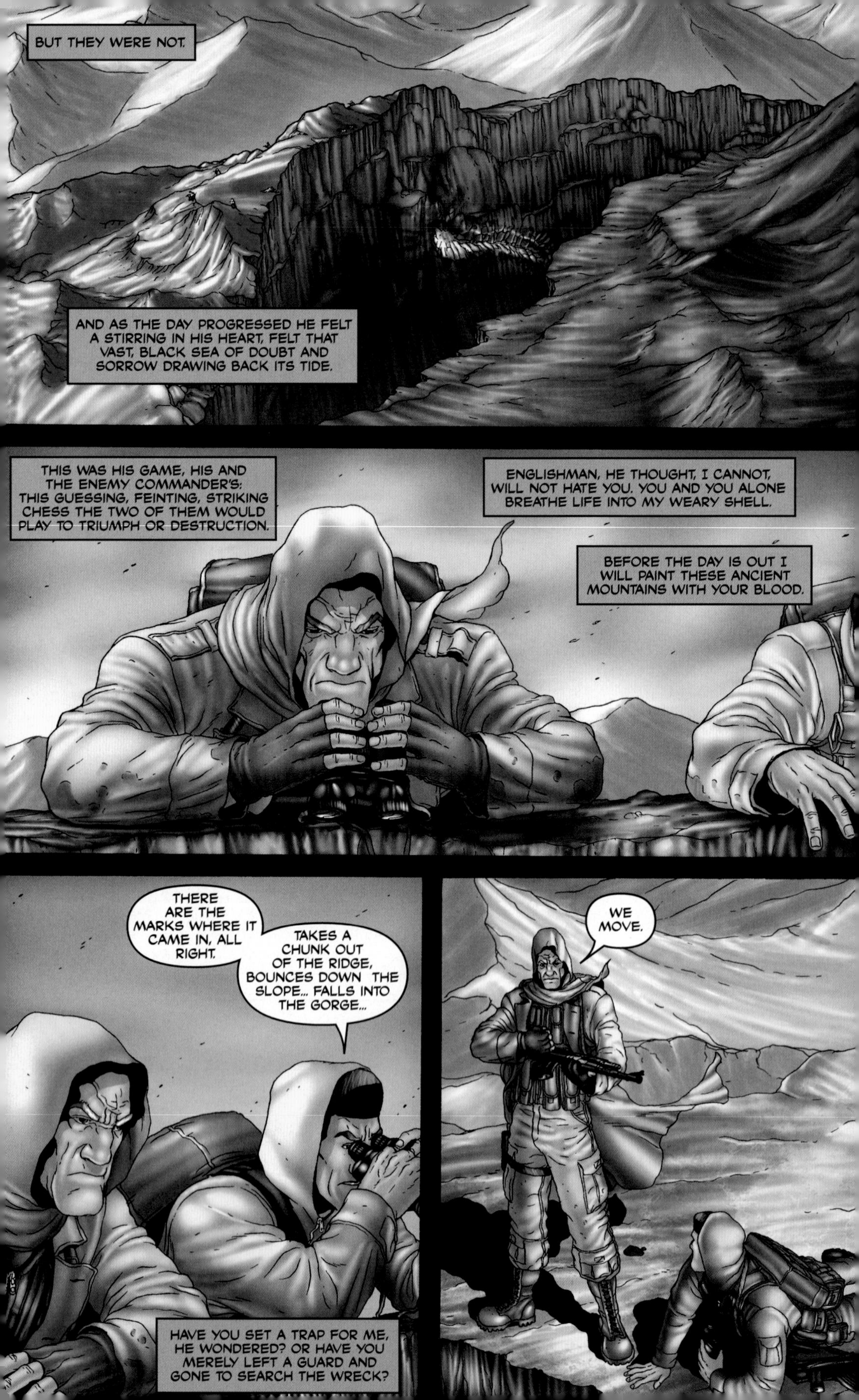
BUT THEY WERE NOT.
AND AS THE DAY PROGRESSED HE FELT A STIRRING IN HIS HEART, FELT THAT VAST, BLACK SEA OF DOUBT AND SORROW DRAWING BACK ITS TIDE.
THIS WAS HIS GAME, HIS AND THE ENEMY COMMANDER'S: THIS GUESSING, FEINTING, STRIKING CHESS THE TWO OF THEM WOULD PLAY TO TRIUMPH OR DESTRUCTION.
ENGLISHMAN, HE THOUGHT, I CANNOT, WILL NOT HATE YOU. YOU AND YOU ALONE BREATHE LIFE INTO MY WEARY SHELL.
BEFORE THE DAY IS OUT I WILL PAINT THESE ANCIENT MOUNTAINS WITH YOUR BLOOD.
THERE ARE THE MARKS WHERE IT CAME IN, ALL RIGHT.
TAKES A CHUNK OUT OF THE RIDGE, BOUNCES DOWN THE SLOPE... FALLS INTO THE GORGE...
HAVE YOU SET A TRAP FOR ME, HE WONDERED? OR HAVE YOU MERELY LEFT A GUARD AND GONE TO SEARCH THE WRECK?
WE MOVE.

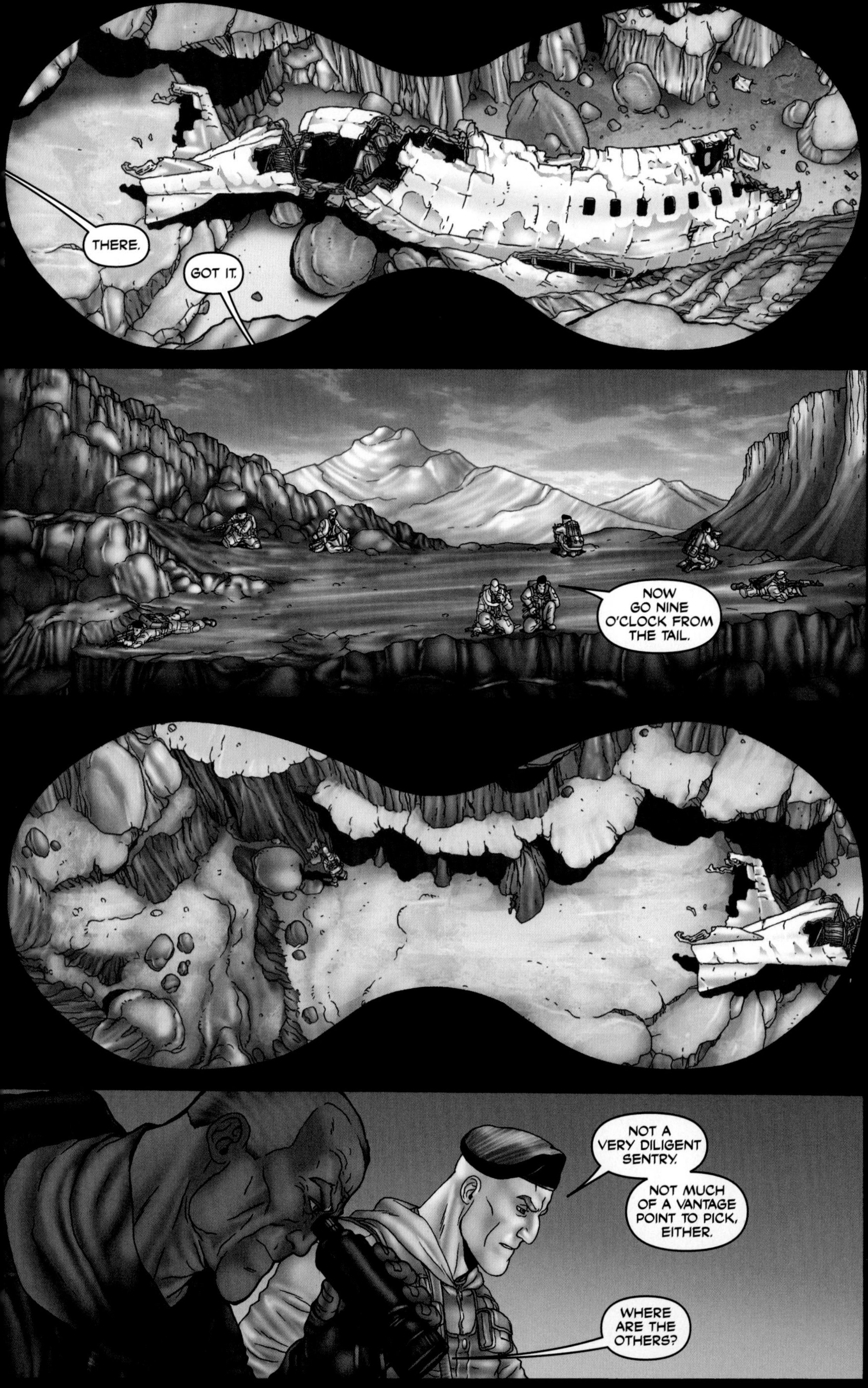
THERE.
GOT IT.
NOW GO NINE O'CLOCK FROM THE TAIL.
NOT A VERY DILIGENT SENTRY.
NOT MUCH OF A VANTAGE POINT TO PICK, EITHER.
WHERE ARE THE OTHERS?

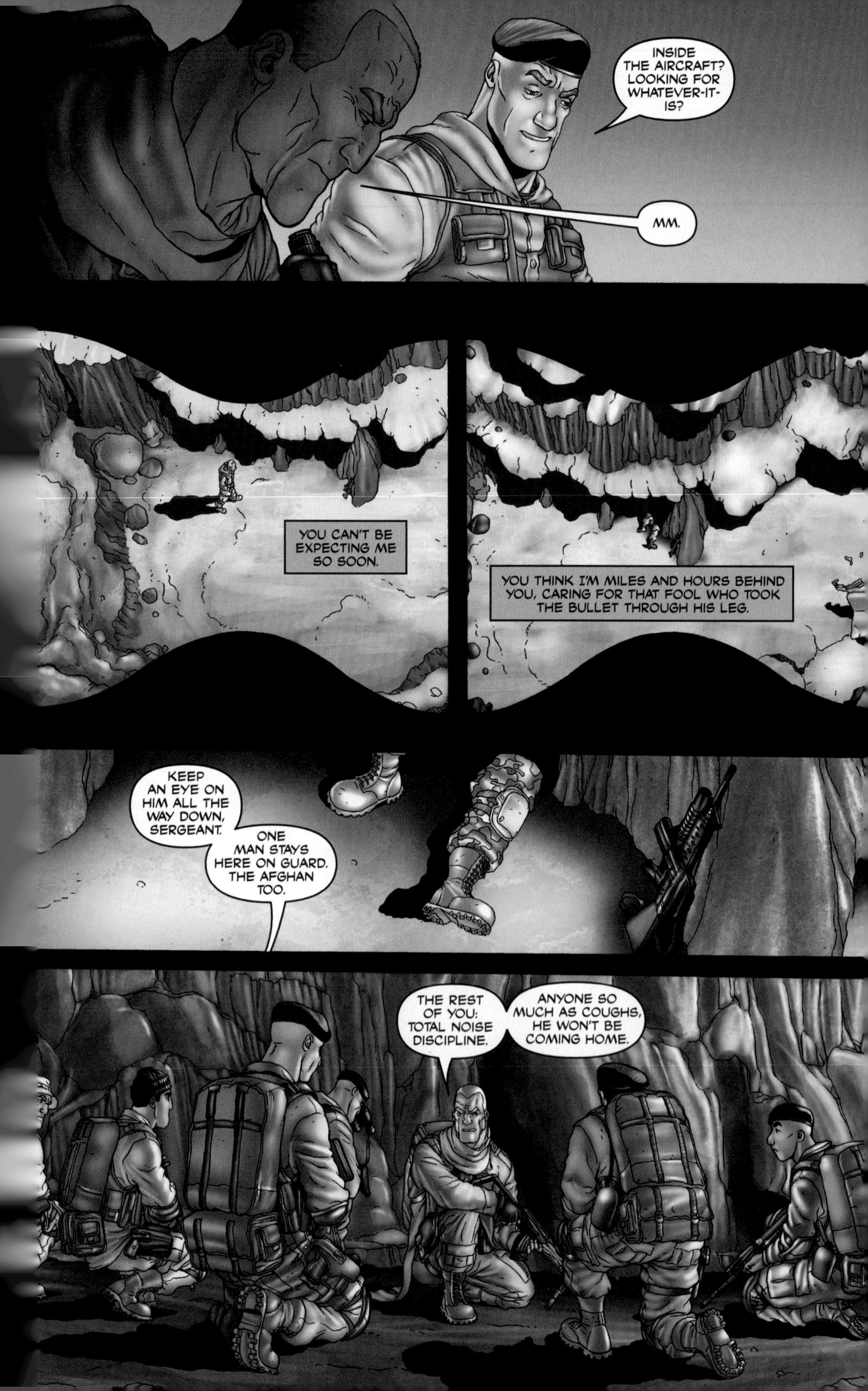
INSIDE THE AIRCRAFT? LOOKING FOR WHATEVER-IT-IS?
MM.
YOU CAN'T BE EXPECTING ME SO SOON.
YOU THINK I'M MILES AND HOURS BEHIND YOU, CARING FOR THAT FOOL WHO TOOK THE BULLET THROUGH HIS LEG.
KEEP AN EYE ON HIM ALL THE WAY DOWN, SERGEANT.
ONE MAN STAYS HERE ON GUARD. THE AFGHAN TOO.
THE REST OF YOU: TOTAL NOISE DISCIPLINE.
ANYONE SO MUCH AS COUGHS, HE WON'T BE COMING HOME.

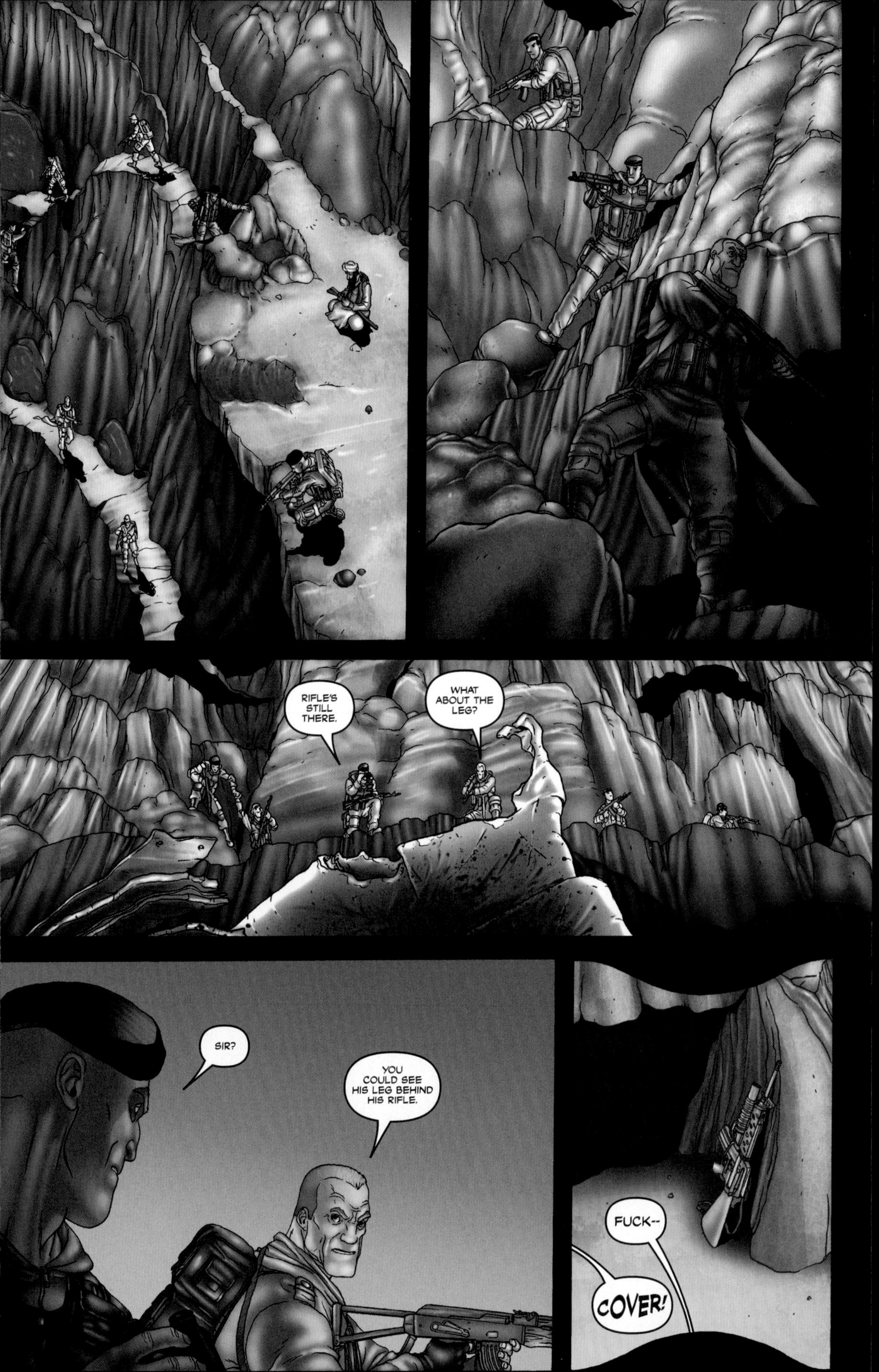
RIFLE'S STILL THERE.
WHAT ABOUT THE LEG?
SIR?
YOU COULD SEE HIS LEG BEHIND HIS RIFLE.
FUCK--
COVER!

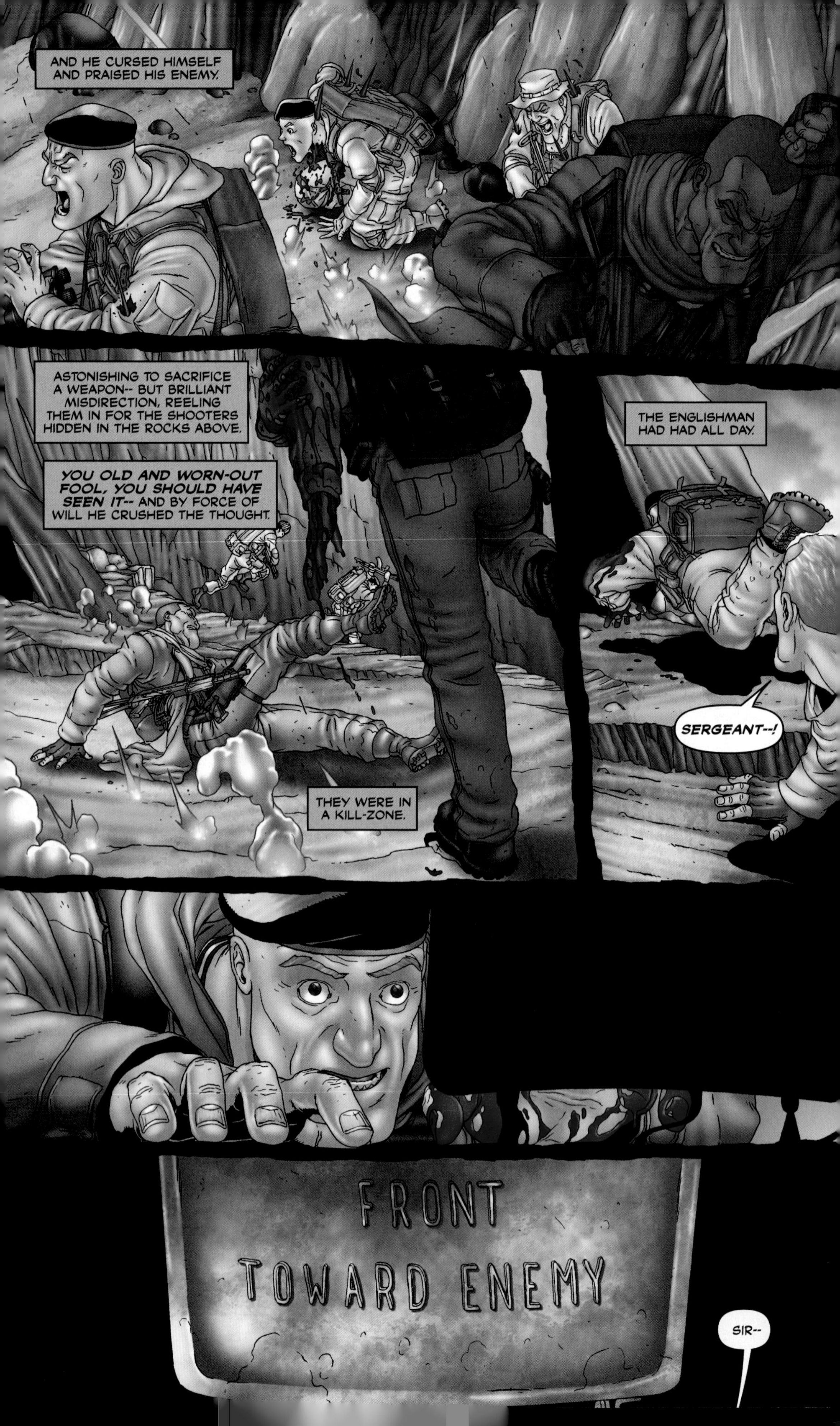

AND HE CURSED HIMSELF AND PRAISED HIS ENEMY.
ASTONISHING TO SACRIFICE A WEAPON-- BUT BRILLIANT MISDIRECTION, REELING THEM IN FOR THE SHOOTERS HIDDEN IN THE ROCKS ABOVE.
YOU OLD AND WORN-OUT FOOL, YOU SHOULD HAVE SEEN IT-- AND BY FORCE OF WILL HE CRUSHED THE THOUGHT.
THEY WERE IN A KILL-ZONE.
THE ENGLISHMAN HAD HAD ALL DAY.
SERGEANT--!
FRONT
TOWARD ENEMY
SIR--

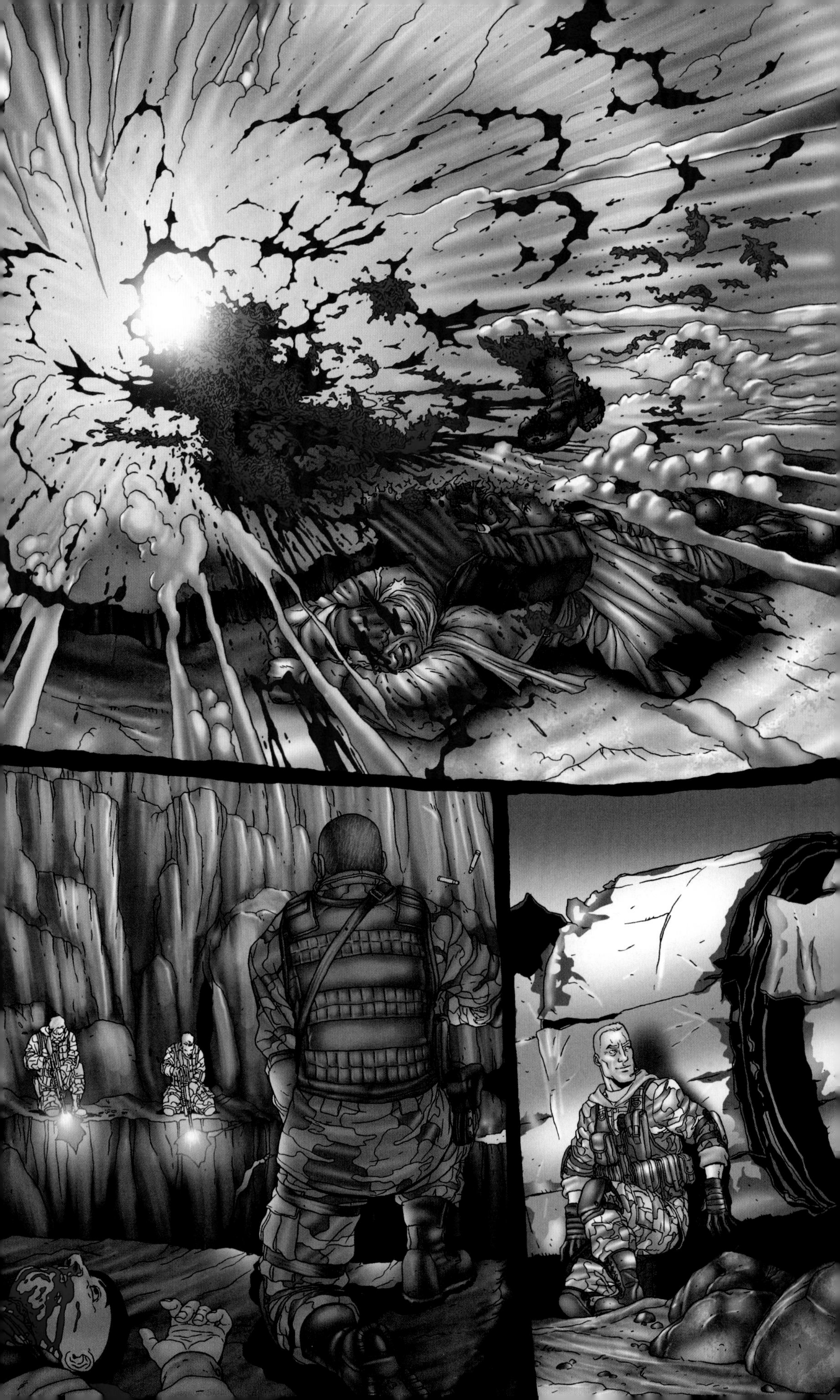

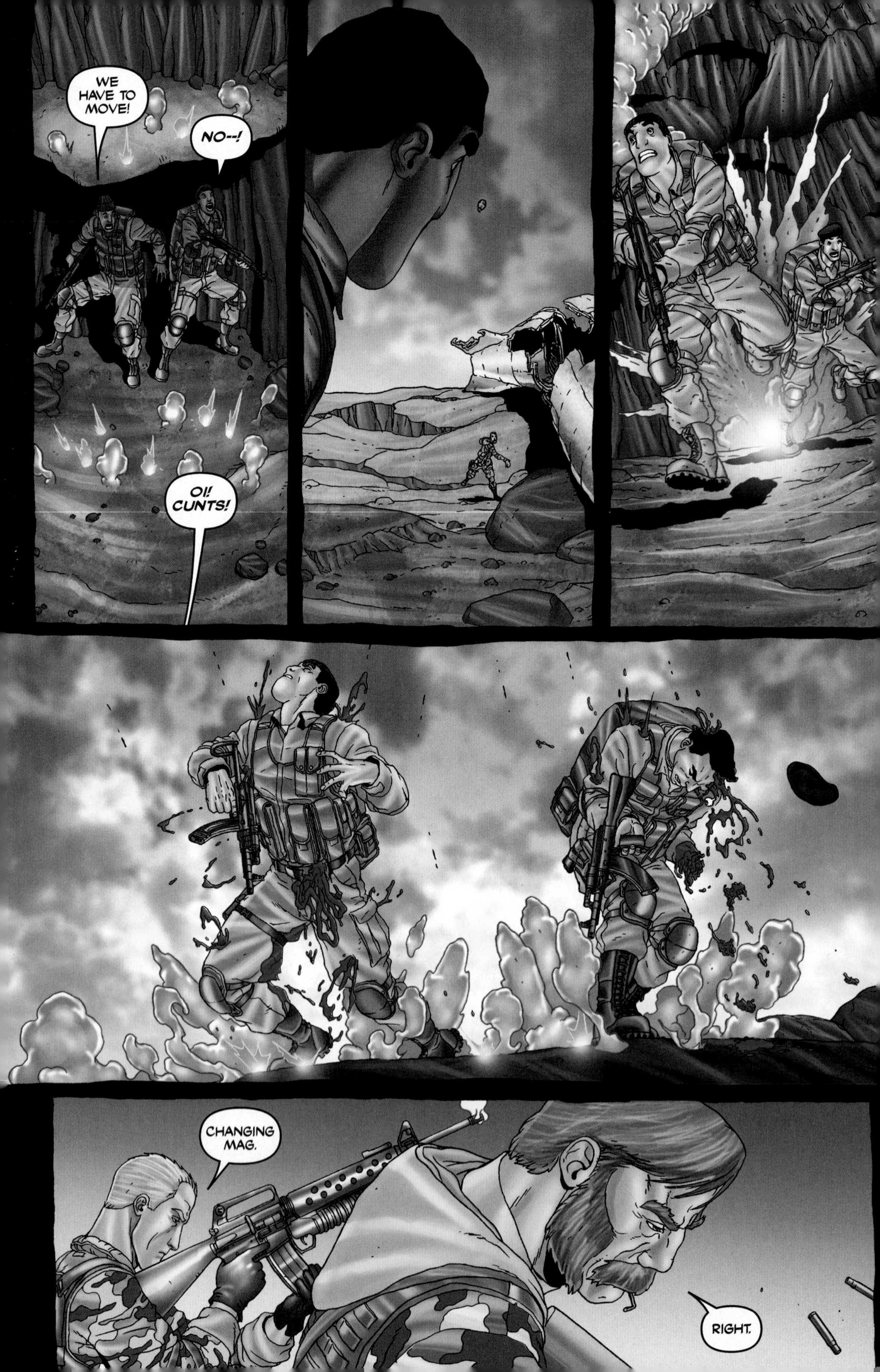
WE HAVE TO MOVE!
NO--!
OI! CUNTS!
CHANGING MAG.
RIGHT.

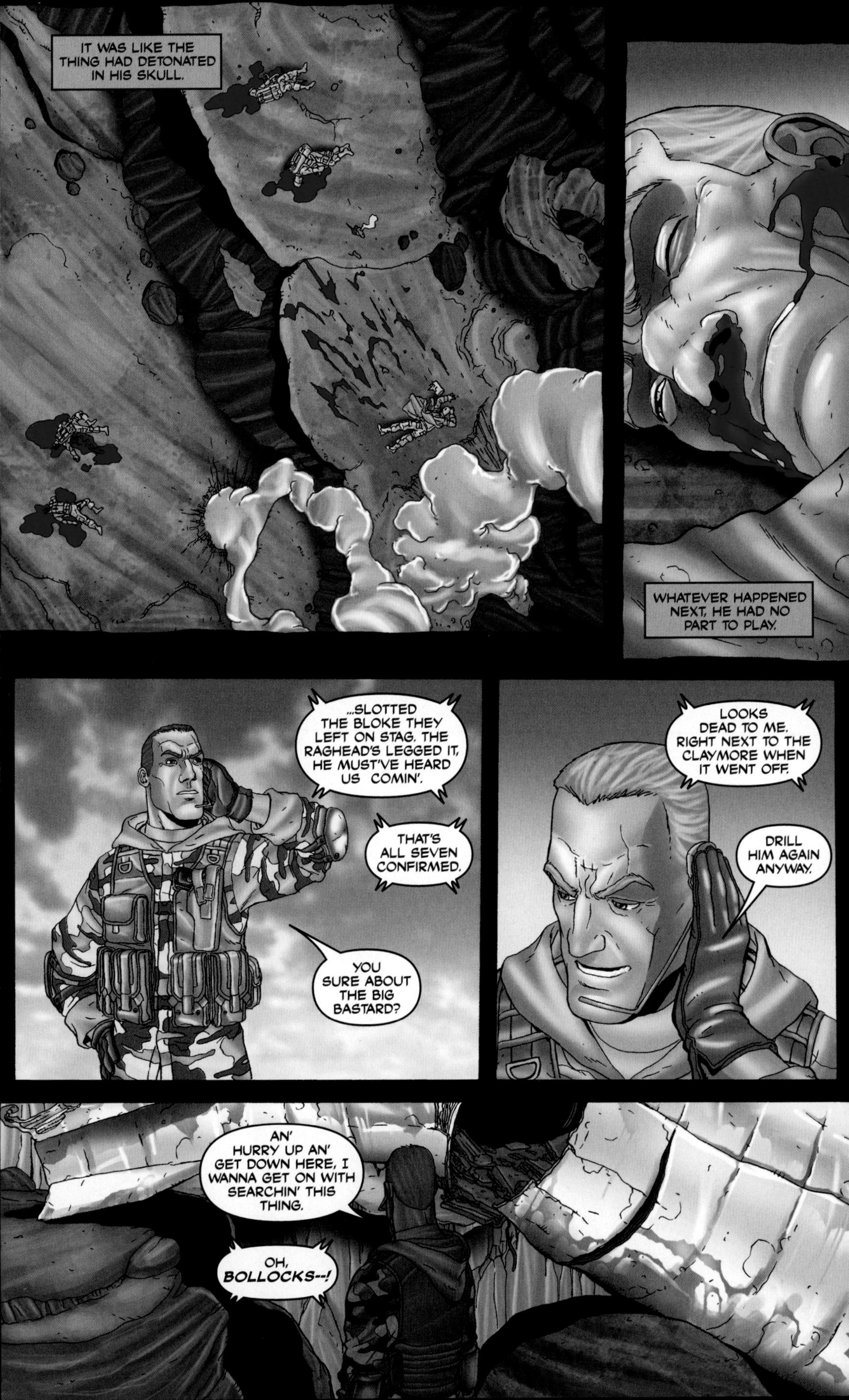
IT WAS LIKE THE THING HAD DETONATED IN HIS SKULL.
WHATEVER HAPPENED NEXT, HE HAD NO PART TO PLAY.
...SLOTTED THE BLOKE THEY LEFT ON STAG. THE RAGHEAD'S LEGGED IT, HE MUST'VE HEARD US COMIN'.
THAT'S ALL SEVEN CONFIRMED.
YOU SURE ABOUT THE BIG BASTARD?
LOOKS DEAD TO ME. RIGHT NEXT TO THE CLAYMORE WHEN IT WENT OFF.
DRILL HIM AGAIN ANYWAY.
AN' HURRY UP AN' GET DOWN HERE, I WANNA GET ON WITH SEARCHIN' THIS THING.
OH, BOLLOCKS--!

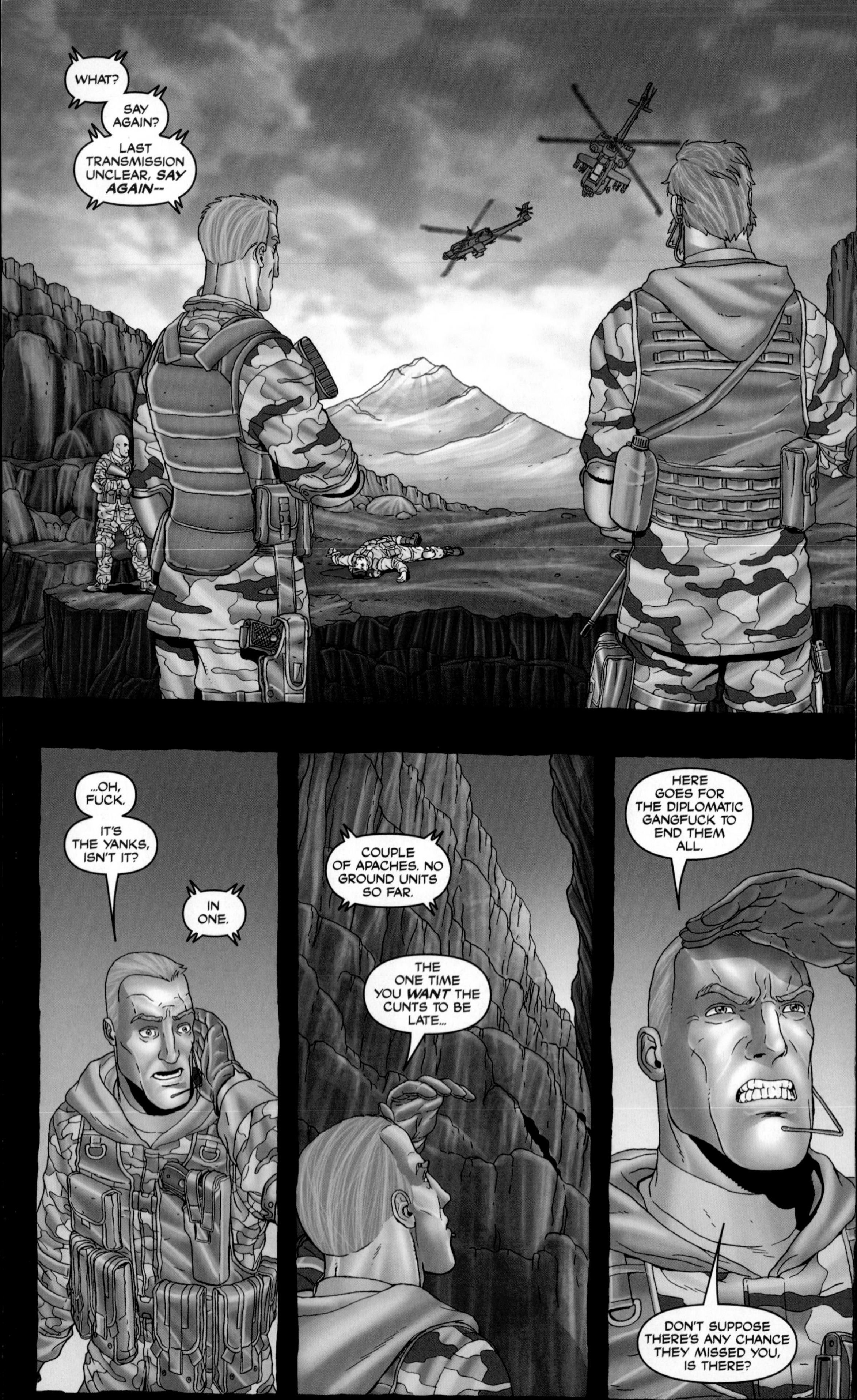
WHAT?
SAY AGAIN?
LAST TRANSMISSION UNCLEAR, *SAY AGAIN--*
...OH, FUCK.
IT'S THE YANKS, ISN'T IT?
IN ONE.
COUPLE OF APACHES. NO GROUND UNITS SO FAR.
THE ONE TIME YOU *WANT* THE CUNTS TO BE LATE...
HERE GOES FOR THE DIPLOMATIC GANGFUCK TO END THEM ALL.
DON'T SUPPOSE THERE'S ANY CHANCE THEY MISSED YOU, IS THERE?

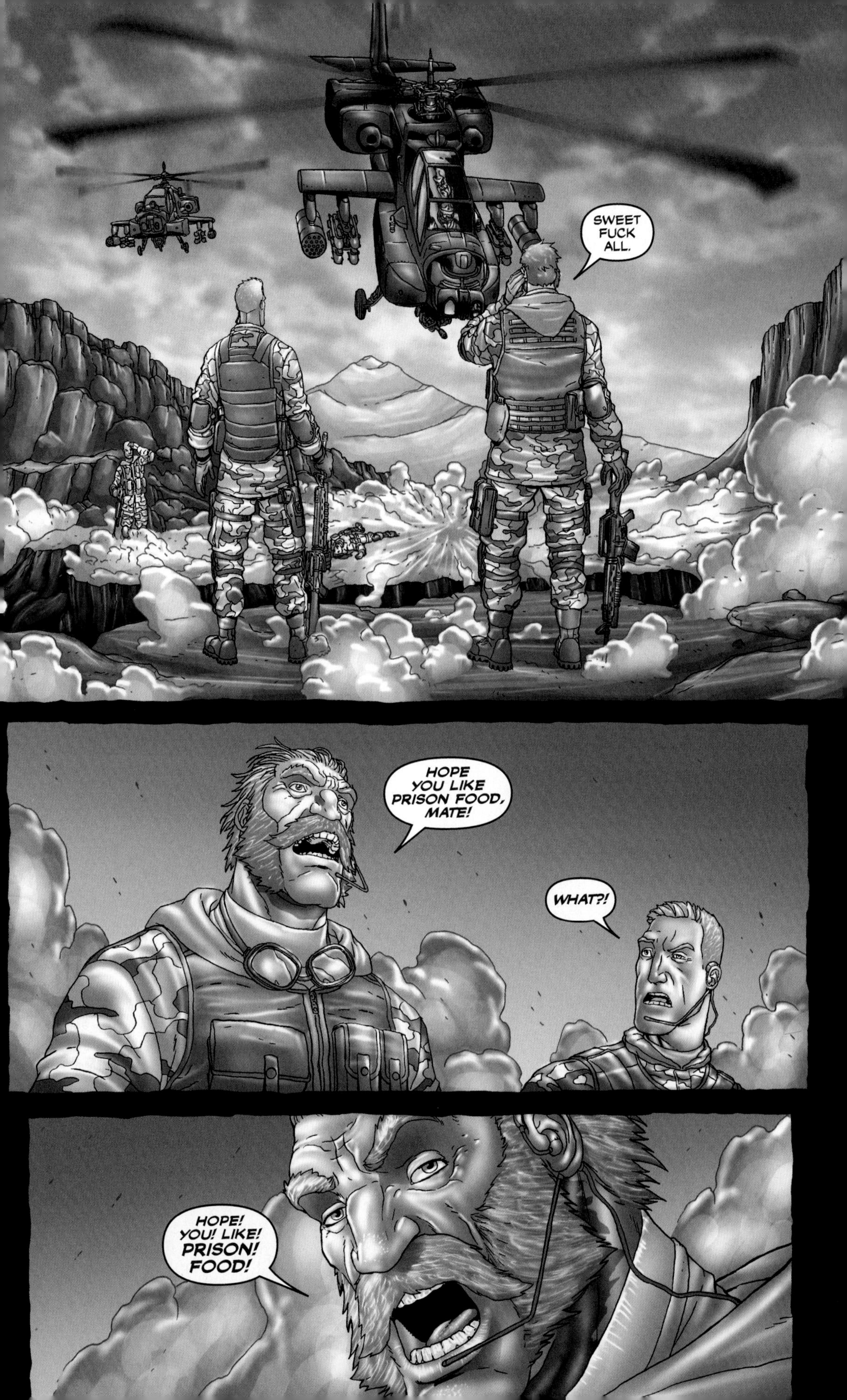
SWEET FUCK ALL.
HOPE YOU LIKE PRISON FOOD, MATE!
WHAT?!
HOPE! YOU! LIKE! PRISON! FOOD!

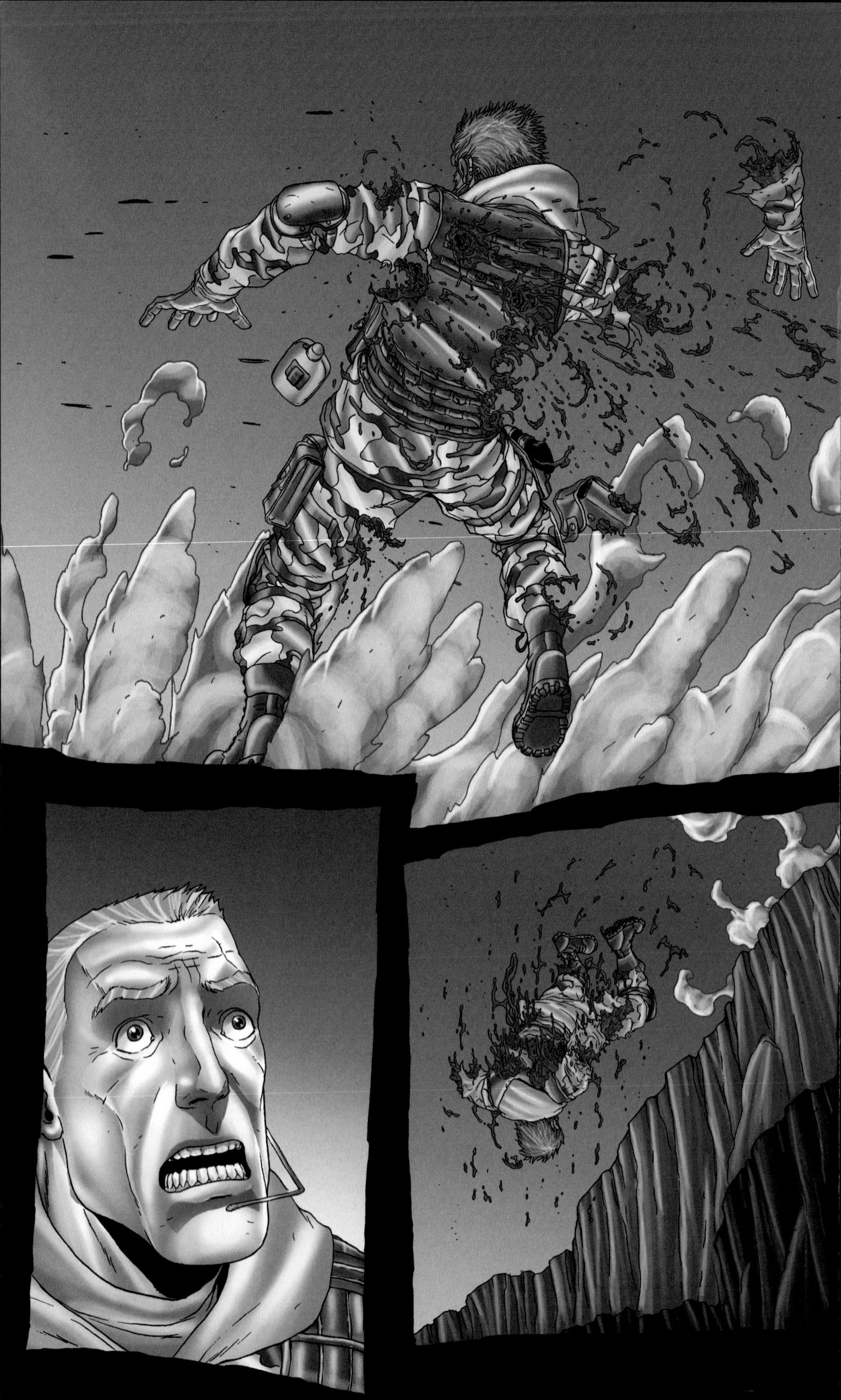

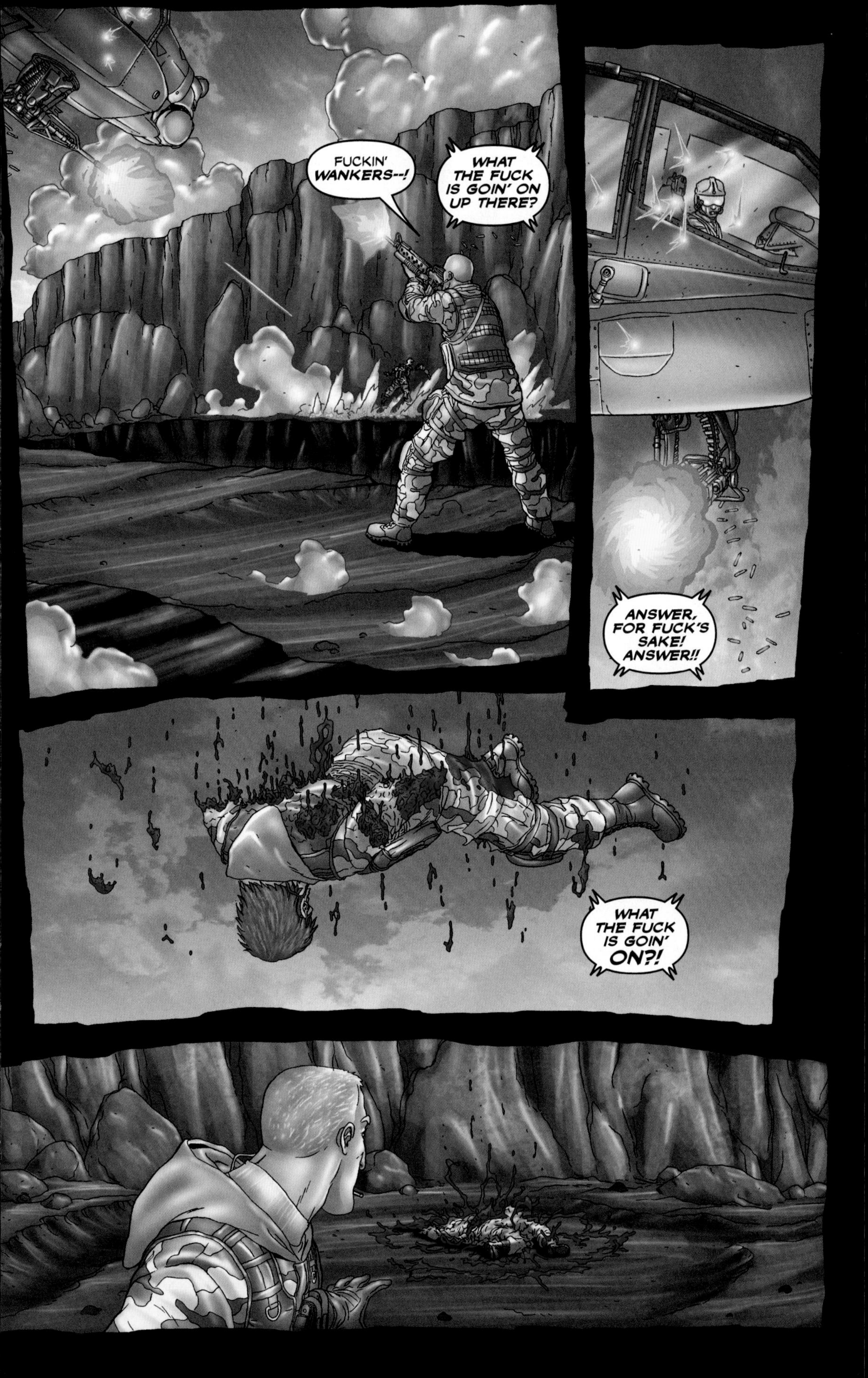
FUCKIN' WANKERS--!
WHAT THE FUCK IS GOIN' ON UP THERE?
ANSWER, FOR FUCK'S SAKE! ANSWER!!
WHAT THE FUCK IS GOIN' ON?!

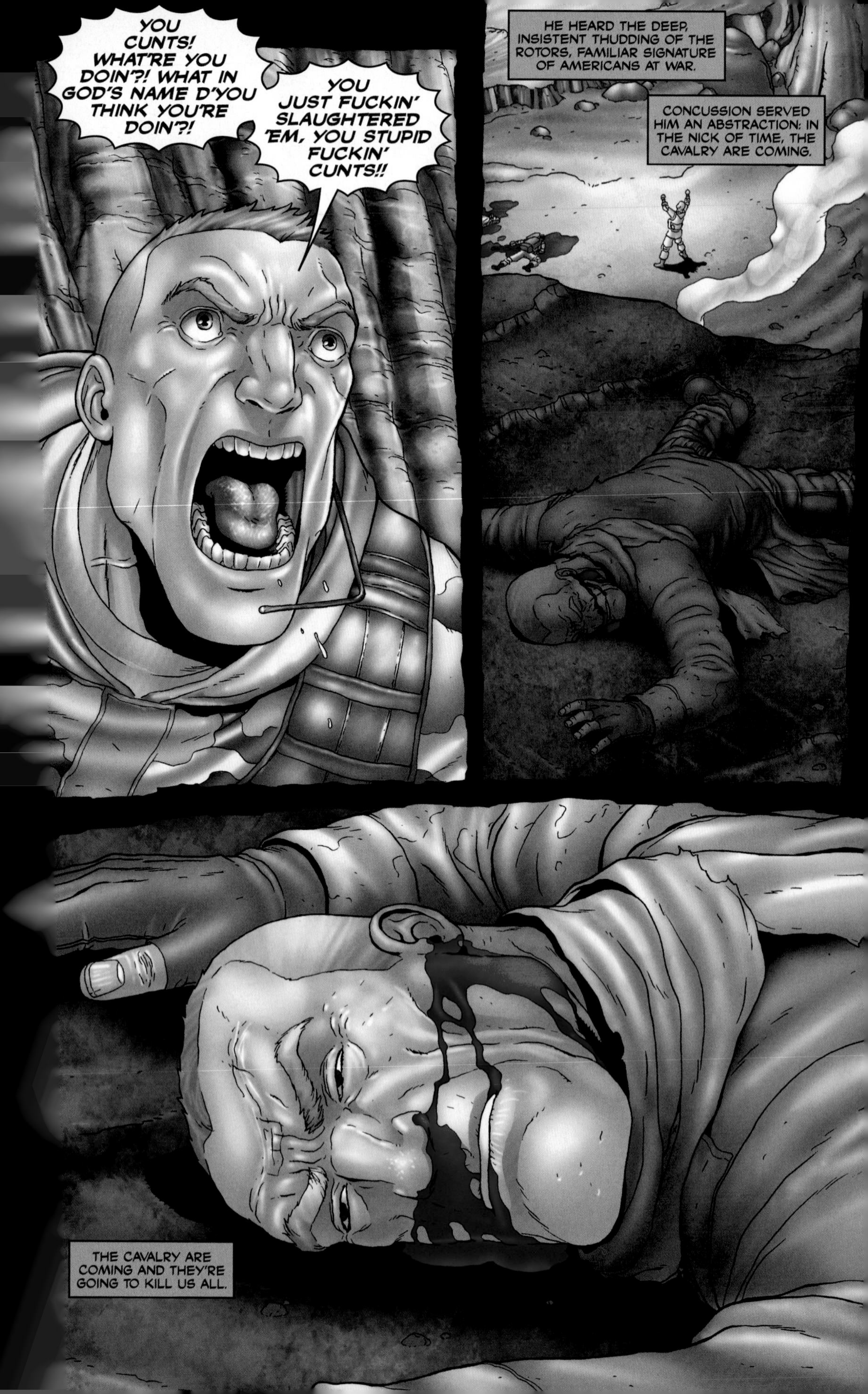
YOU CUNTS! WHAT'RE YOU DOIN'?! WHAT IN GOD'S NAME D'YOU THINK YOU'RE DOIN'?!
YOU JUST FUCKIN' SLAUGHTERED 'EM, YOU STUPID FUCKIN' CUNTS!!
HE HEARD THE DEEP, INSISTENT THUDDING OF THE ROTORS, FAMILIAR SIGNATURE OF AMERICANS AT WAR.
CONCUSSION SERVED HIM AN ABSTRACTION: IN THE NICK OF TIME, THE CAVALRY ARE COMING.
THE CAVALRY ARE COMING AND THEY'RE GOING TO KILL US ALL.

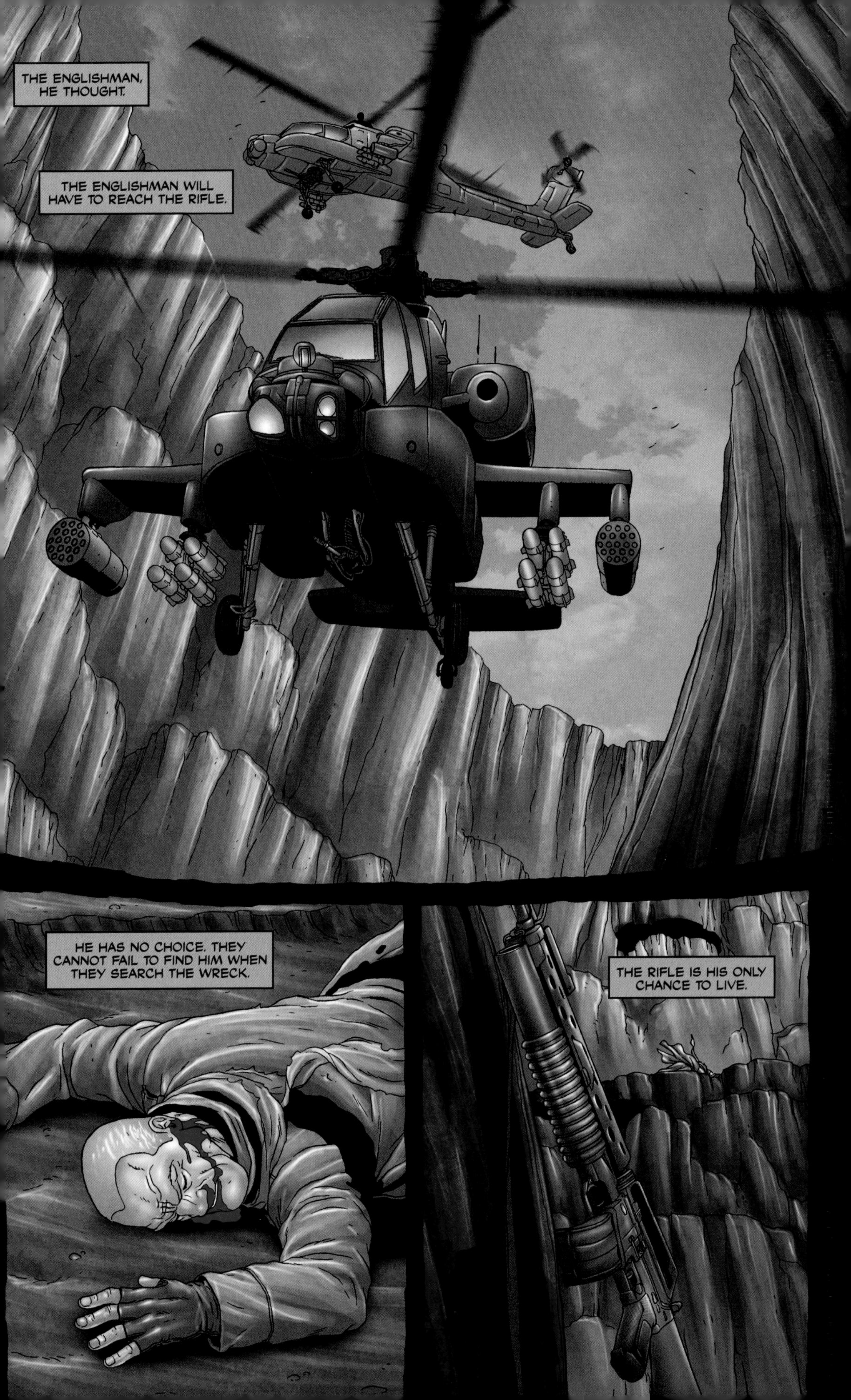
THE ENGLISHMAN, HE THOUGHT.
THE ENGLISHMAN WILL HAVE TO REACH THE RIFLE.
HE HAS NO CHOICE. THEY CANNOT FAIL TO FIND HIM WHEN THEY SEARCH THE WRECK.
THE RIFLE IS HIS ONLY CHANCE TO LIVE.

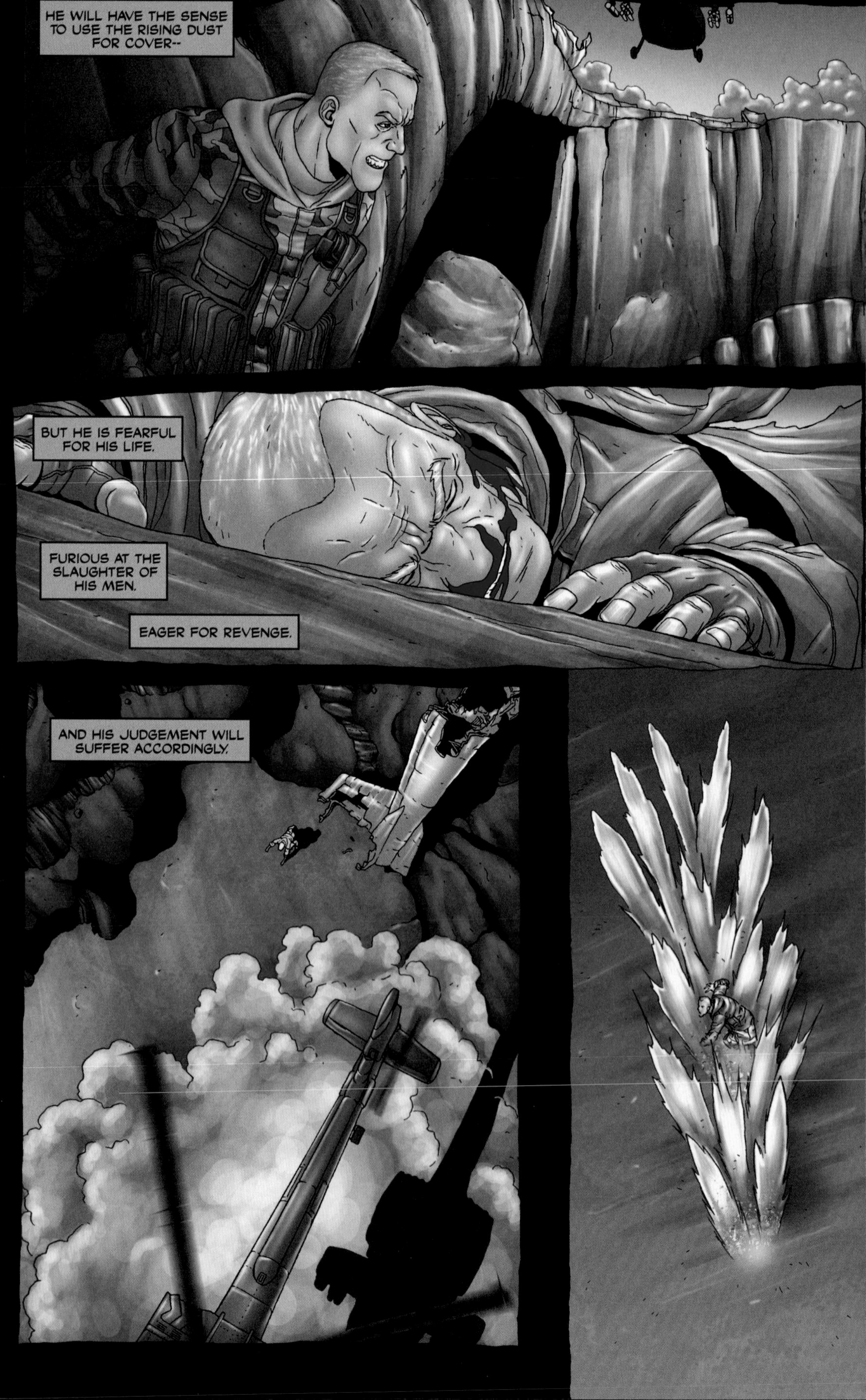
HE WILL HAVE THE SENSE TO USE THE RISING DUST FOR COVER--
BUT HE IS FEARFUL FOR HIS LIFE.
FURIOUS AT THE SLAUGHTER OF HIS MEN.
EAGER FOR REVENGE.
AND HIS JUDGEMENT WILL SUFFER ACCORDINGLY.

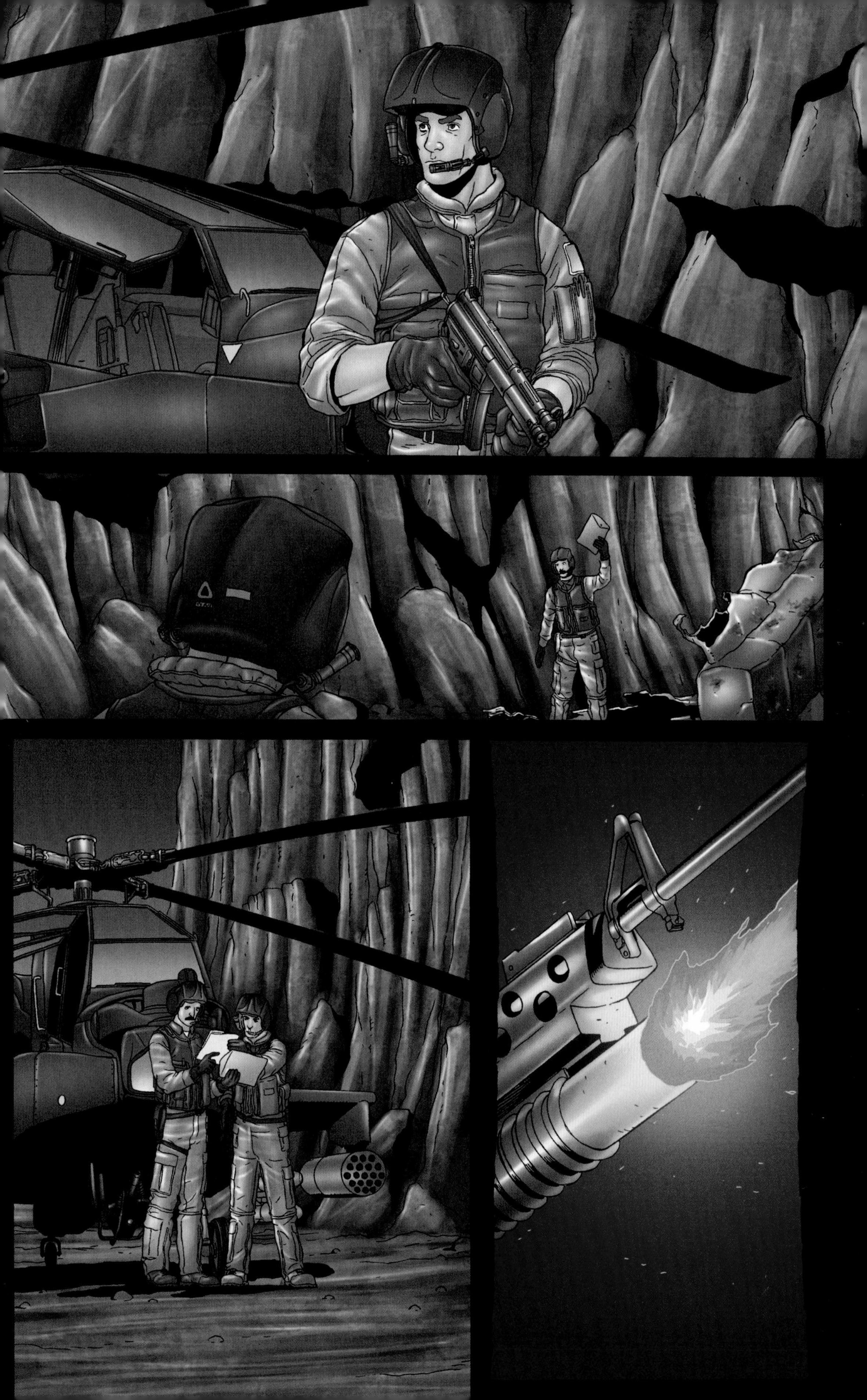

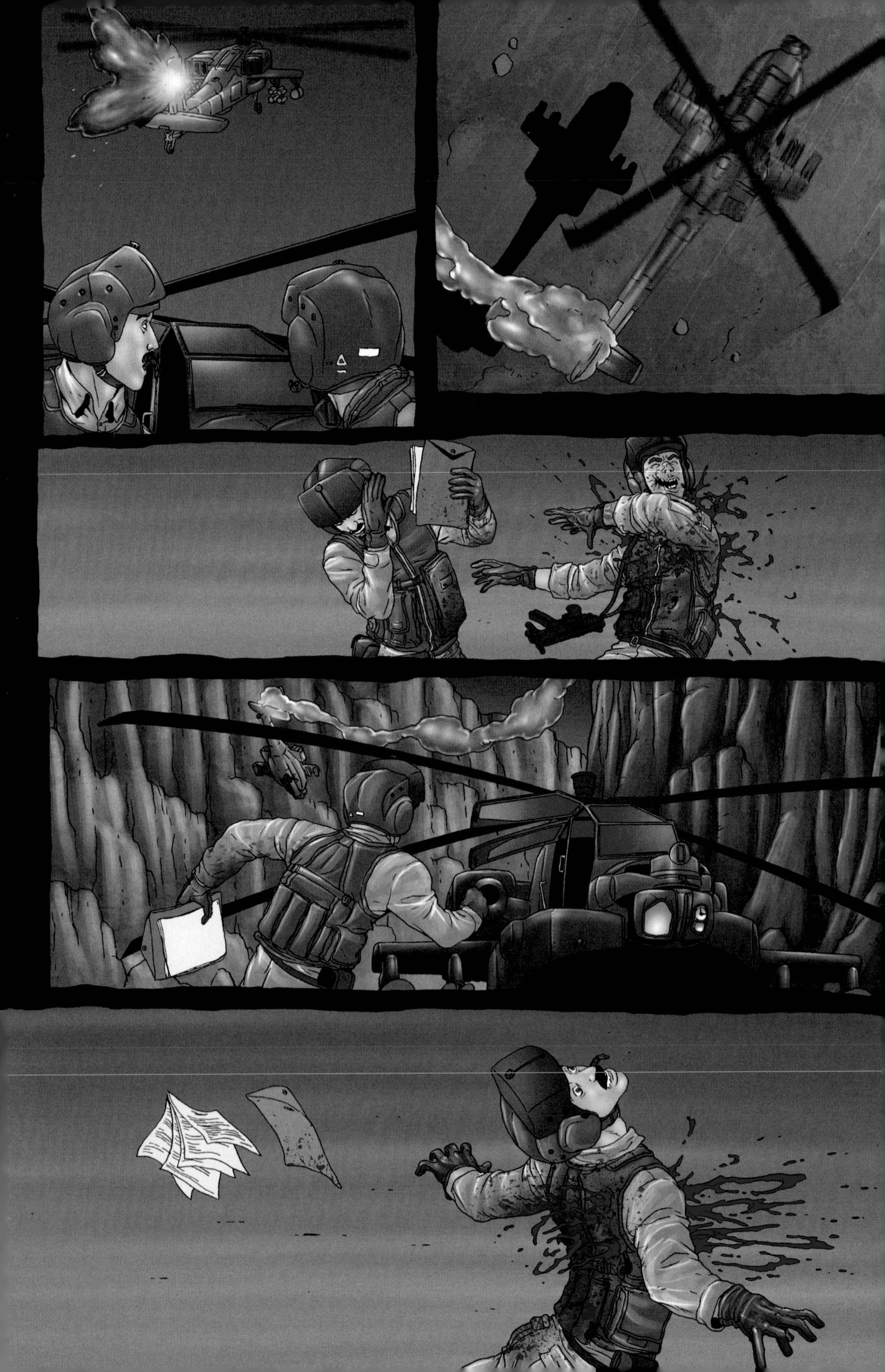

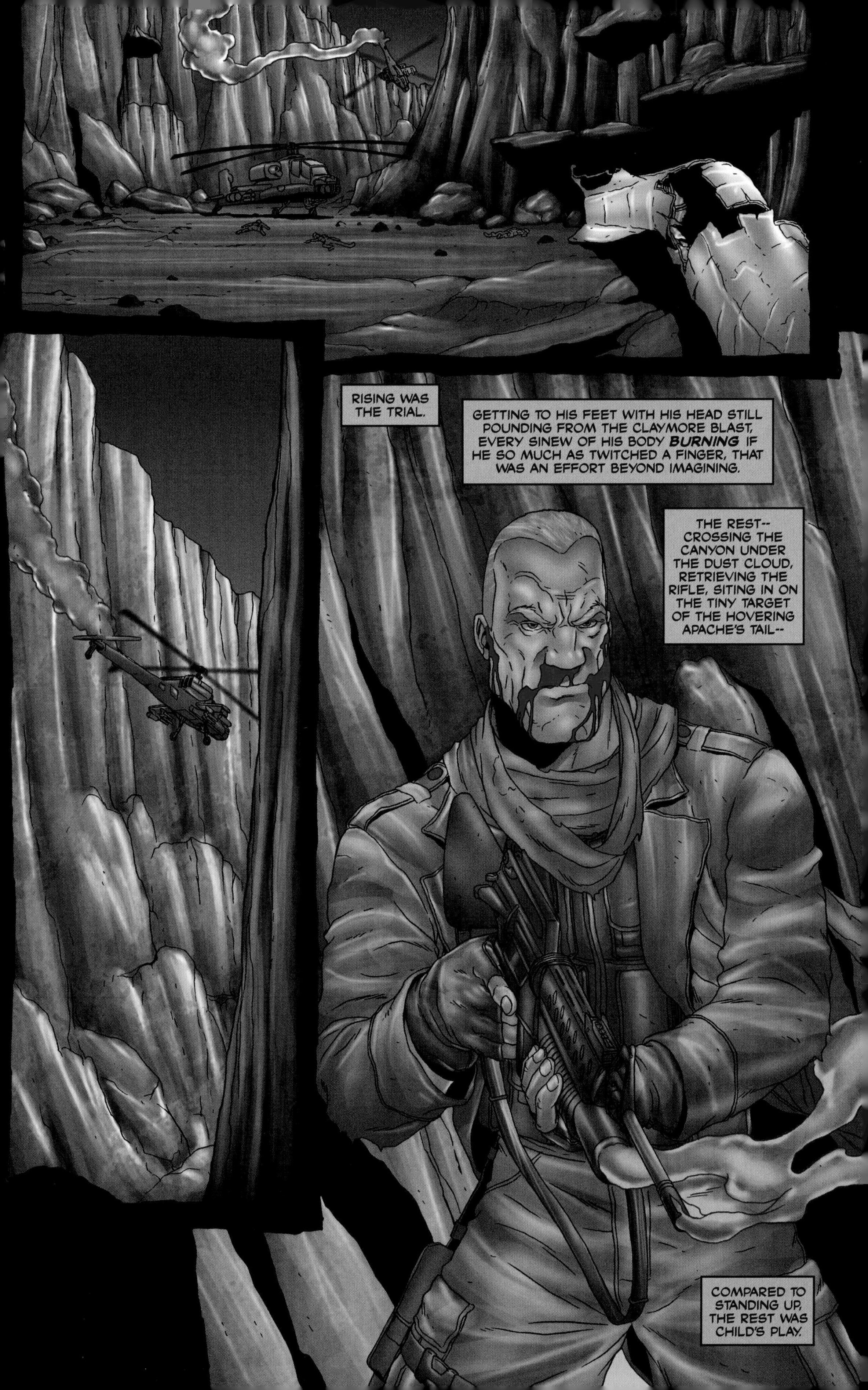
RISING WAS THE TRIAL.
GETTING TO HIS FEET WITH HIS HEAD STILL POUNDING FROM THE CLAYMORE BLAST, EVERY SINEW OF HIS BODY *BURNING* IF HE SO MUCH AS TWITCHED A FINGER, THAT WAS AN EFFORT BEYOND IMAGINING.
THE REST-- CROSSING THE CANYON UNDER THE DUST CLOUD, RETRIEVING THE RIFLE, SITING IN ON THE TINY TARGET OF THE HOVERING APACHE'S TAIL--
COMPARED TO STANDING UP, THE REST WAS CHILD'S PLAY.

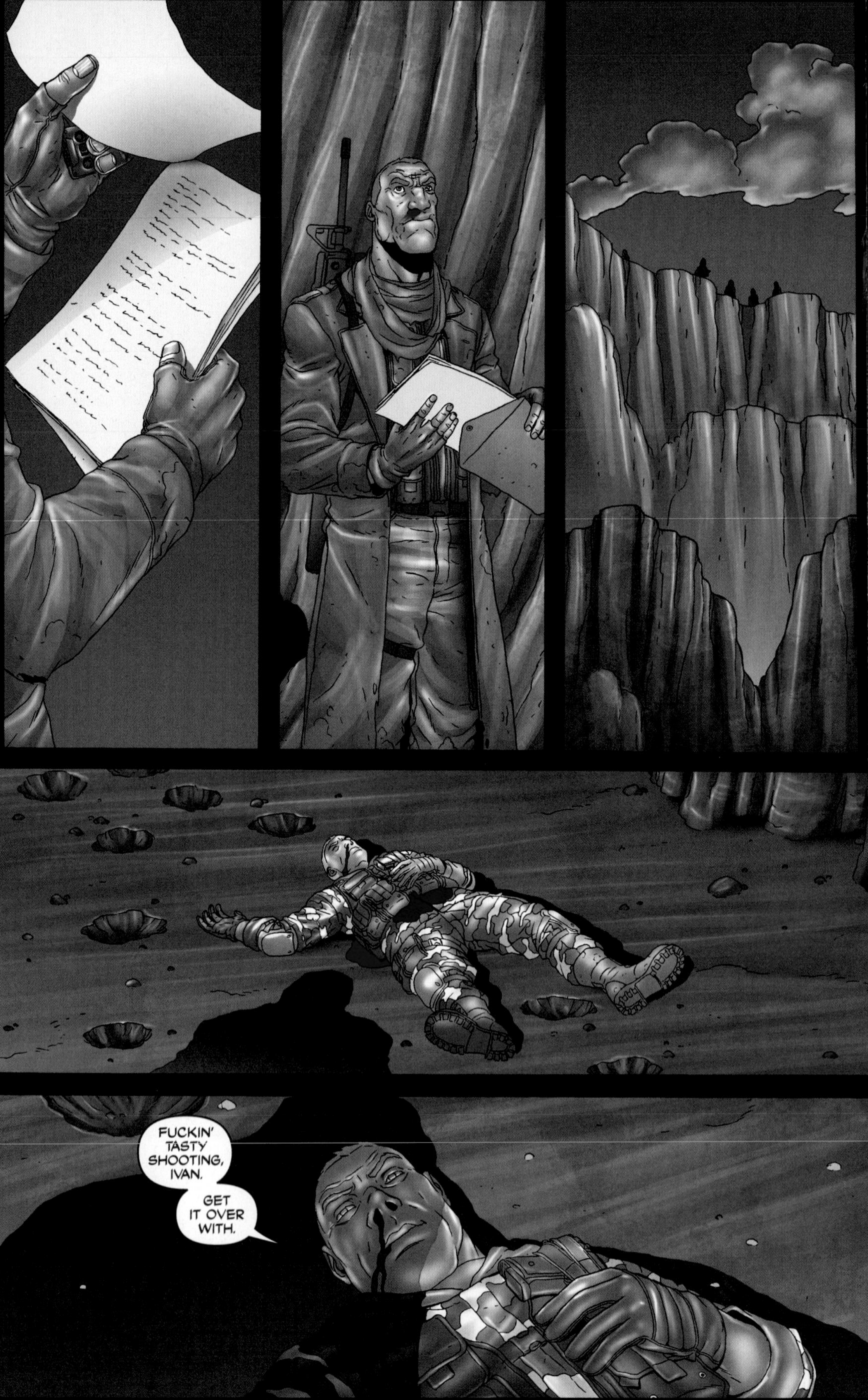
FUCKIN' TASTY SHOOTING, IVAN.
GET IT OVER WITH.

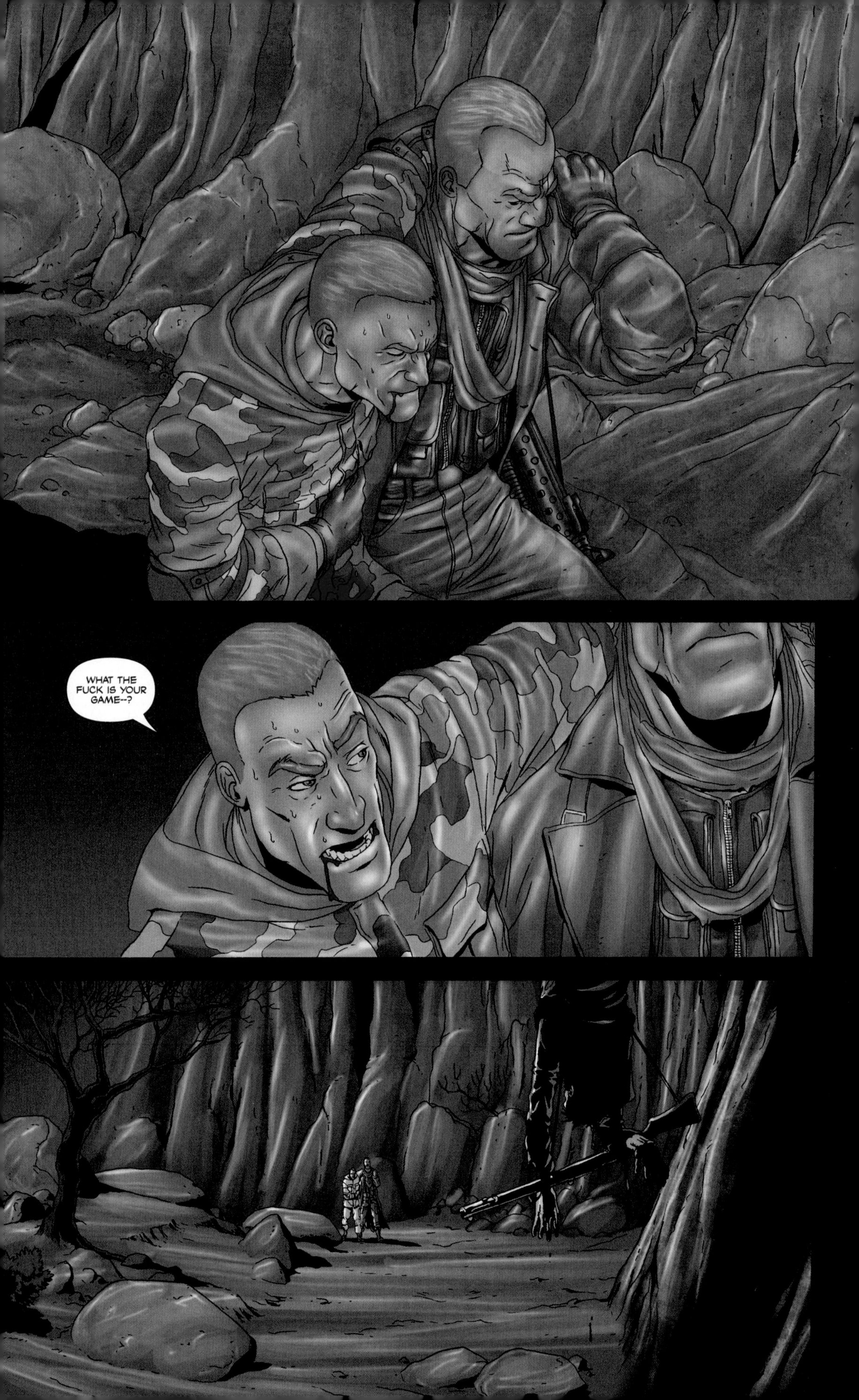
WHAT THE
FUCK IS YOUR
GAME--?

BLOKE YOU HAD WITH YOU, INNIT?

MY LADS PANICKED HIM, HE MUST'VE RUN RIGHT OFF THE EDGE OF THE CLIFF.

FUCK ME, A LEE-ENFIELD, WOULD YOU BLOODY BELIEVE IT.

MY GRANDAD HAD ONE OF THEM.

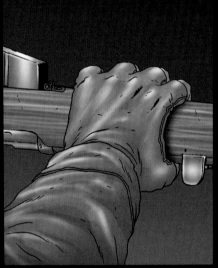

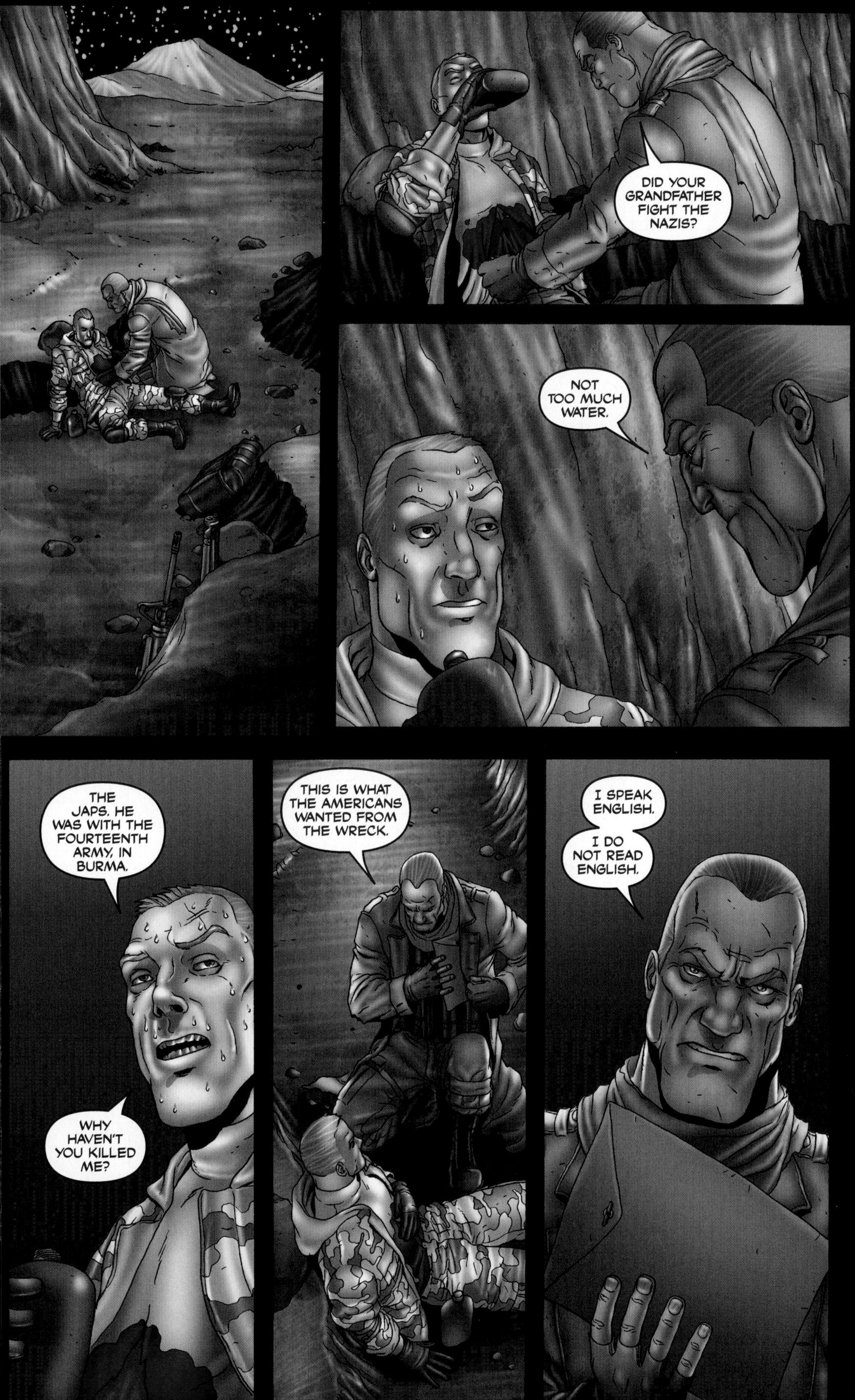
DID YOUR GRANDFATHER FIGHT THE NAZIS?
NOT TOO MUCH WATER.
THE JAPS. HE WAS WITH THE FOURTEENTH ARMY, IN BURMA.
WHY HAVEN'T YOU KILLED ME?
THIS IS WHAT THE AMERICANS WANTED FROM THE WRECK.
I SPEAK ENGLISH.
I DO NOT READ ENGLISH.

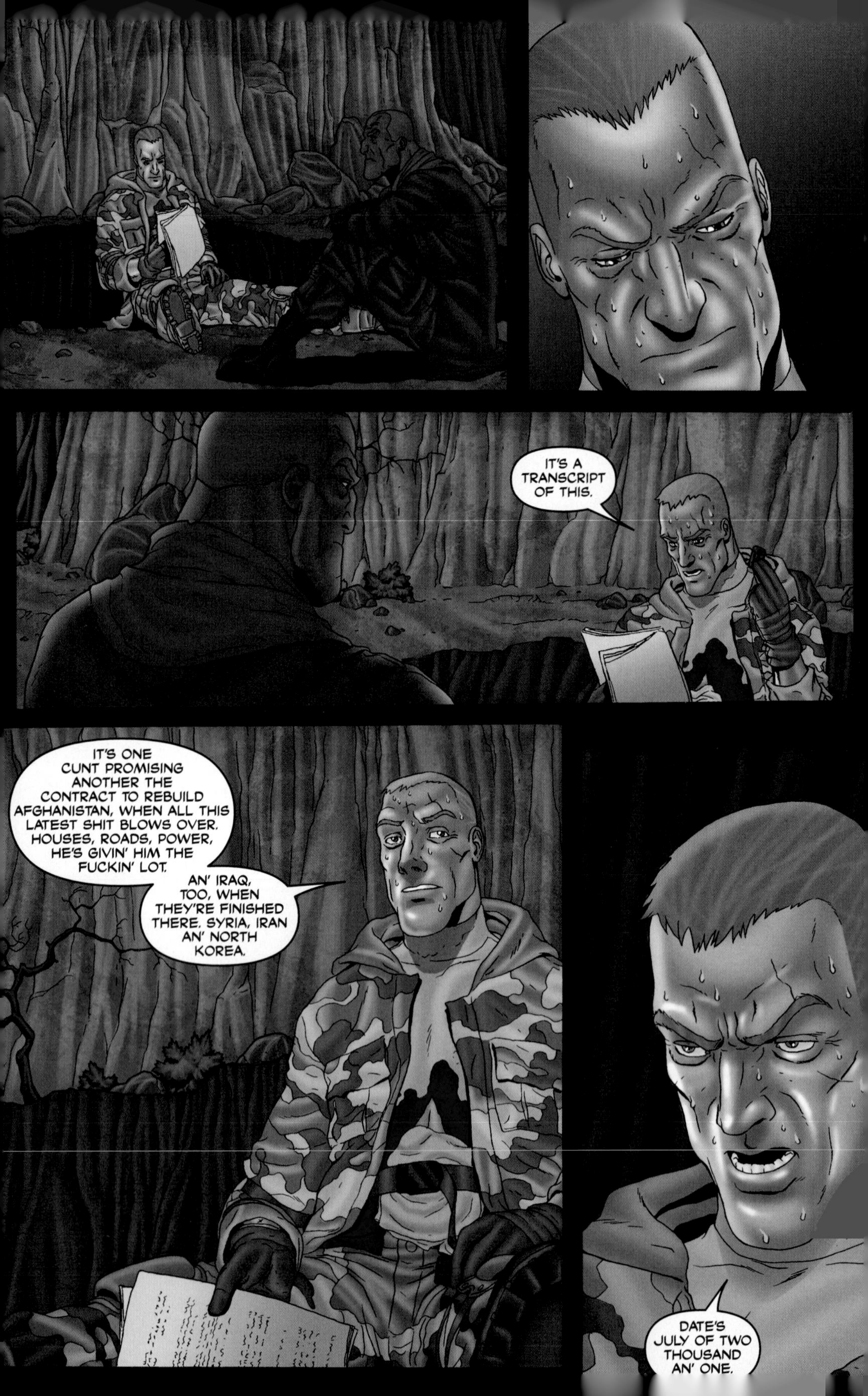
IT'S A TRANSCRIPT OF THIS.
IT'S ONE CUNT PROMISING ANOTHER THE CONTRACT TO REBUILD AFGHANISTAN, WHEN ALL THIS LATEST SHIT BLOWS OVER. HOUSES, ROADS, POWER, HE'S GIVIN' HIM THE FUCKIN' LOT.
AN' IRAQ, TOO, WHEN THEY'RE FINISHED THERE. SYRIA, IRAN AN' NORTH KOREA.
DATE'S JULY OF TWO THOUSAND AN' ONE.

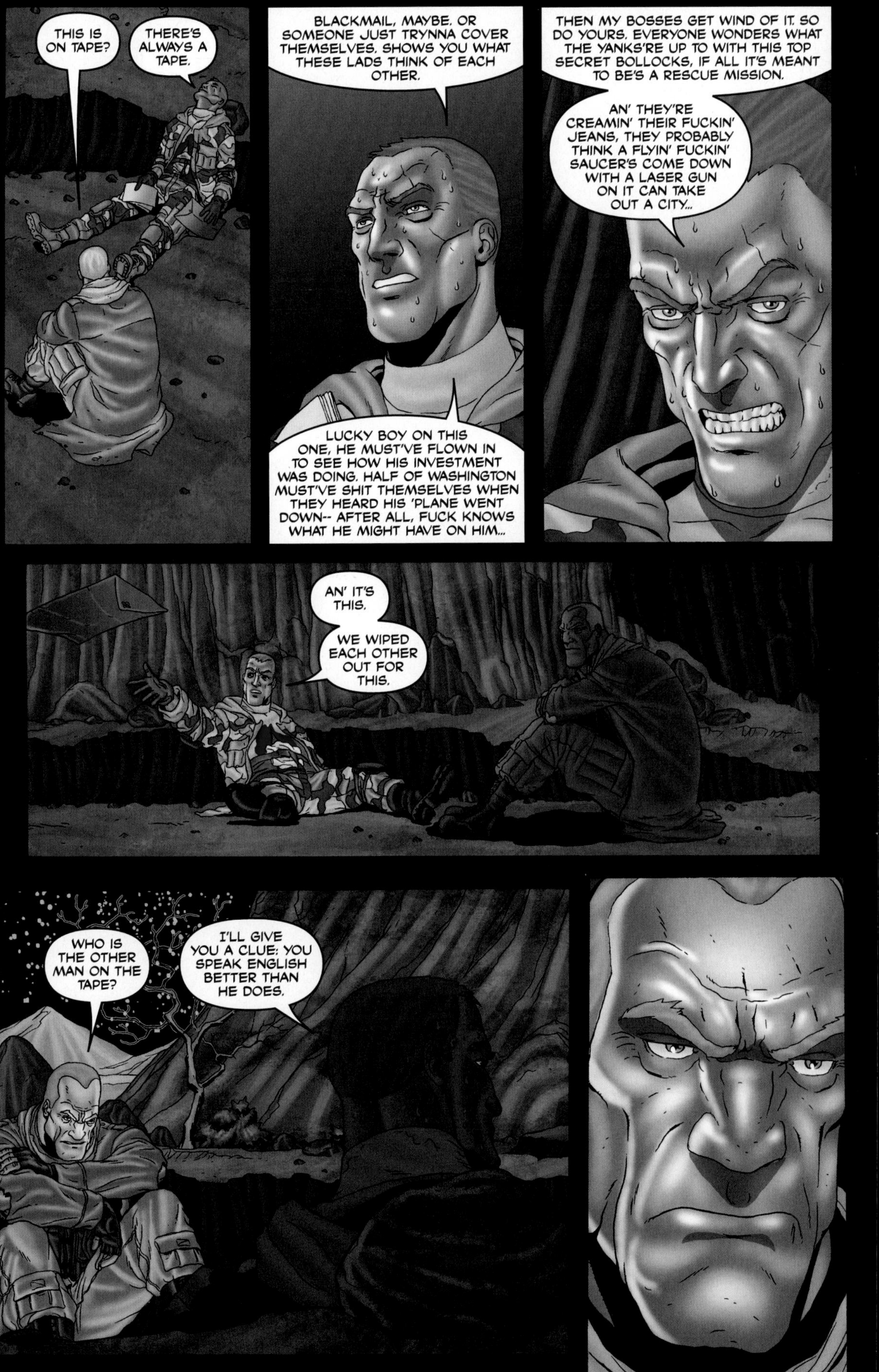
THIS IS ON TAPE?
THERE'S ALWAYS A TAPE.
BLACKMAIL, MAYBE, OR SOMEONE JUST TRYNNA COVER THEMSELVES. SHOWS YOU WHAT THESE LADS THINK OF EACH OTHER.
LUCKY BOY ON THIS ONE, HE MUST'VE FLOWN IN TO SEE HOW HIS INVESTMENT WAS DOING. HALF OF WASHINGTON MUST'VE SHIT THEMSELVES WHEN THEY HEARD HIS 'PLANE WENT DOWN-- AFTER ALL, FUCK KNOWS WHAT HE MIGHT HAVE ON HIM...
THEN MY BOSSES GET WIND OF IT. SO DO YOURS. EVERYONE WONDERS WHAT THE YANKS'RE UP TO WITH THIS TOP SECRET BOLLOCKS, IF ALL IT'S MEANT TO BE'S A RESCUE MISSION.
AN' THEY'RE CREAMIN' THEIR FUCKIN' JEANS, THEY PROBABLY THINK A FLYIN' FUCKIN' SAUCER'S COME DOWN WITH A LASER GUN ON IT CAN TAKE OUT A CITY...
AN' IT'S THIS.
WE WIPED EACH OTHER OUT FOR THIS.
WHO IS THE OTHER MAN ON THE TAPE?
I'LL GIVE YOU A CLUE: YOU SPEAK ENGLISH BETTER THAN HE DOES.

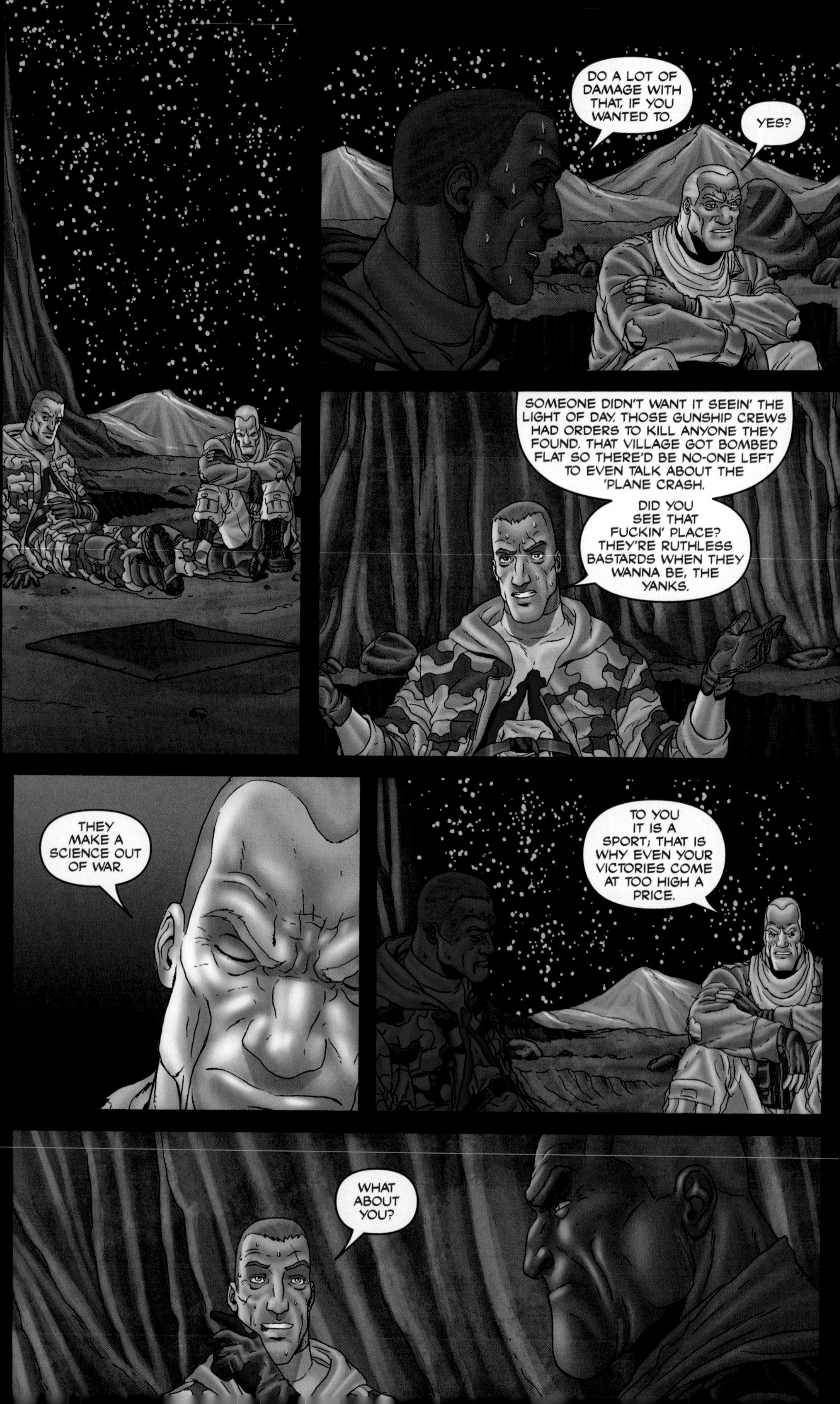
DO A LOT OF DAMAGE WITH THAT, IF YOU WANTED TO.
YES?
SOMEONE DIDN'T WANT IT SEEIN' THE LIGHT OF DAY. THOSE GUNSHIP CREWS HAD ORDERS TO KILL ANYONE THEY FOUND. THAT VILLAGE GOT BOMBED FLAT SO THERE'D BE NO-ONE LEFT TO EVEN TALK ABOUT THE 'PLANE CRASH.
DID YOU SEE THAT FUCKIN' PLACE? THEY'RE RUTHLESS BASTARDS WHEN THEY WANNA BE, THE YANKS.
THEY MAKE A SCIENCE OUT OF WAR.
TO YOU IT IS A SPORT; THAT IS WHY EVEN YOUR VICTORIES COME AT TOO HIGH A PRICE.
WHAT ABOUT YOU?

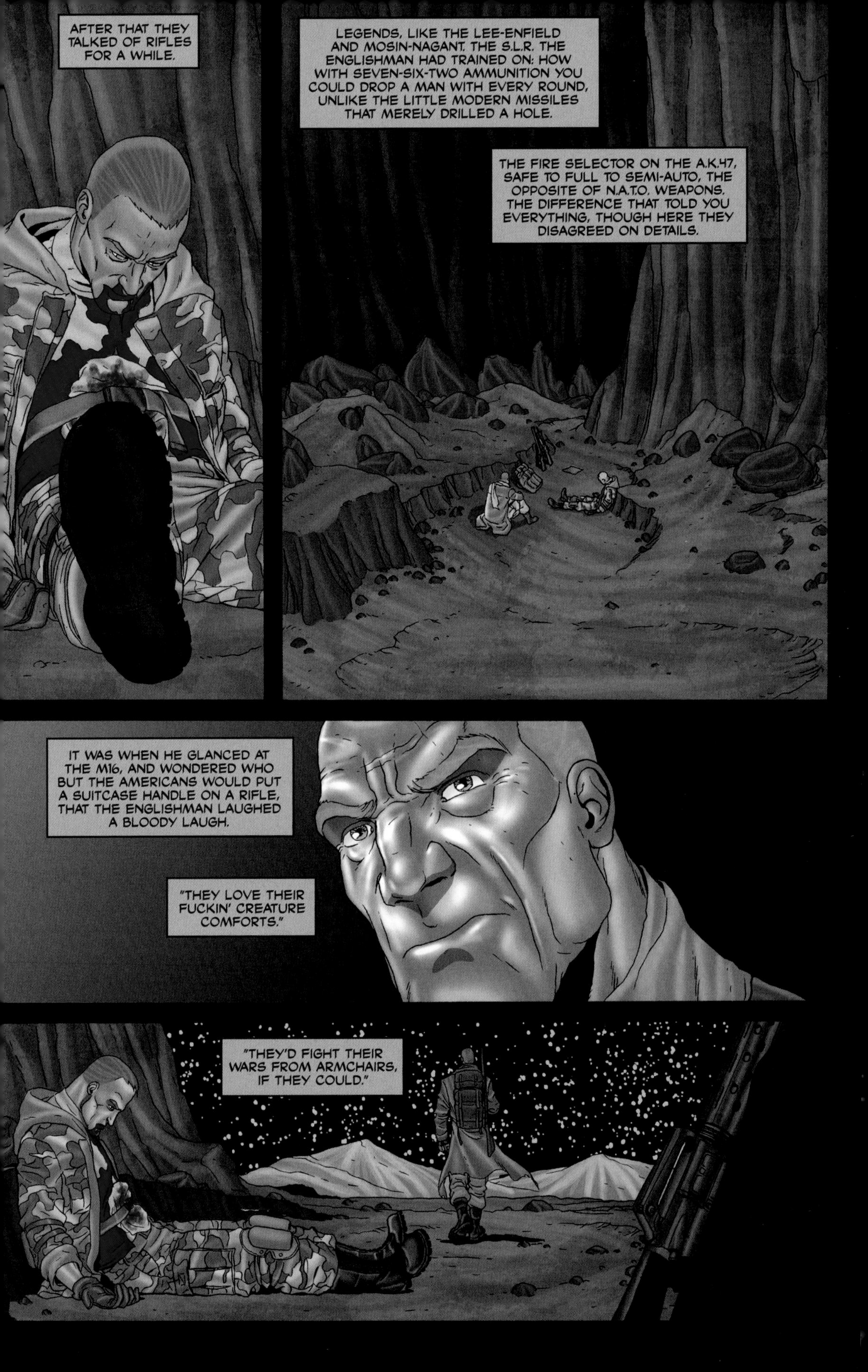
AFTER THAT THEY TALKED OF RIFLES FOR A WHILE.
LEGENDS, LIKE THE LEE-ENFIELD AND MOSIN-NAGANT. THE S.L.R. THE ENGLISHMAN HAD TRAINED ON: HOW WITH SEVEN-SIX-TWO AMMUNITION YOU COULD DROP A MAN WITH EVERY ROUND, UNLIKE THE LITTLE MODERN MISSILES THAT MERELY DRILLED A HOLE.
THE FIRE SELECTOR ON THE A.K.47, SAFE TO FULL TO SEMI-AUTO, THE OPPOSITE OF N.A.T.O. WEAPONS. THE DIFFERENCE THAT TOLD YOU EVERYTHING, THOUGH HERE THEY DISAGREED ON DETAILS.
IT WAS WHEN HE GLANCED AT THE M16, AND WONDERED WHO BUT THE AMERICANS WOULD PUT A SUITCASE HANDLE ON A RIFLE, THAT THE ENGLISHMAN LAUGHED A BLOODY LAUGH.
"THEY LOVE THEIR FUCKIN' CREATURE COMFORTS."
"THEY'D FIGHT THEIR WARS FROM ARMCHAIRS, IF THEY COULD."

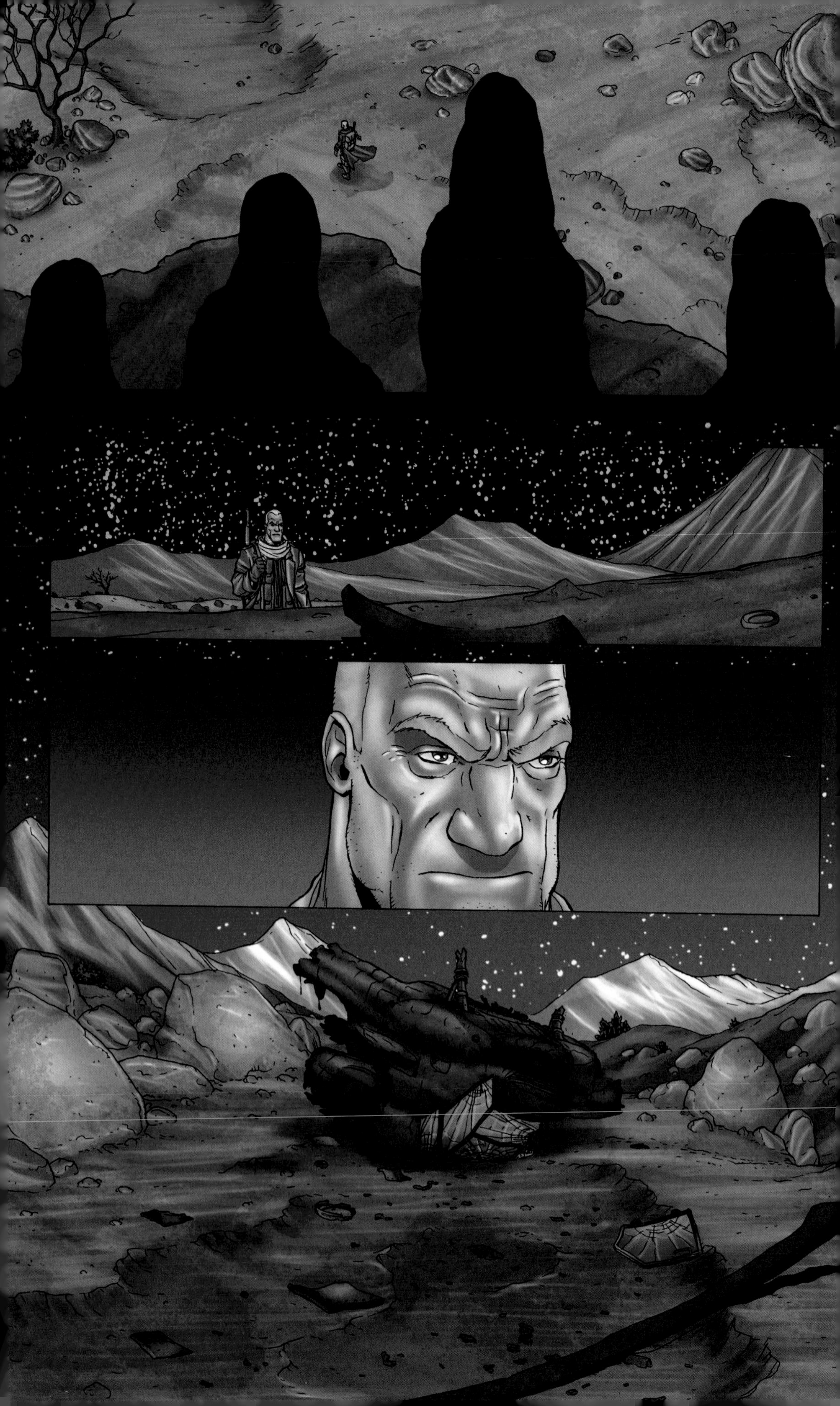

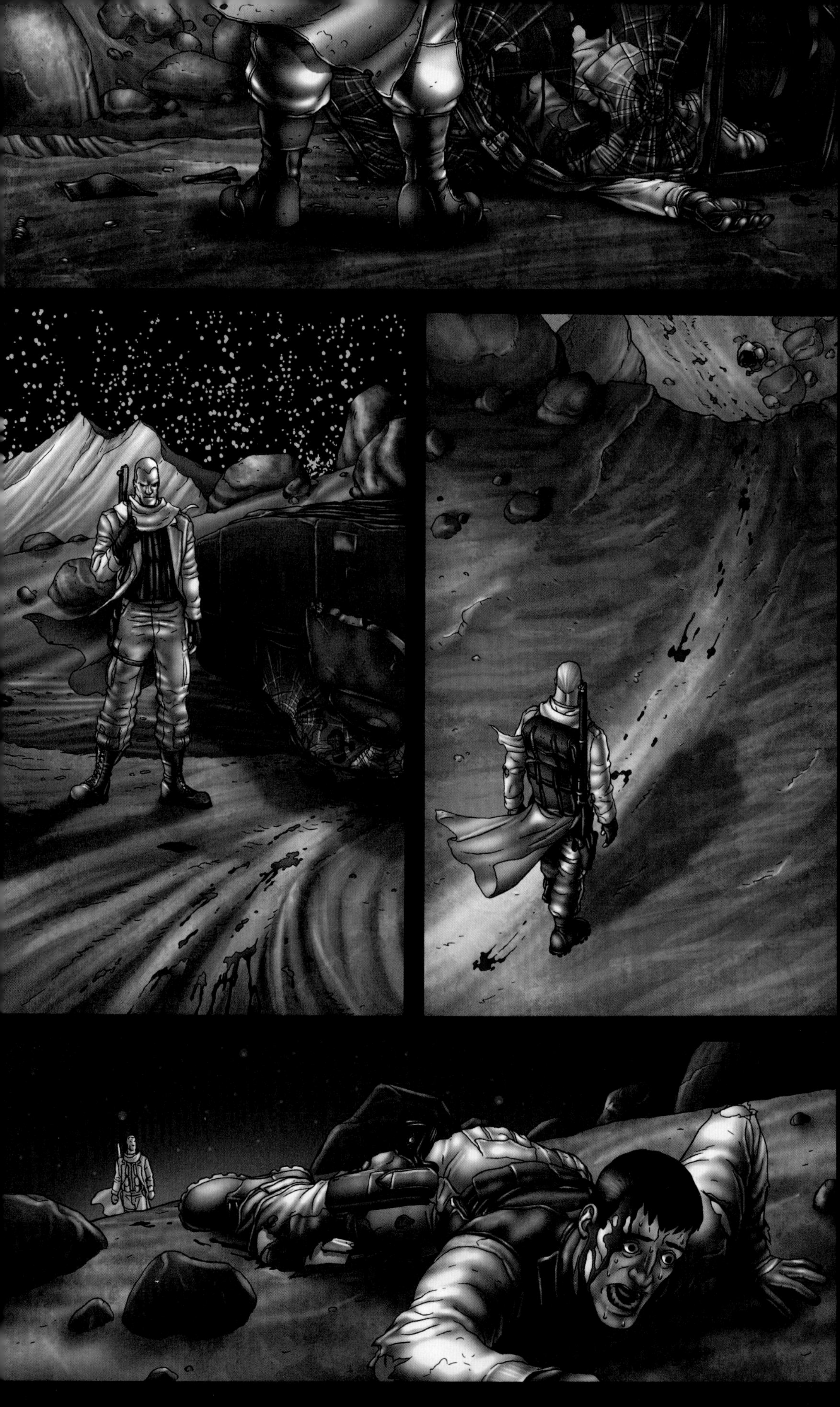

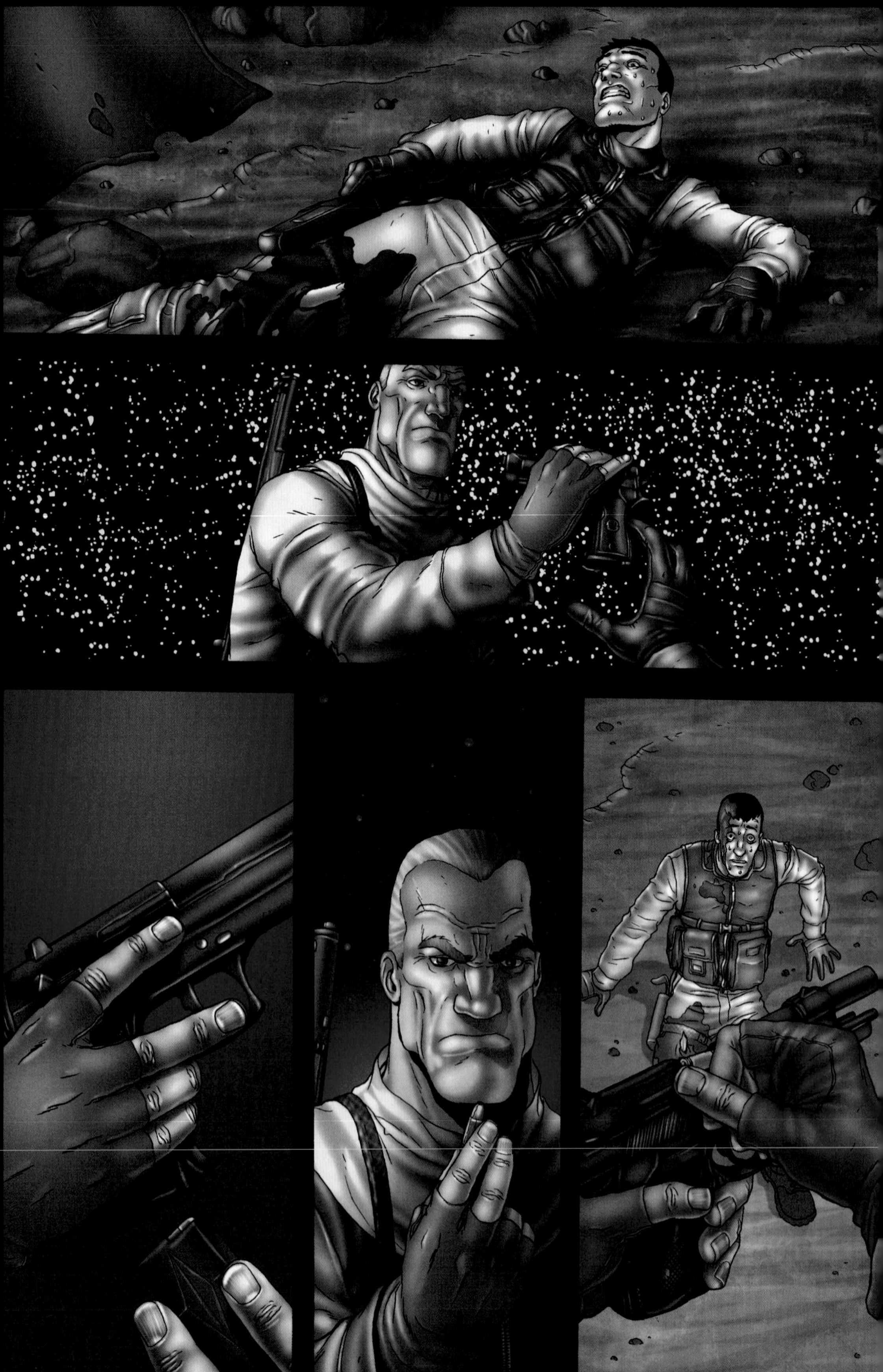

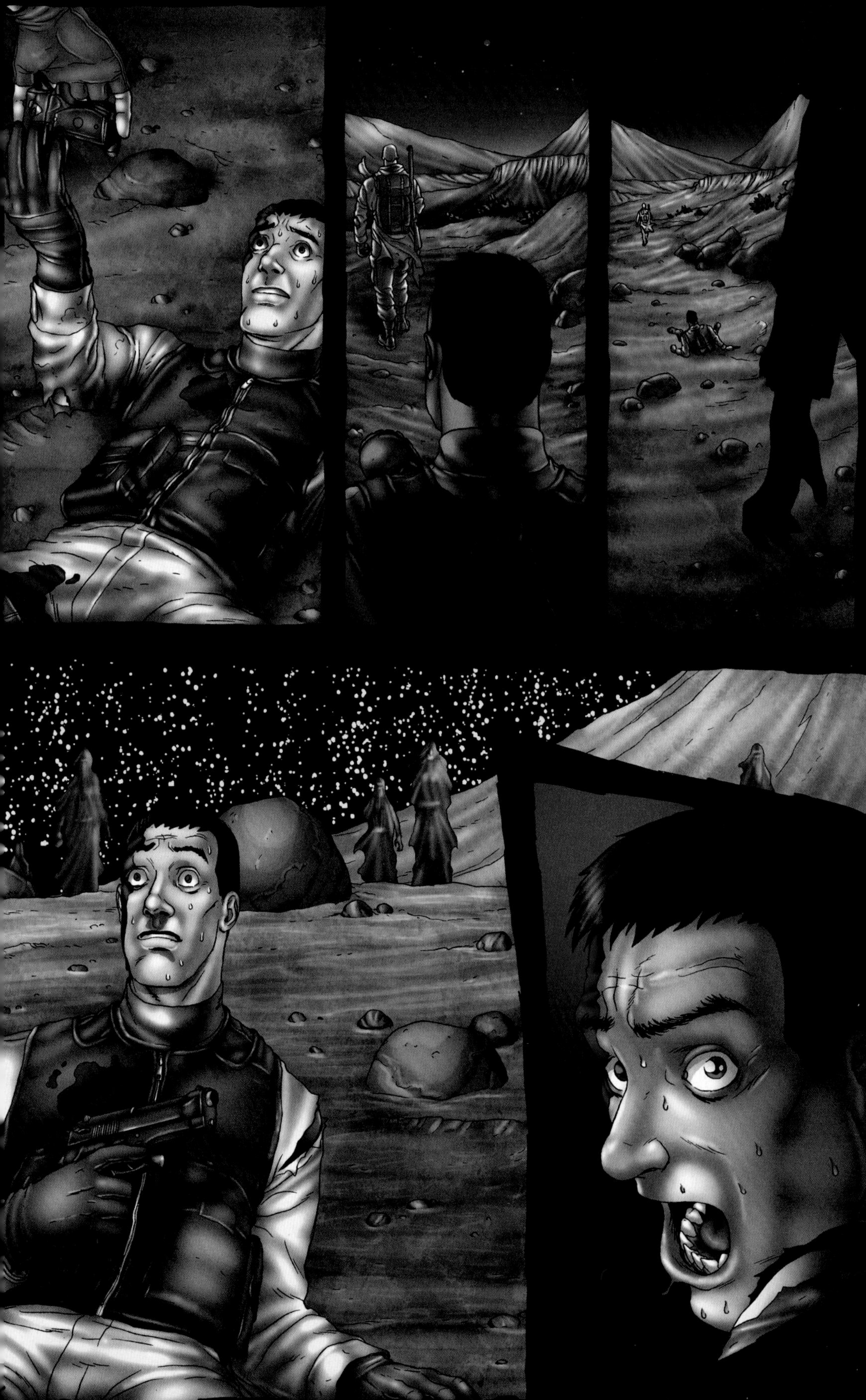

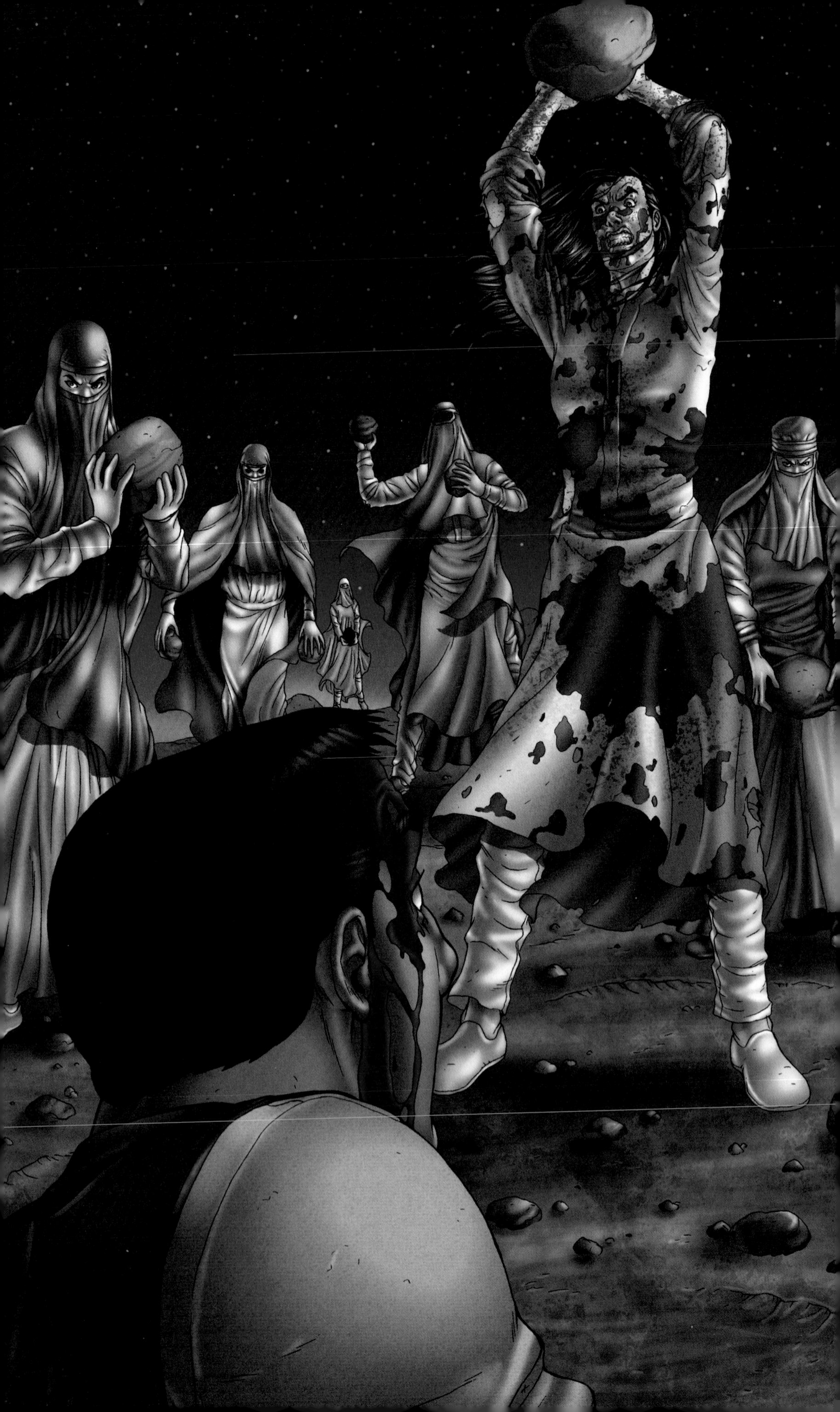

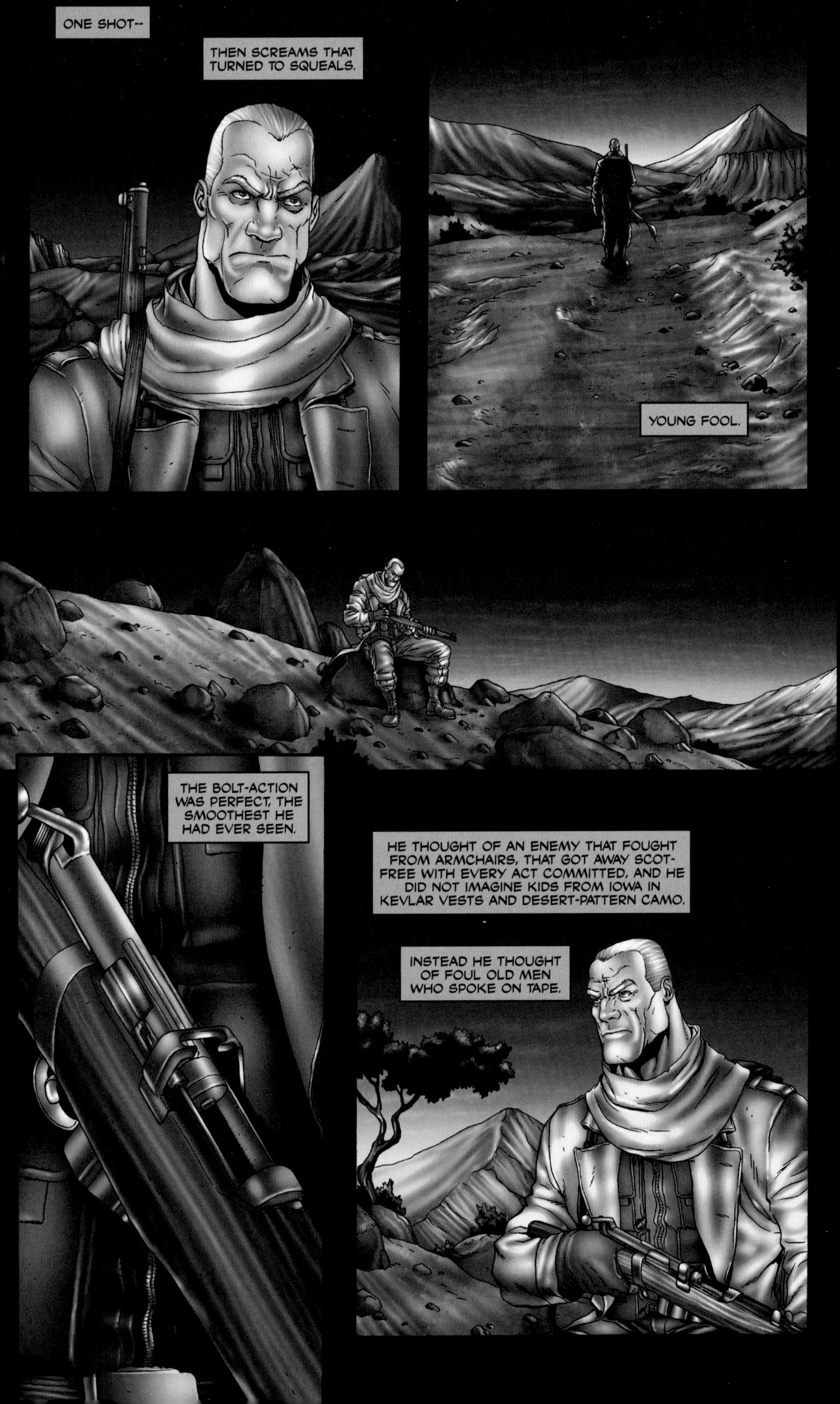
ONE SHOT--
THEN SCREAMS THAT TURNED TO SQUEALS.
YOUNG FOOL.
THE BOLT-ACTION WAS PERFECT, THE SMOOTHEST HE HAD EVER SEEN.
HE THOUGHT OF AN ENEMY THAT FOUGHT FROM ARMCHAIRS, THAT GOT AWAY SCOT-FREE WITH EVERY ACT COMMITTED, AND HE DID NOT IMAGINE KIDS FROM IOWA IN KEVLAR VESTS AND DESERT-PATTERN CAMO.
INSTEAD HE THOUGHT OF FOUL OLD MEN WHO SPOKE ON TAPE.

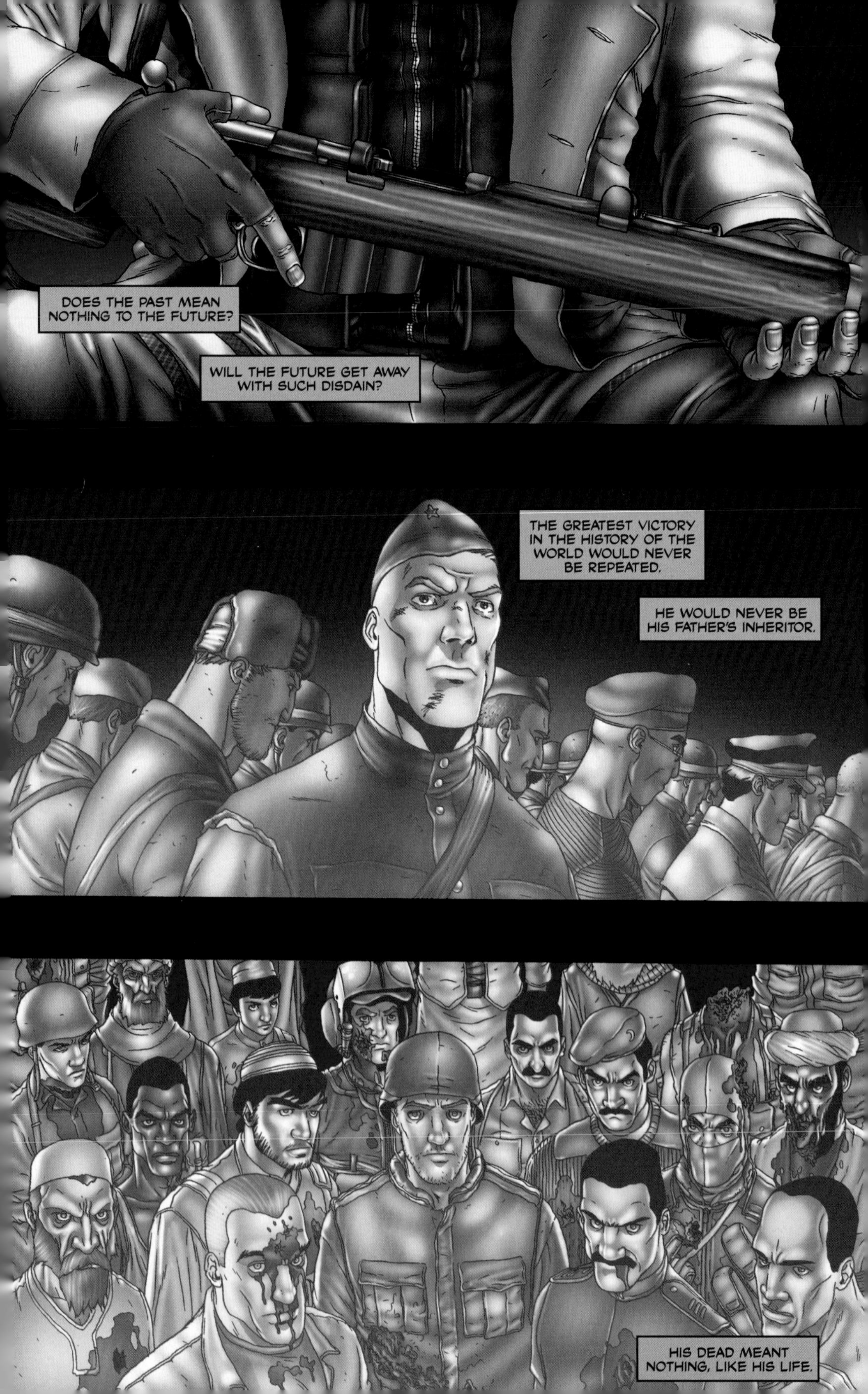
DOES THE PAST MEAN NOTHING TO THE FUTURE?
WILL THE FUTURE GET AWAY WITH SUCH DISDAIN?
THE GREATEST VICTORY IN THE HISTORY OF THE WORLD WOULD NEVER BE REPEATED.
HE WOULD NEVER BE HIS FATHER'S INHERITOR.
HIS DEAD MEANT NOTHING, LIKE HIS LIFE.

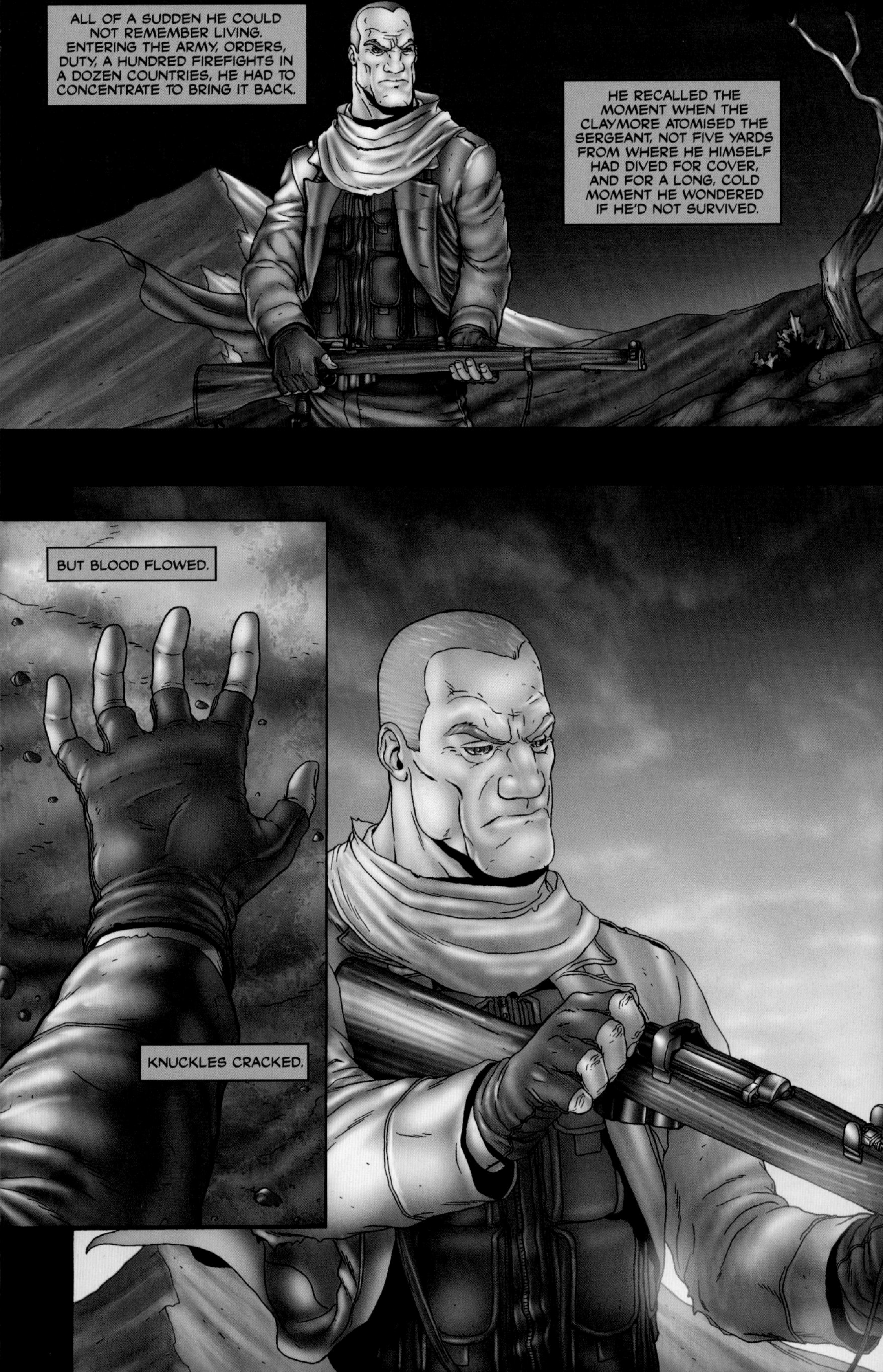
ALL OF A SUDDEN HE COULD NOT REMEMBER LIVING. ENTERING THE ARMY, ORDERS, DUTY, A HUNDRED FIREFIGHTS IN A DOZEN COUNTRIES, HE HAD TO CONCENTRATE TO BRING IT BACK.
HE RECALLED THE MOMENT WHEN THE CLAYMORE ATOMISED THE SERGEANT, NOT FIVE YARDS FROM WHERE HE HIMSELF HAD DIVED FOR COVER, AND FOR A LONG, COLD MOMENT HE WONDERED IF HE'D NOT SURVIVED.
BUT BLOOD FLOWED.
KNUCKLES CRACKED.

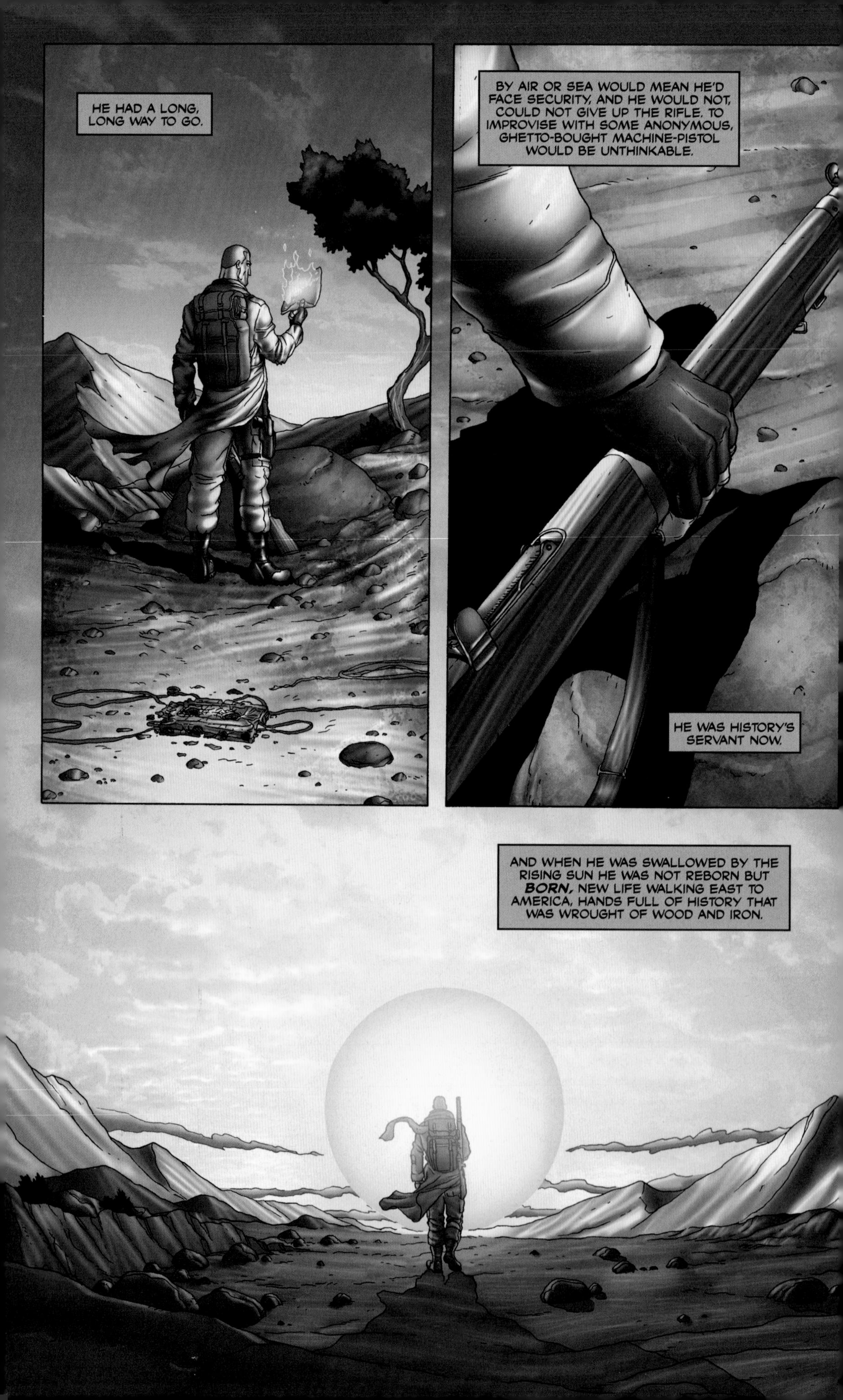
HE HAD A LONG, LONG WAY TO GO.
BY AIR OR SEA WOULD MEAN HE'D FACE SECURITY, AND HE WOULD NOT, COULD NOT GIVE UP THE RIFLE. TO IMPROVISE WITH SOME ANONYMOUS, GHETTO-BOUGHT MACHINE-PISTOL WOULD BE UNTHINKABLE.
HE WAS HISTORY'S SERVANT NOW.
AND WHEN HE WAS SWALLOWED BY THE RISING SUN HE WAS NOT REBORN BUT BORN, NEW LIFE WALKING EAST TO AMERICA, HANDS FULL OF HISTORY THAT WAS WROUGHT OF WOOD AND IRON.

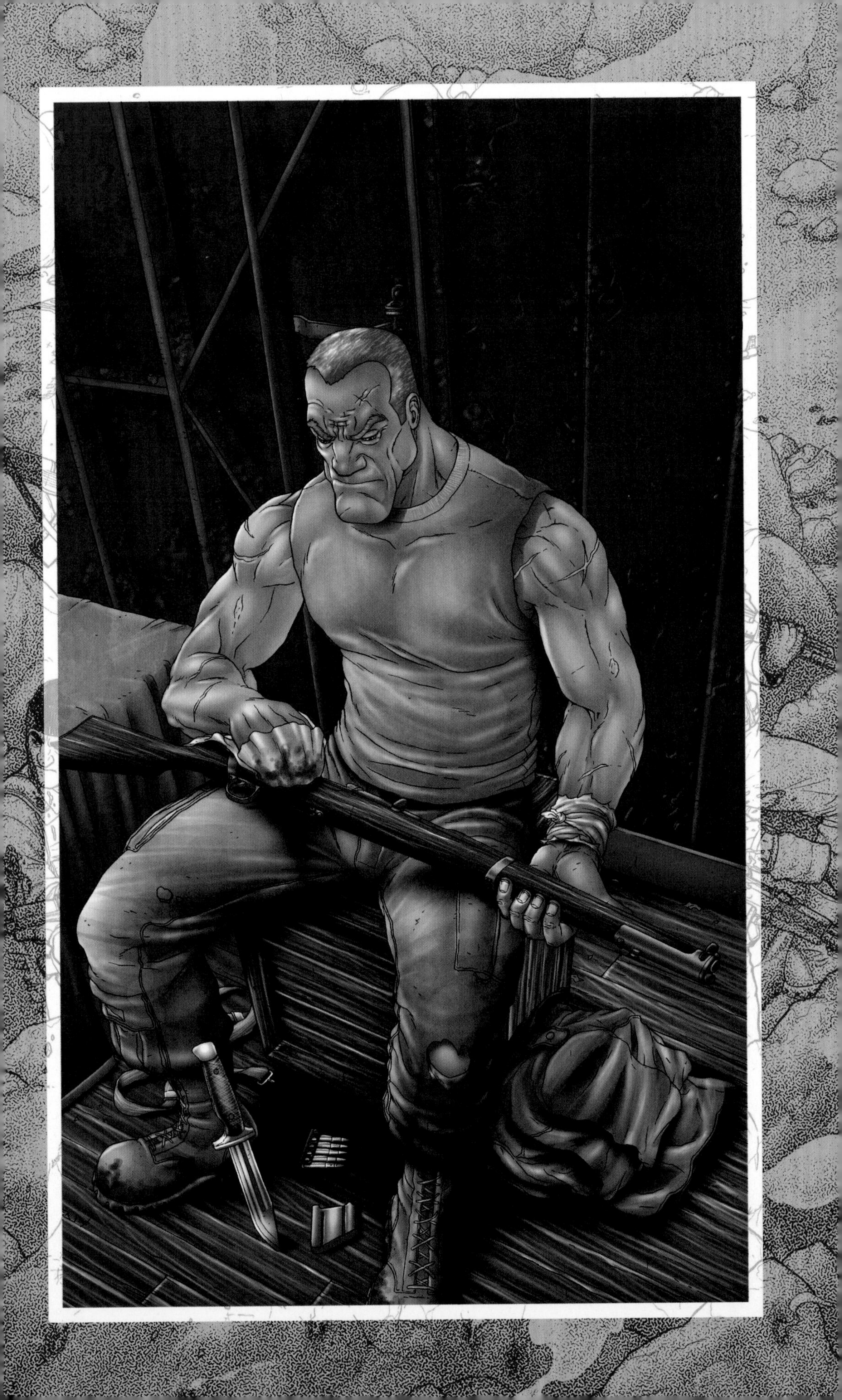

part two

BLACK ARROW

"Arrow!" said the bowman. "Black arrow! I have saved you to the last. You have never failed me and always I have recovered you. I had you from my father and he from of old. If ever you came from the forges of the true king under the Mountain, go now and speed well!"

—J.R.R. Tolkien, *The Hobbit*

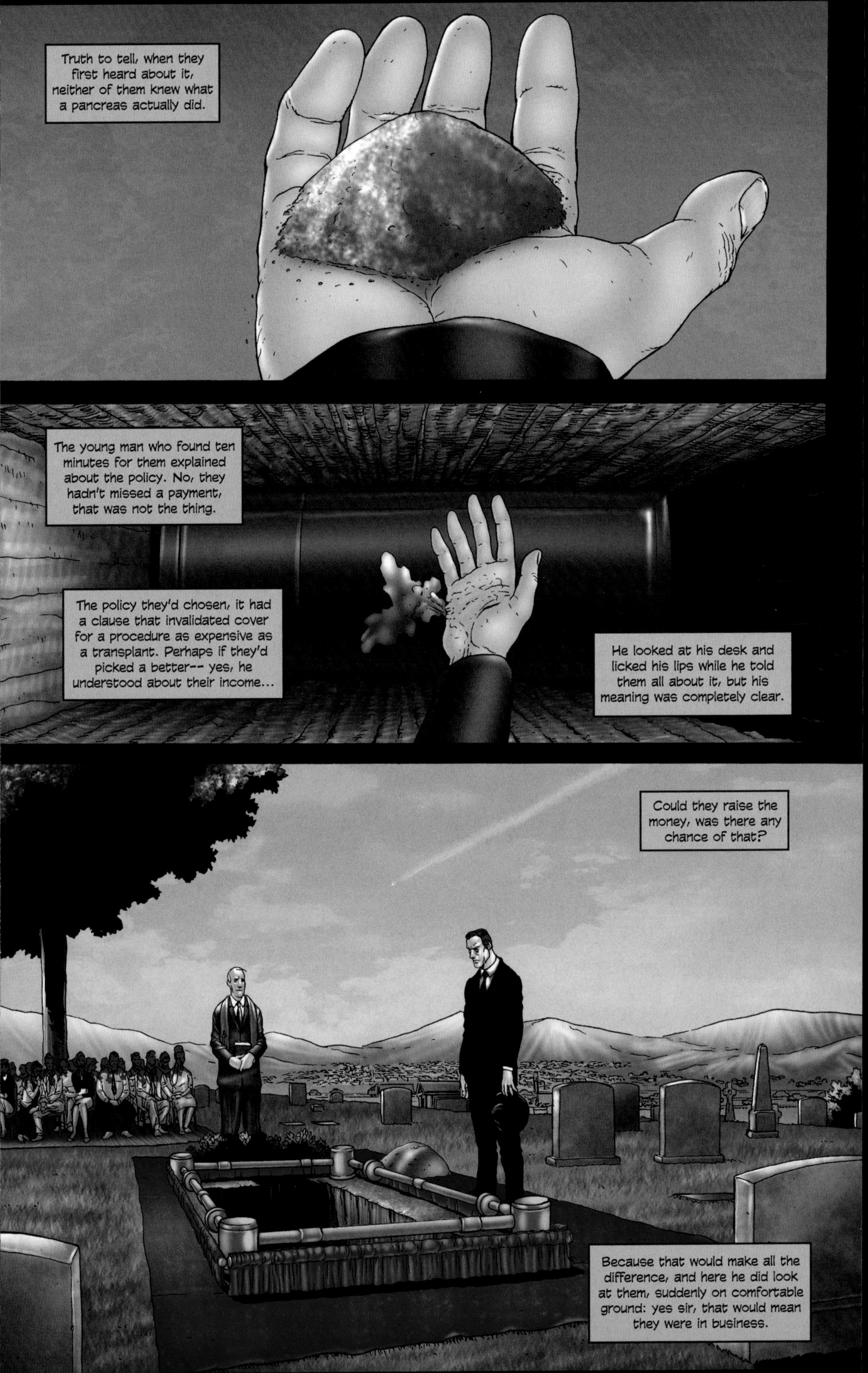

Truth to tell, when they first heard about it, neither of them knew what a pancreas actually did.
The young man who found ten minutes for them explained about the policy. No, they hadn't missed a payment, that was not the thing.
The policy they'd chosen, it had a clause that invalidated cover for a procedure as expensive as a transplant. Perhaps if they'd picked a better-- yes, he understood about their income...
He looked at his desk and licked his lips while he told them all about it, but his meaning was completely clear.
Could they raise the money, was there any chance of that?
Because that would make all the difference, and here he did look at them, suddenly on comfortable ground: yes sir, that would mean they were in business.

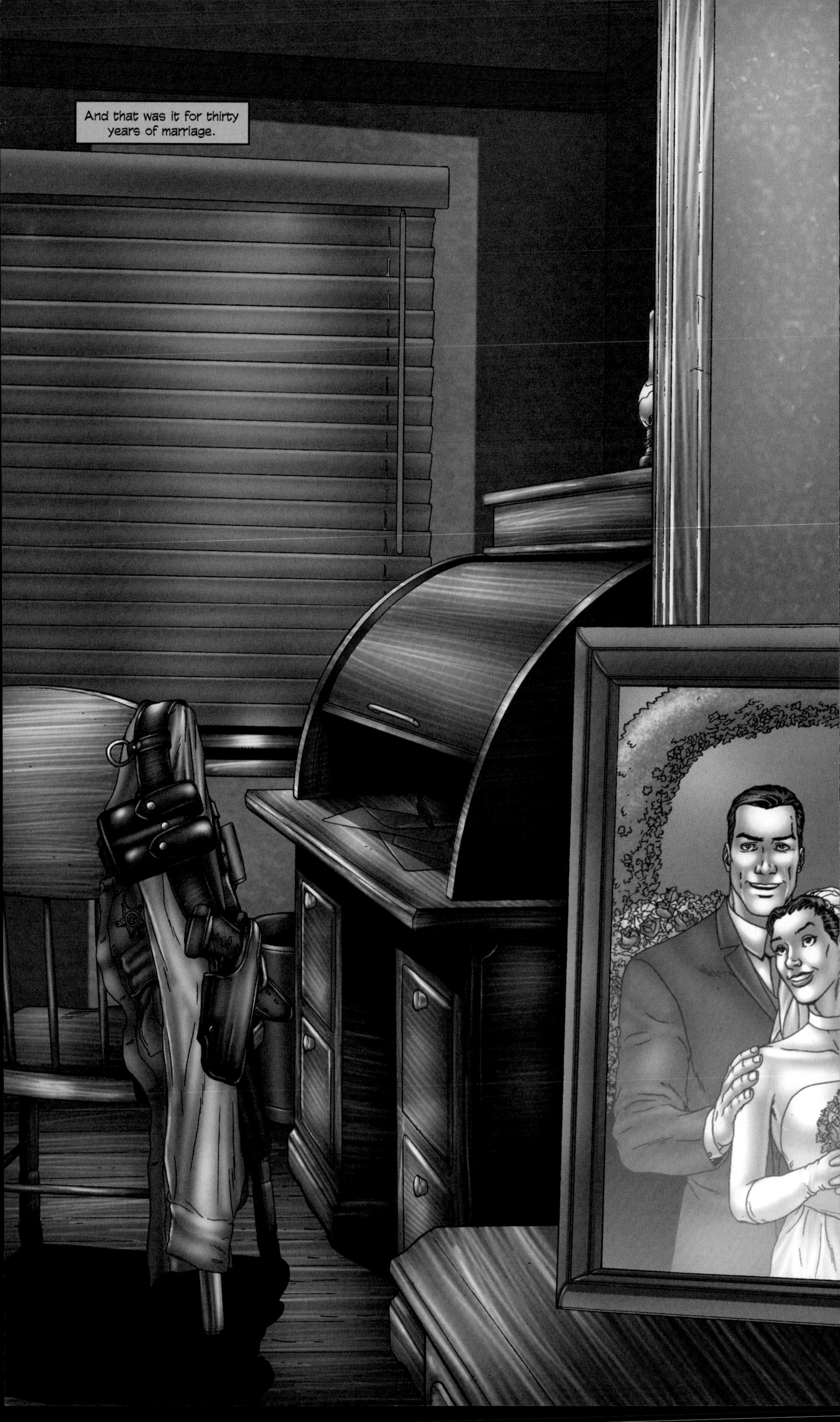
And that was it for thirty years of marriage.

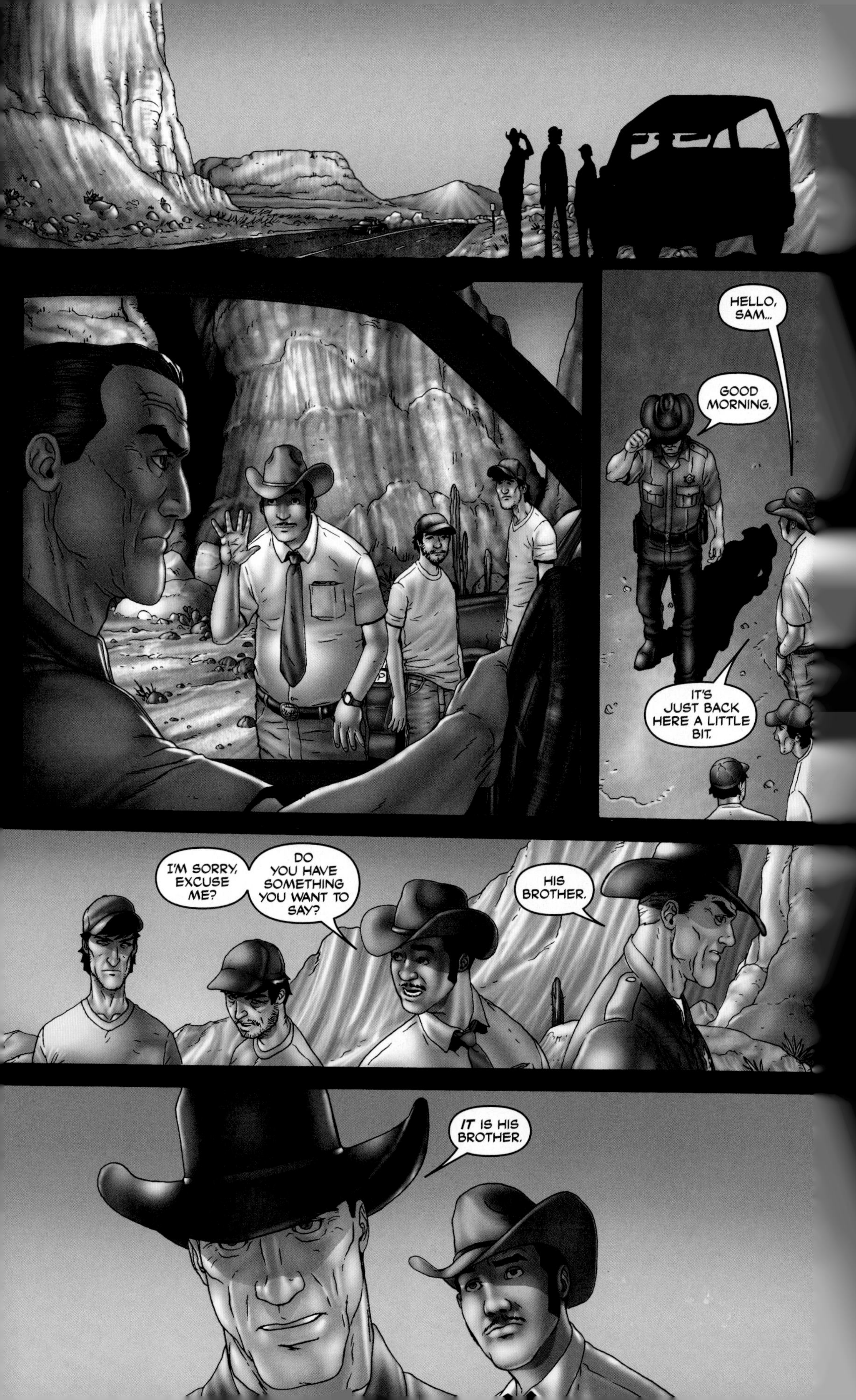
HELLO, SAM...
GOOD MORNING.
IT'S JUST BACK HERE A LITTLE BIT.
I'M SORRY, EXCUSE ME?
DO YOU HAVE SOMETHING YOU WANT TO SAY?
HIS BROTHER.
IT IS HIS BROTHER.

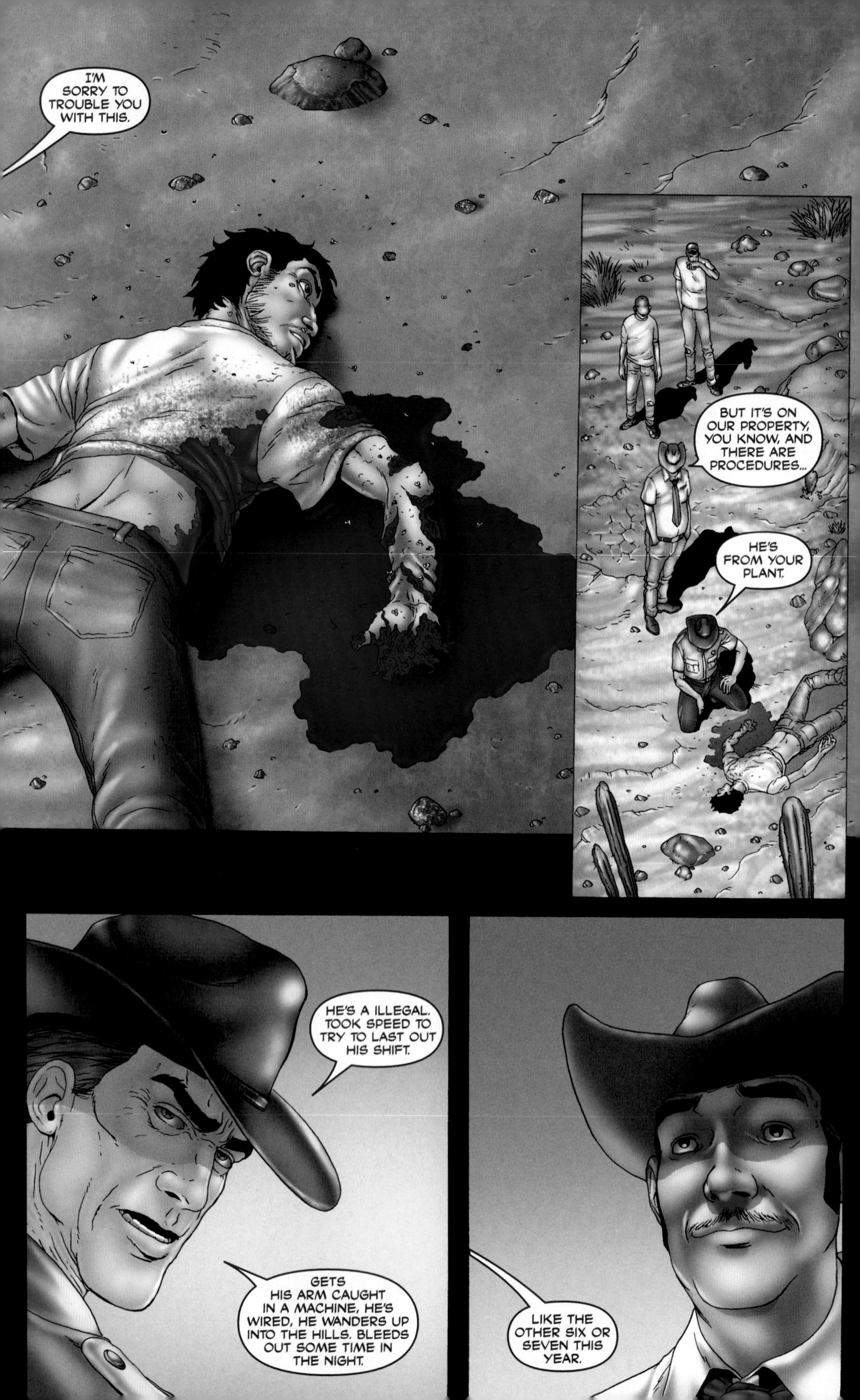
I'M SORRY TO TROUBLE YOU WITH THIS.
BUT IT'S ON OUR PROPERTY, YOU KNOW, AND THERE ARE PROCEDURES...
HE'S FROM YOUR PLANT.
HE'S A ILLEGAL. TOOK SPEED TO TRY TO LAST OUT HIS SHIFT.
GETS HIS ARM CAUGHT IN A MACHINE, HE'S WIRED, HE WANDERS UP INTO THE HILLS. BLEEDS OUT SOME TIME IN THE NIGHT.
LIKE THE OTHER SIX OR SEVEN THIS YEAR.

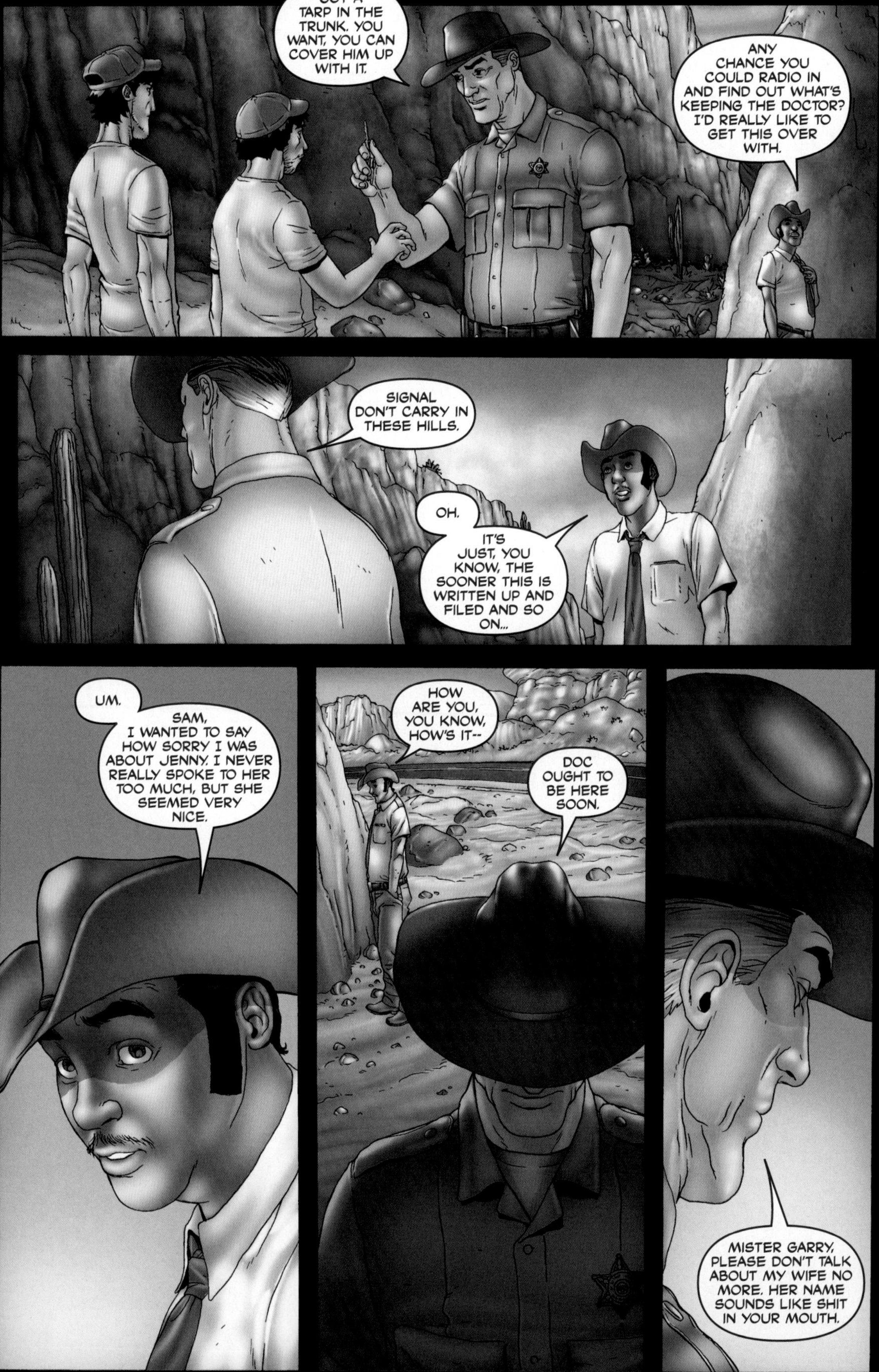
GOT A TARP IN THE TRUNK. YOU WANT, YOU CAN COVER HIM UP WITH IT.
ANY CHANCE YOU COULD RADIO IN AND FIND OUT WHAT'S KEEPING THE DOCTOR? I'D REALLY LIKE TO GET THIS OVER WITH.
SIGNAL DON'T CARRY IN THESE HILLS.
OH.
IT'S JUST, YOU KNOW, THE SOONER THIS IS WRITTEN UP AND FILED AND SO ON...
UM.
SAM, I WANTED TO SAY HOW SORRY I WAS ABOUT JENNY. I NEVER REALLY SPOKE TO HER TOO MUCH, BUT SHE SEEMED VERY NICE.
HOW ARE YOU, YOU KNOW, HOW'S IT--
DOC OUGHT TO BE HERE SOON.
MISTER GARRY, PLEASE DON'T TALK ABOUT MY WIFE NO MORE. HER NAME SOUNDS LIKE SHIT IN YOUR MOUTH.

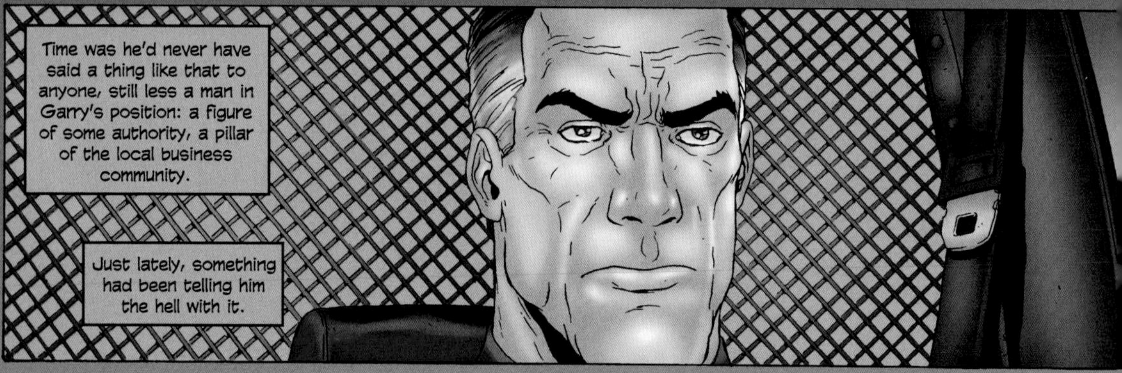
Time was he'd never have said a thing like that to anyone, still less a man in Garry's position: a figure of some authority, a pillar of the local business community.
Just lately, something had been telling him the hell with it.

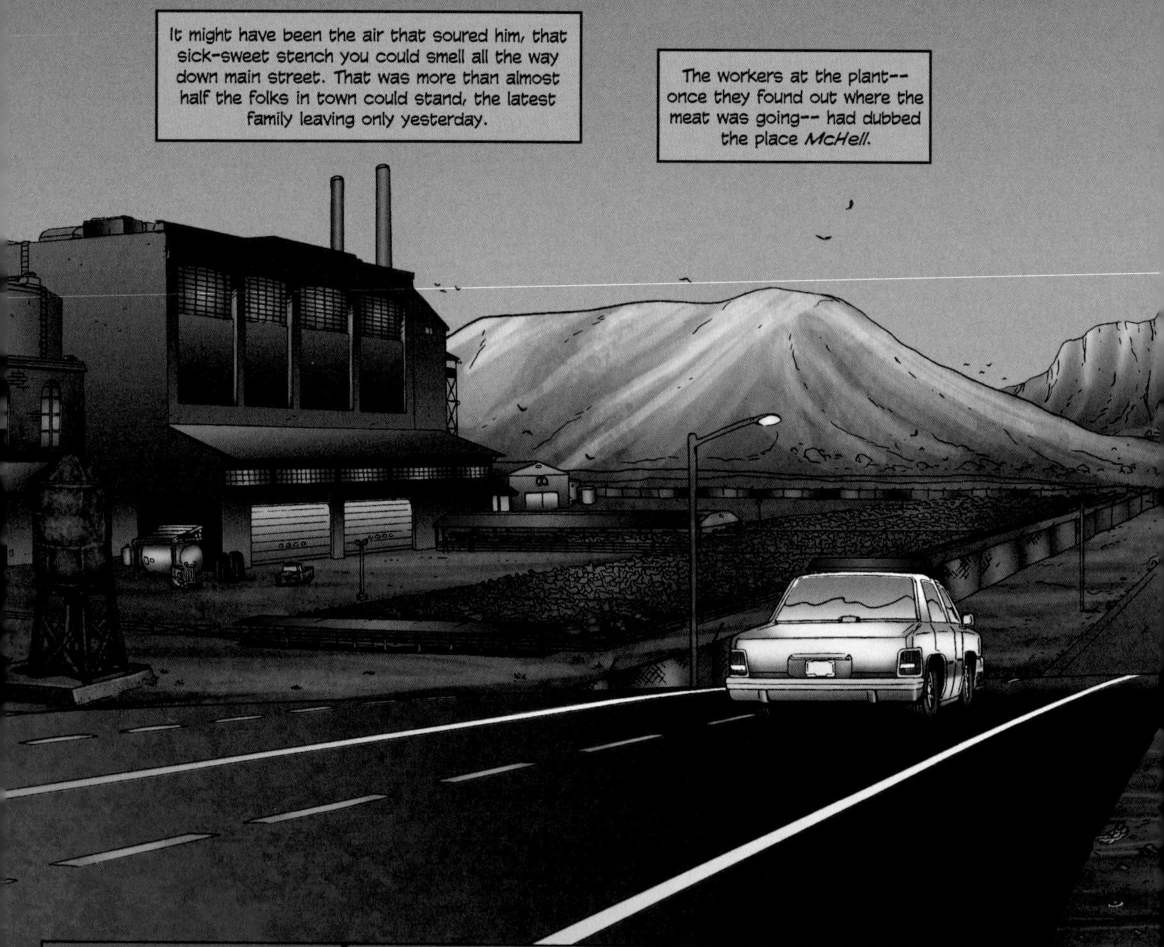
It might have been the air that soured him, that sick-sweet stench you could smell all the way down main street. That was more than almost half the folks in town could stand, the latest family leaving only yesterday.
The workers at the plant-- once they found out where the meat was going-- had dubbed the place *McHell*.

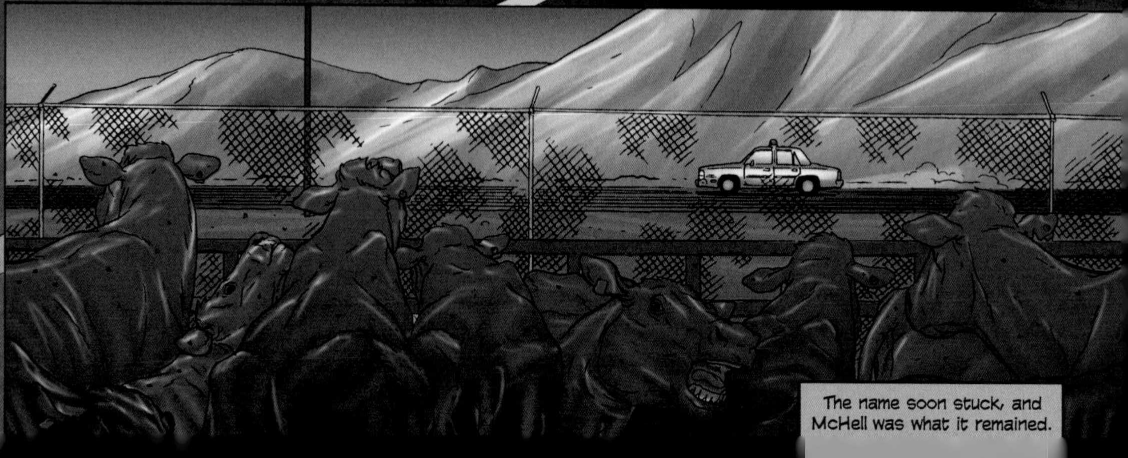
The name soon stuck, and McHell was what it remained.

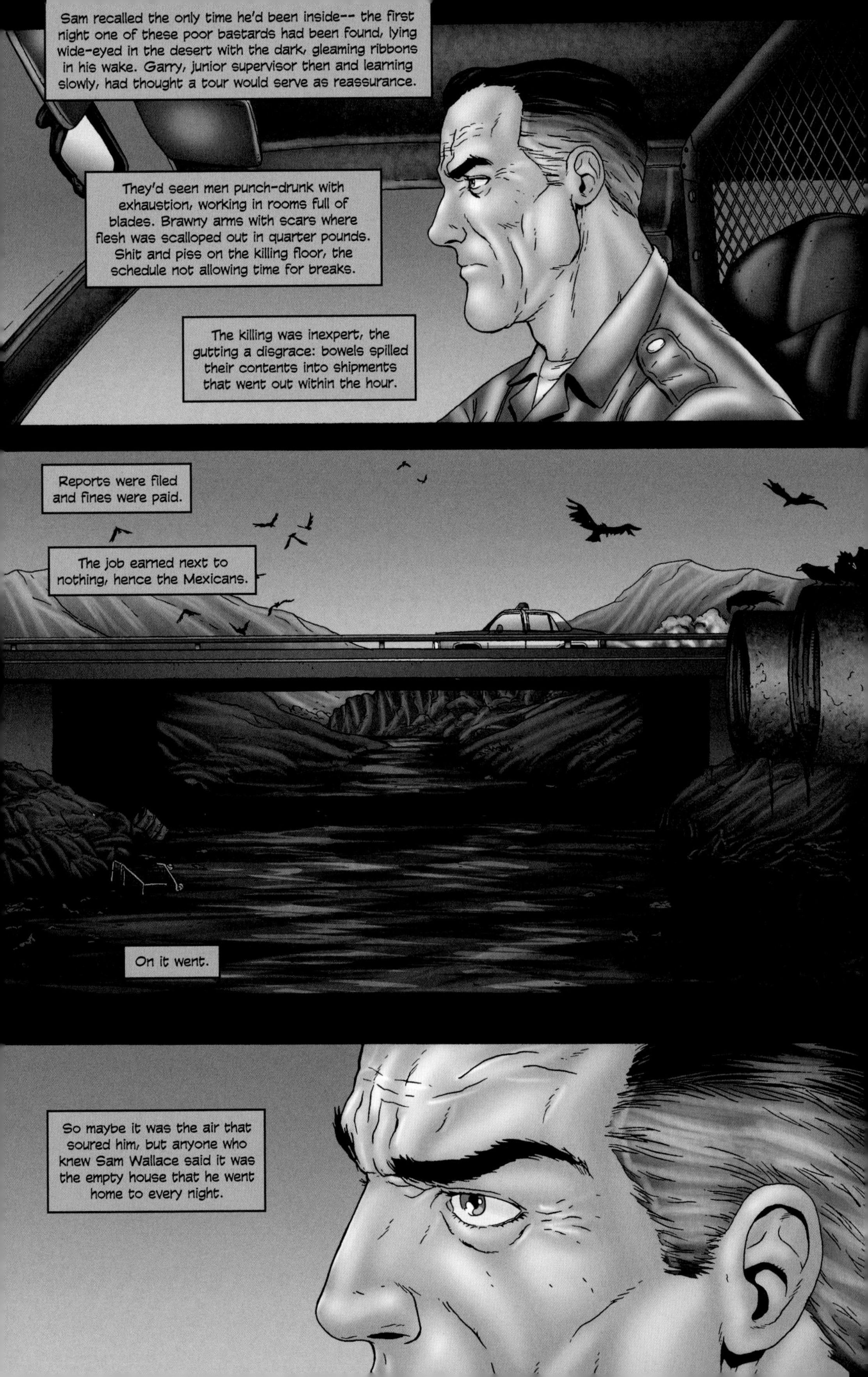
Sam recalled the only time he'd been inside-- the first night one of these poor bastards had been found, lying wide-eyed in the desert with the dark, gleaming ribbons in his wake. Garry, junior supervisor then and learning slowly, had thought a tour would serve as reassurance.
They'd seen men punch-drunk with exhaustion, working in rooms full of blades. Brawny arms with scars where flesh was scalloped out in quarter pounds. Shit and piss on the killing floor, the schedule not allowing time for breaks.
The killing was inexpert, the gutting a disgrace: bowels spilled their contents into shipments that went out within the hour.
Reports were filed and fines were paid.
The job earned next to nothing, hence the Mexicans.
On it went.
So maybe it was the air that soured him, but anyone who knew Sam Wallace said it was the empty house that he went home to every night.

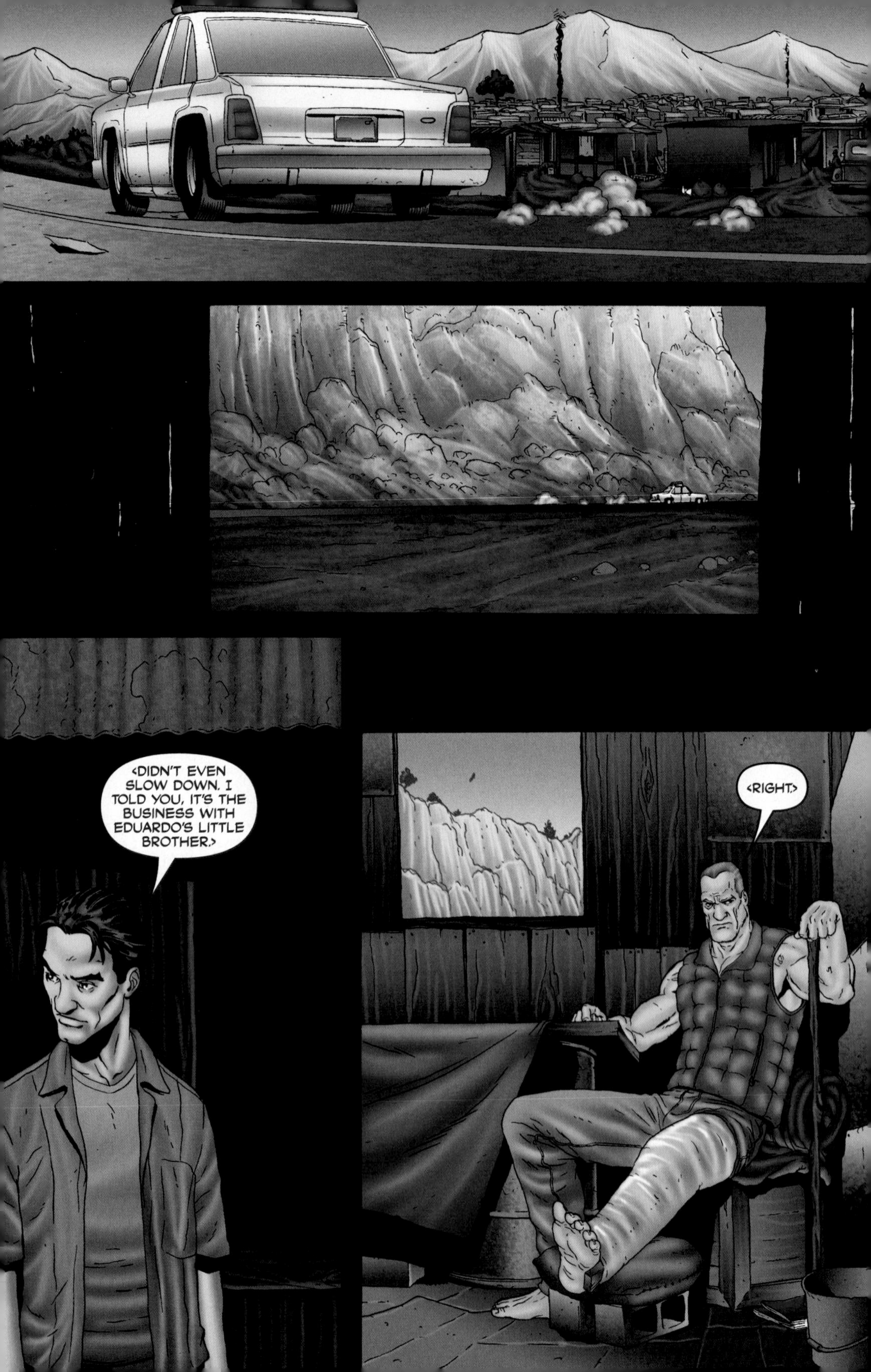
<DIDN'T EVEN SLOW DOWN. I TOLD YOU, IT'S THE BUSINESS WITH EDUARDO'S LITTLE BROTHER.>
<RIGHT.>

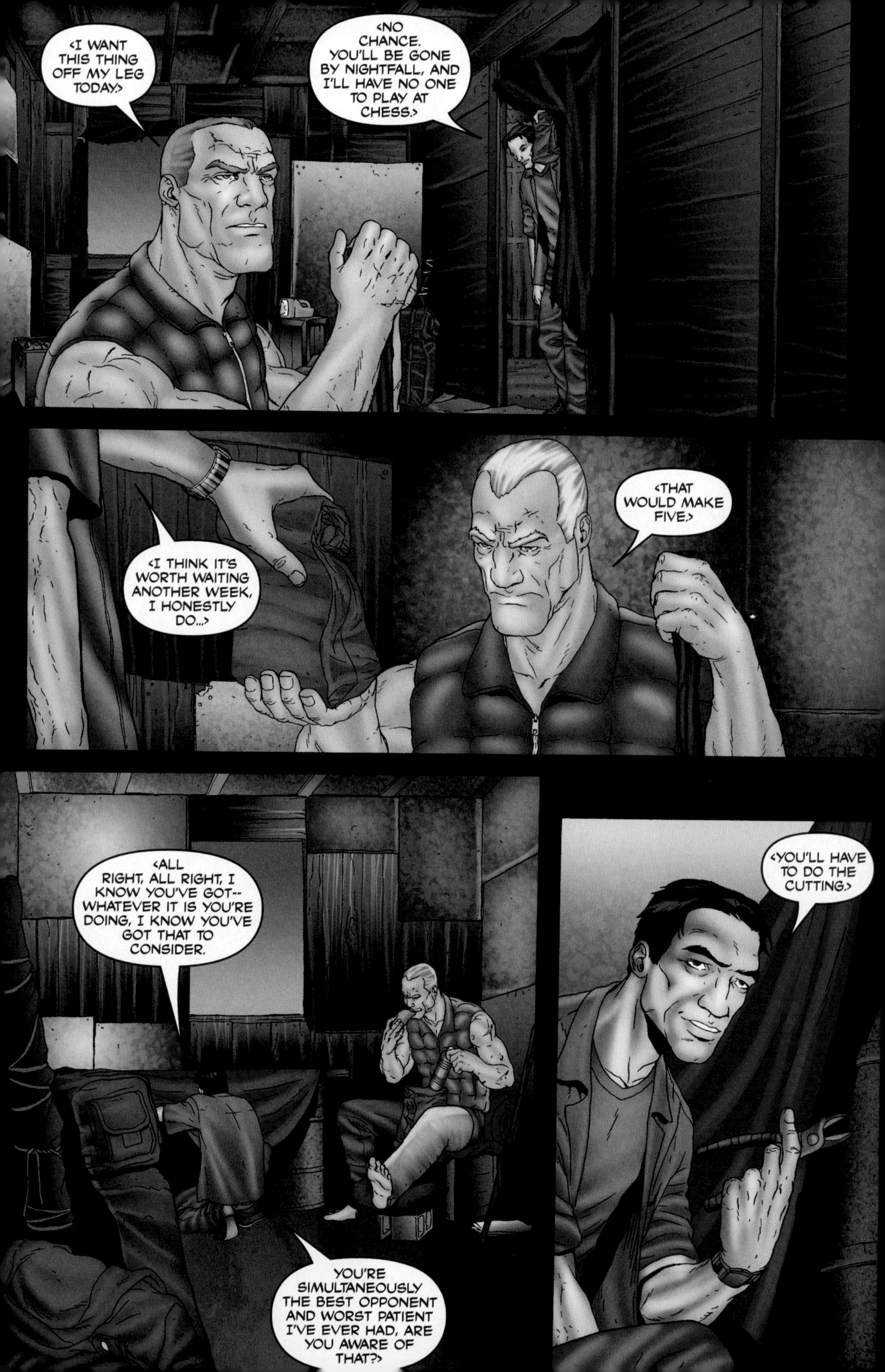

<I WANT THIS THING OFF MY LEG TODAY>
<NO CHANCE. YOU'LL BE GONE BY NIGHTFALL, AND I'LL HAVE NO ONE TO PLAY AT CHESS.>
<I THINK IT'S WORTH WAITING ANOTHER WEEK, I HONESTLY DO...>
<THAT WOULD MAKE FIVE.>
<ALL RIGHT, ALL RIGHT, I KNOW YOU'VE GOT-- WHATEVER IT IS YOU'RE DOING, I KNOW YOU'VE GOT THAT TO CONSIDER.
YOU'RE SIMULTANEOUSLY THE BEST OPPONENT AND WORST PATIENT I'VE EVER HAD, ARE YOU AWARE OF THAT?>
<YOU'LL HAVE TO DO THE CUTTING.>

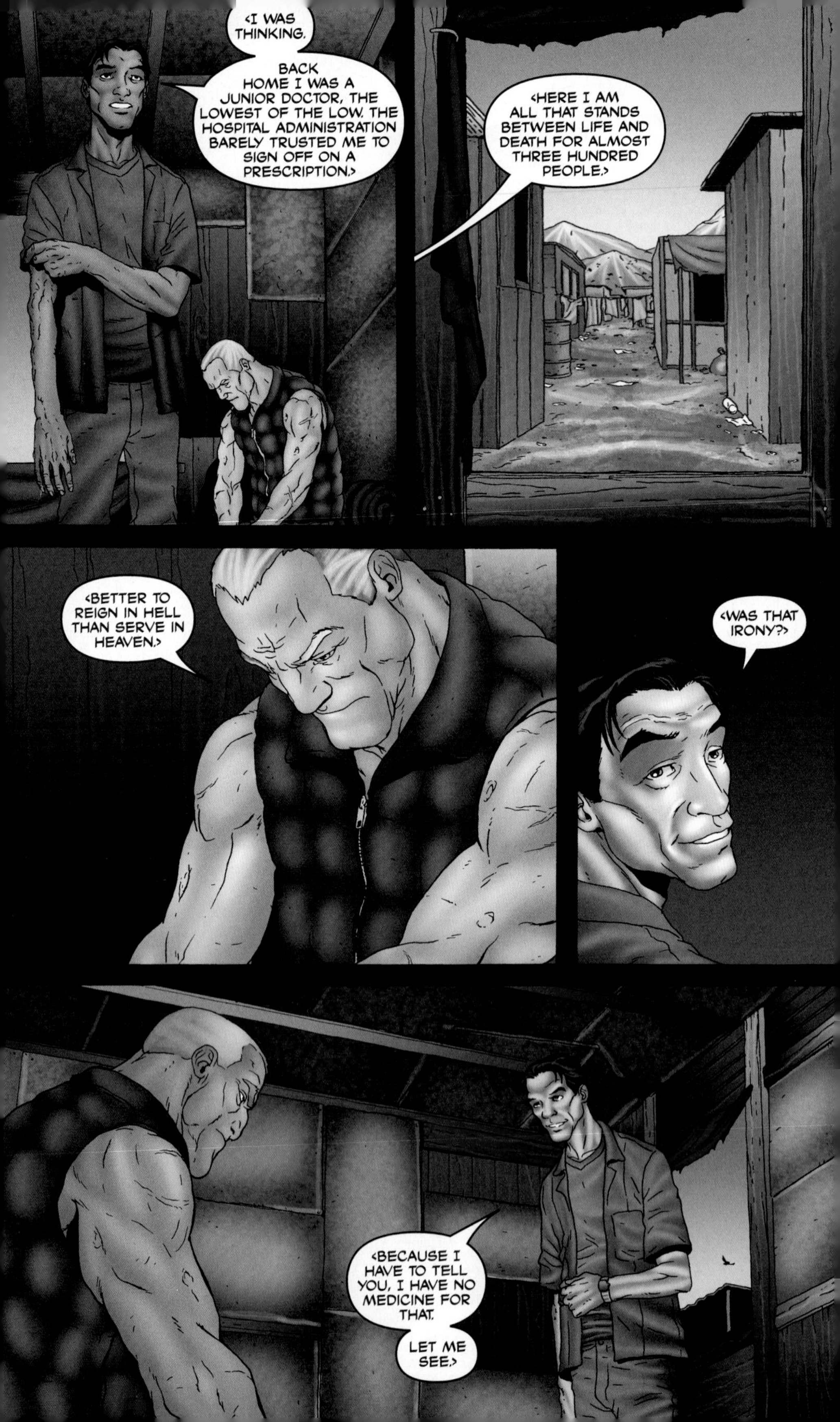

<I WAS THINKING.
BACK HOME I WAS A JUNIOR DOCTOR, THE LOWEST OF THE LOW. THE HOSPITAL ADMINISTRATION BARELY TRUSTED ME TO SIGN OFF ON A PRESCRIPTION.>
<HERE I AM ALL THAT STANDS BETWEEN LIFE AND DEATH FOR ALMOST THREE HUNDRED PEOPLE.>
<BETTER TO REIGN IN HELL THAN SERVE IN HEAVEN.>
<WAS THAT IRONY?>
<BECAUSE I HAVE TO TELL YOU, I HAVE NO MEDICINE FOR THAT.
LET ME SEE.>

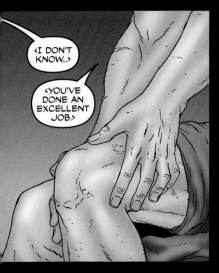

‹I DON'T KNOW...›

‹YOU'VE DONE AN EXCELLENT JOB.›

‹MY WIFE DID AN EXCELLENT JOB. I SIMPLY TOLD HER WHAT TO DO.›

‹I HAVE SOME MONEY.›

‹NO.›

‹AT LEAST FOR THE FOOD.›

‹I WILL NOT TAKE MONEY FROM YOU.›

‹YOU KNOW YOU NEED IT.›

‹ALL I KNOW IS THAT I AM SICK TO MY STOMACH OF THINGS BEING SOLD.›

‹NOW, THERE IS PLENTY OF TIME.›

‹I KNOW YOU HAVE AN AVERSION TO TRAVELLING IN DAYLIGHT.›

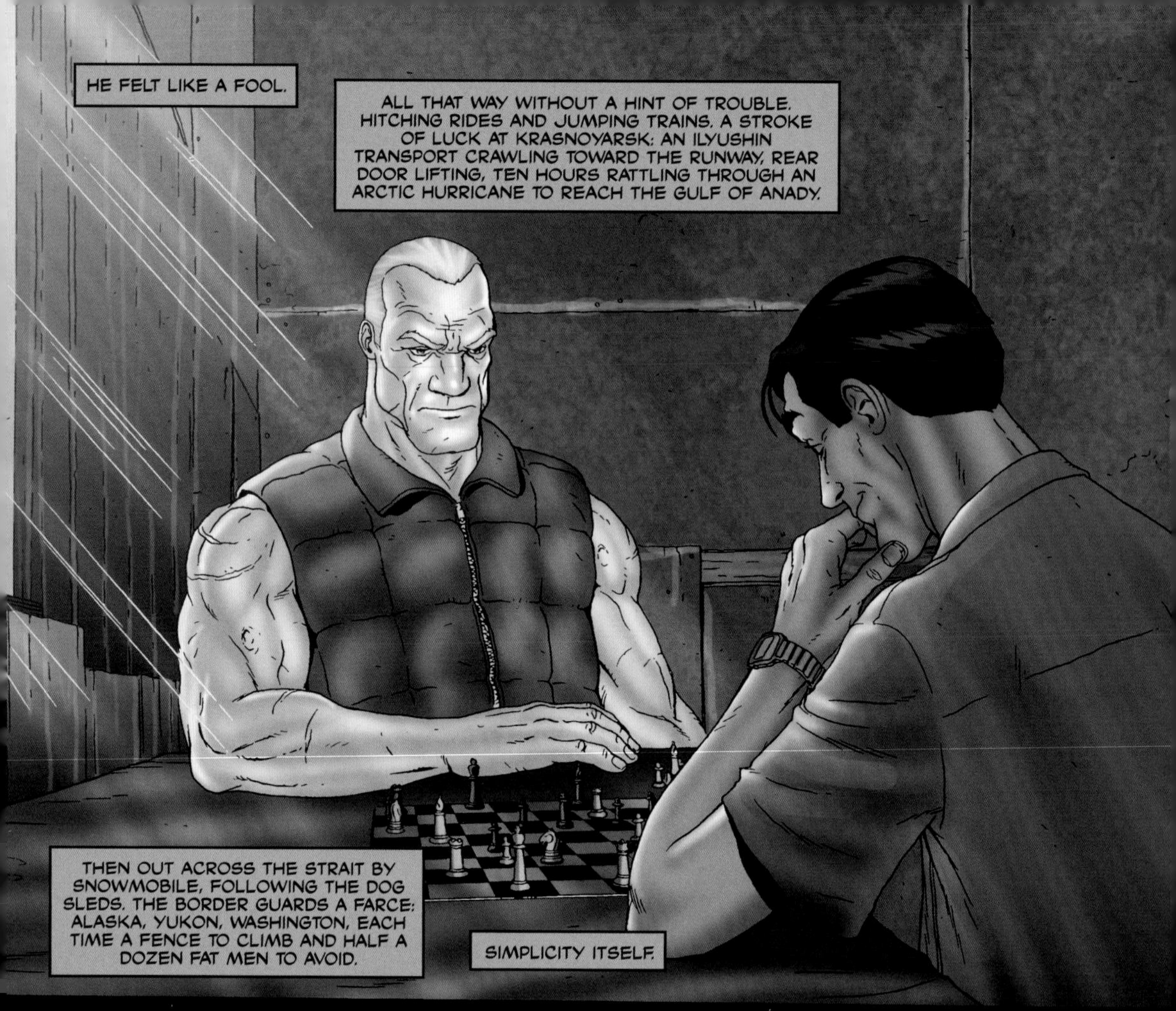
HE FELT LIKE A FOOL.
ALL THAT WAY WITHOUT A HINT OF TROUBLE. HITCHING RIDES AND JUMPING TRAINS. A STROKE OF LUCK AT KRASNOYARSK: AN ILYUSHIN TRANSPORT CRAWLING TOWARD THE RUNWAY, REAR DOOR LIFTING, TEN HOURS RATTLING THROUGH AN ARCTIC HURRICANE TO REACH THE GULF OF ANADY.
THEN OUT ACROSS THE STRAIT BY SNOWMOBILE, FOLLOWING THE DOG SLEDS. THE BORDER GUARDS A FARCE: ALASKA, YUKON, WASHINGTON, EACH TIME A FENCE TO CLIMB AND HALF A DOZEN FAT MEN TO AVOID.
SIMPLICITY ITSELF.

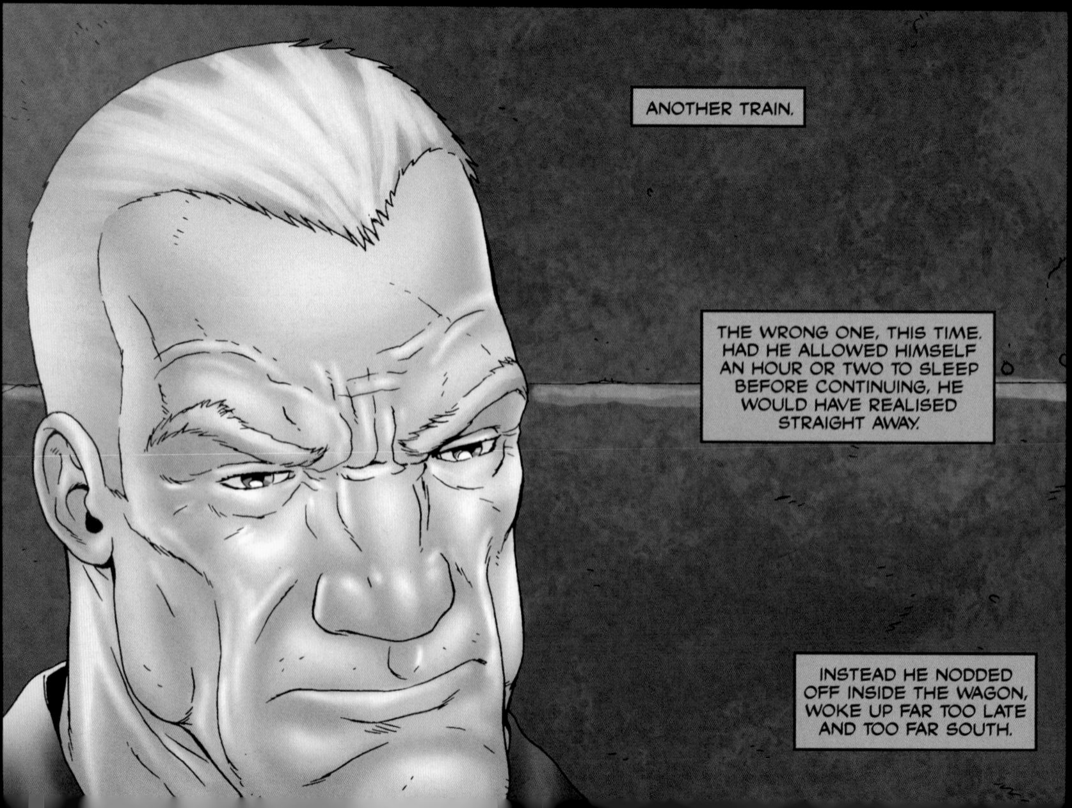
ANOTHER TRAIN.
THE WRONG ONE, THIS TIME. HAD HE ALLOWED HIMSELF AN HOUR OR TWO TO SLEEP BEFORE CONTINUING, HE WOULD HAVE REALISED STRAIGHT AWAY.
INSTEAD HE NODDED OFF INSIDE THE WAGON, WOKE UP FAR TOO LATE AND TOO FAR SOUTH.

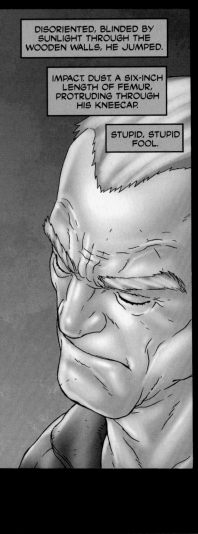

DISORIENTED, BLINDED BY SUNLIGHT THROUGH THE WOODEN WALLS, HE JUMPED.

IMPACT. DUST. A SIX-INCH LENGTH OF FEMUR, PROTRUDING THROUGH HIS KNEECAP.

STUPID, STUPID FOOL.

HE WOKE AGAIN TO DESERT NIGHT, THE STILLNESS BROKEN BY APPROACHING VOICES. HIS SPANISH CAME BACK TO HIM, TWO YEARS' WORTH FROM BLOODY TIMES ON CUBA.

THEY GAVE HIM WATER AND BORE HIM AWAY.

‹CHECKMATE.›

‹FOR OUR NEXT GAME, YOUR UNDIVIDED ATTENTION WOULD BE APPRECIATED.›

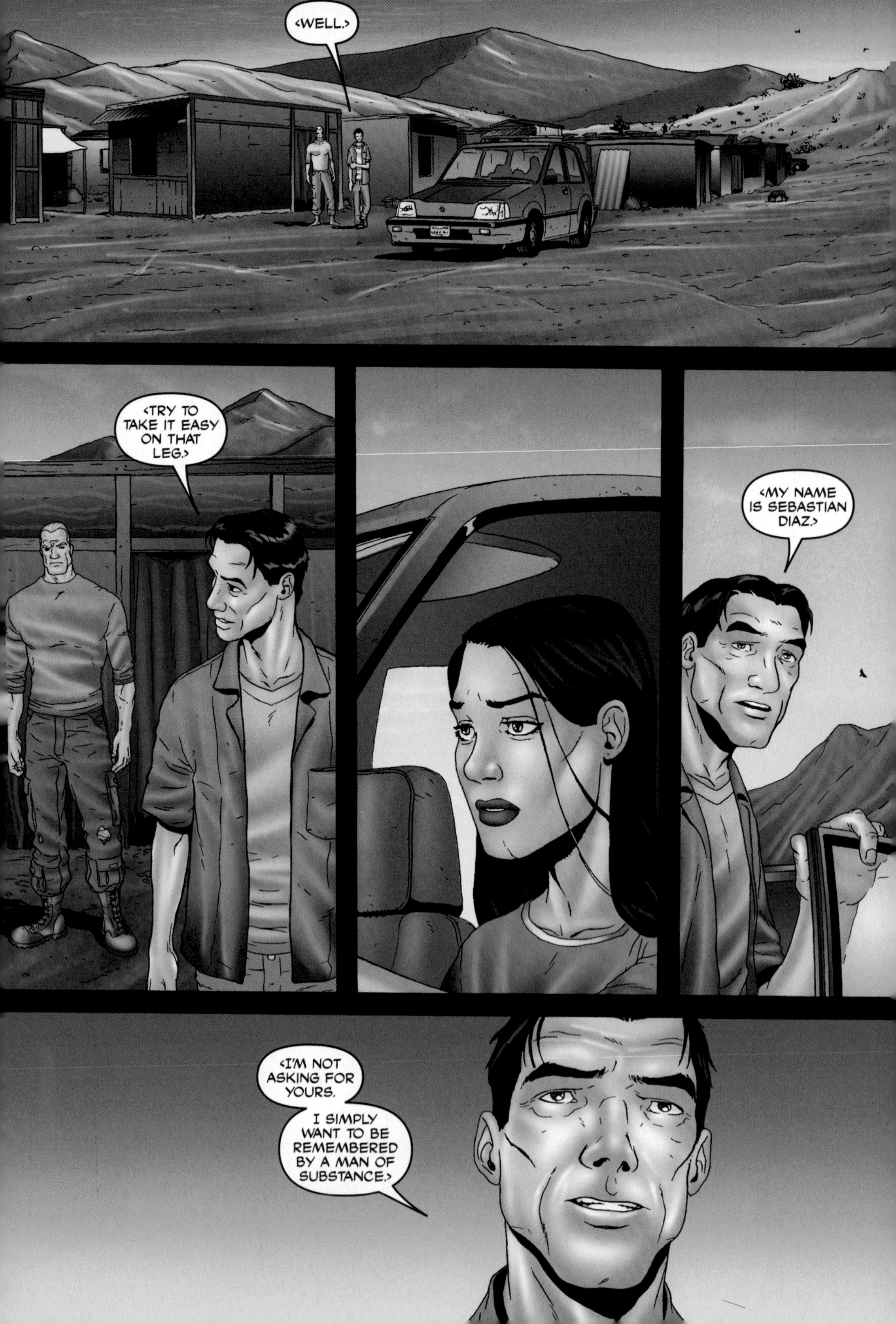

<WELL.>
<TRY TO TAKE IT EASY ON THAT LEG.>
<MY NAME IS SEBASTIAN DIAZ.>
<I'M NOT ASKING FOR YOURS.
I SIMPLY WANT TO BE REMEMBERED BY A MAN OF SUBSTANCE.>

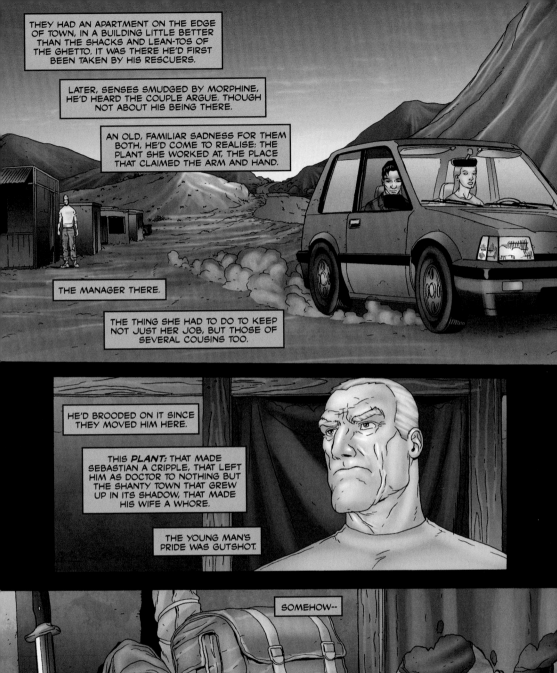

THEY HAD AN APARTMENT ON THE EDGE OF TOWN, IN A BUILDING LITTLE BETTER THAN THE SHACKS AND LEAN-TOS OF THE GHETTO. IT WAS THERE HE'D FIRST BEEN TAKEN BY HIS RESCUERS.

LATER, SENSES SMUDGED BY MORPHINE, HE'D HEARD THE COUPLE ARGUE, THOUGH NOT ABOUT HIS BEING THERE.

AN OLD, FAMILIAR SADNESS FOR THEM BOTH, HE'D COME TO REALISE: THE PLANT SHE WORKED AT, THE PLACE THAT CLAIMED THE ARM AND HAND.

THE MANAGER THERE.

THE THING SHE HAD TO DO TO KEEP NOT JUST HER JOB, BUT THOSE OF SEVERAL COUSINS TOO.

HE'D BROODED ON IT SINCE THEY MOVED HIM HERE.

THIS *PLANT*: THAT MADE SEBASTIAN A CRIPPLE, THAT LEFT HIM AS DOCTOR TO NOTHING BUT THE SHANTY TOWN THAT GREW UP IN ITS SHADOW, THAT MADE HIS WIFE A WHORE.

THE YOUNG MAN'S PRIDE WAS GUTSHOT.

SOMEHOW--

IT STIRRED A MEMORY OF KINDNESS.

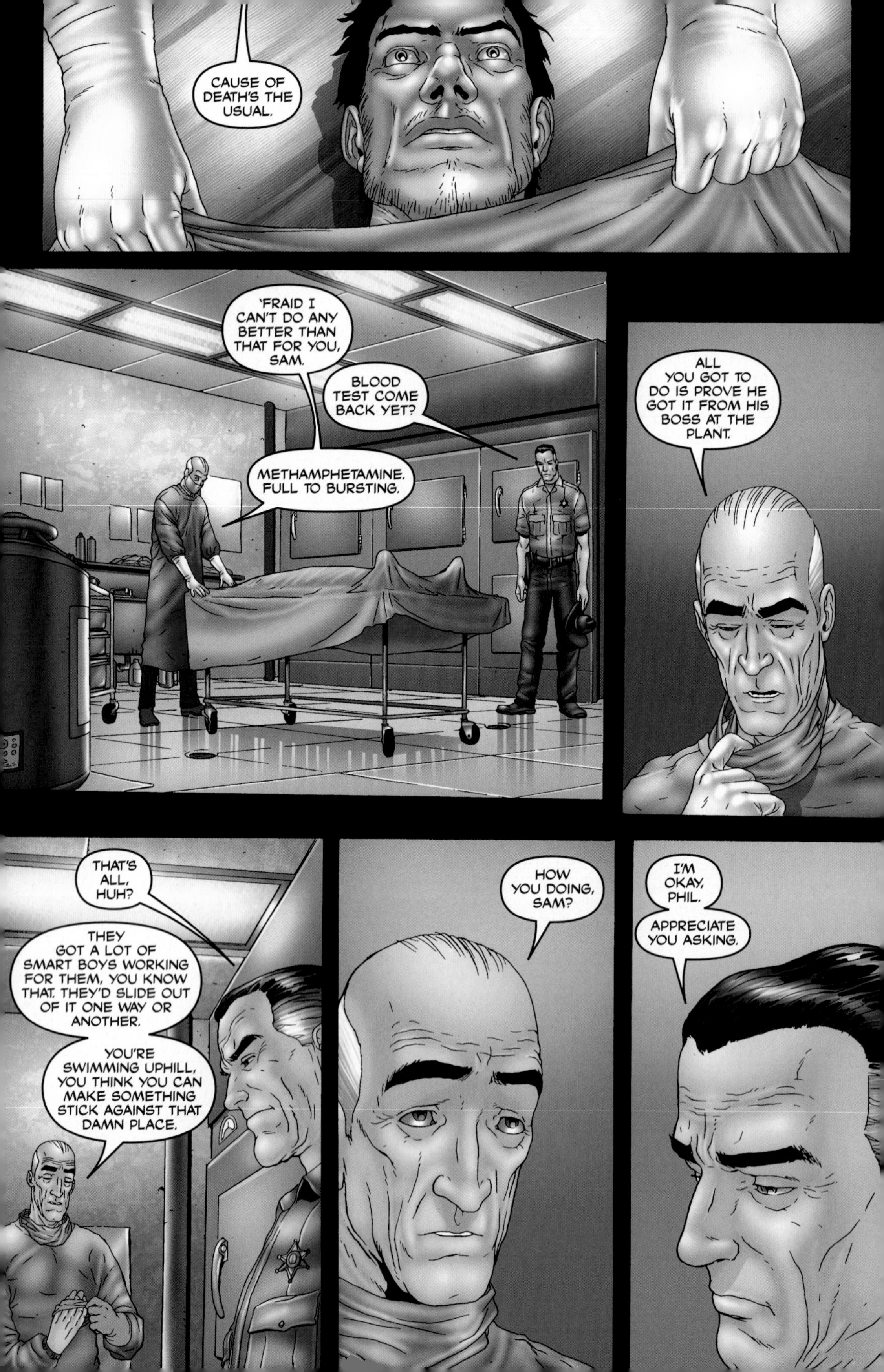
CAUSE OF DEATH'S THE USUAL.
'FRAID I CAN'T DO ANY BETTER THAN THAT FOR YOU, SAM.
BLOOD TEST COME BACK YET?
METHAMPHETAMINE. FULL TO BURSTING.
ALL YOU GOT TO DO IS PROVE HE GOT IT FROM HIS BOSS AT THE PLANT.
THAT'S ALL, HUH?
THEY GOT A LOT OF SMART BOYS WORKING FOR THEM, YOU KNOW THAT. THEY'D SLIDE OUT OF IT ONE WAY OR ANOTHER.
YOU'RE SWIMMING UPHILL, YOU THINK YOU CAN MAKE SOMETHING STICK AGAINST THAT DAMN PLACE.
HOW YOU DOING, SAM?
I'M OKAY, PHIL.
APPRECIATE YOU ASKING.

LOOK, WHY DON'T YOU COME ON BACK WITH ME TONIGHT? NANCY'S FIXING STEAKS, I'LL CALL HER, IT'S AS EASY TO COOK FOR THREE AS IT IS FOR TWO.

BEAT THE HELL OUT OF WHATEVER GODAWFUL MICROWAVABLE CONCOCTION YOU GOT WAITING FOR YOU, DON'T YOU THINK?

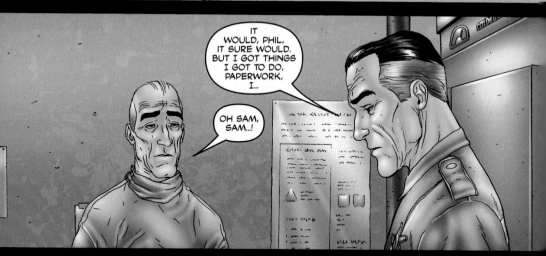

IT WOULD, PHIL, IT SURE WOULD. BUT I GOT THINGS I GOT TO DO, PAPERWORK, I...

OH SAM, SAM...!

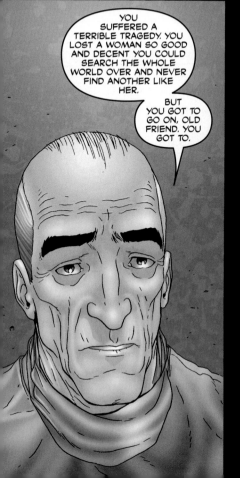

YOU SUFFERED A TERRIBLE TRAGEDY. YOU LOST A WOMAN SO GOOD AND DECENT YOU COULD SEARCH THE WHOLE WORLD OVER AND NEVER FIND ANOTHER LIKE HER.

BUT YOU GOT TO GO ON, OLD FRIEND. YOU GOT TO.

PHIL--

I FEAR FOR YOU, SAM.

I THINK OF YOU ALONE IN THAT HOUSE WITH JUST THOSE GUNS OF YOURS, AND I FEAR FOR YOU.

PHIL, I AIN'T ABOUT TO SHOOT MYSELF.

I PROMISE YOU.

OH, HELL.

FORGET ABOUT IT.

THANK YOU FOR THE INVITE TO DINNER. GIVE NANCY MY APOLOGIES, OKAY?

I WAS THINKING WE COULD MAYBE TAKE A LITTLE HUNTING TRIP, ONE OF THESE WEEKENDS. OUT BY THE PEAK WHERE THE DEER COME, YOU KNOW?

THAT WOULD BE JUST FINE. I'LL GIVE YOU A CALL ABOUT THAT.

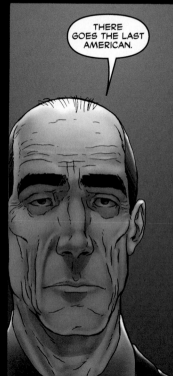

THERE GOES THE LAST AMERICAN.

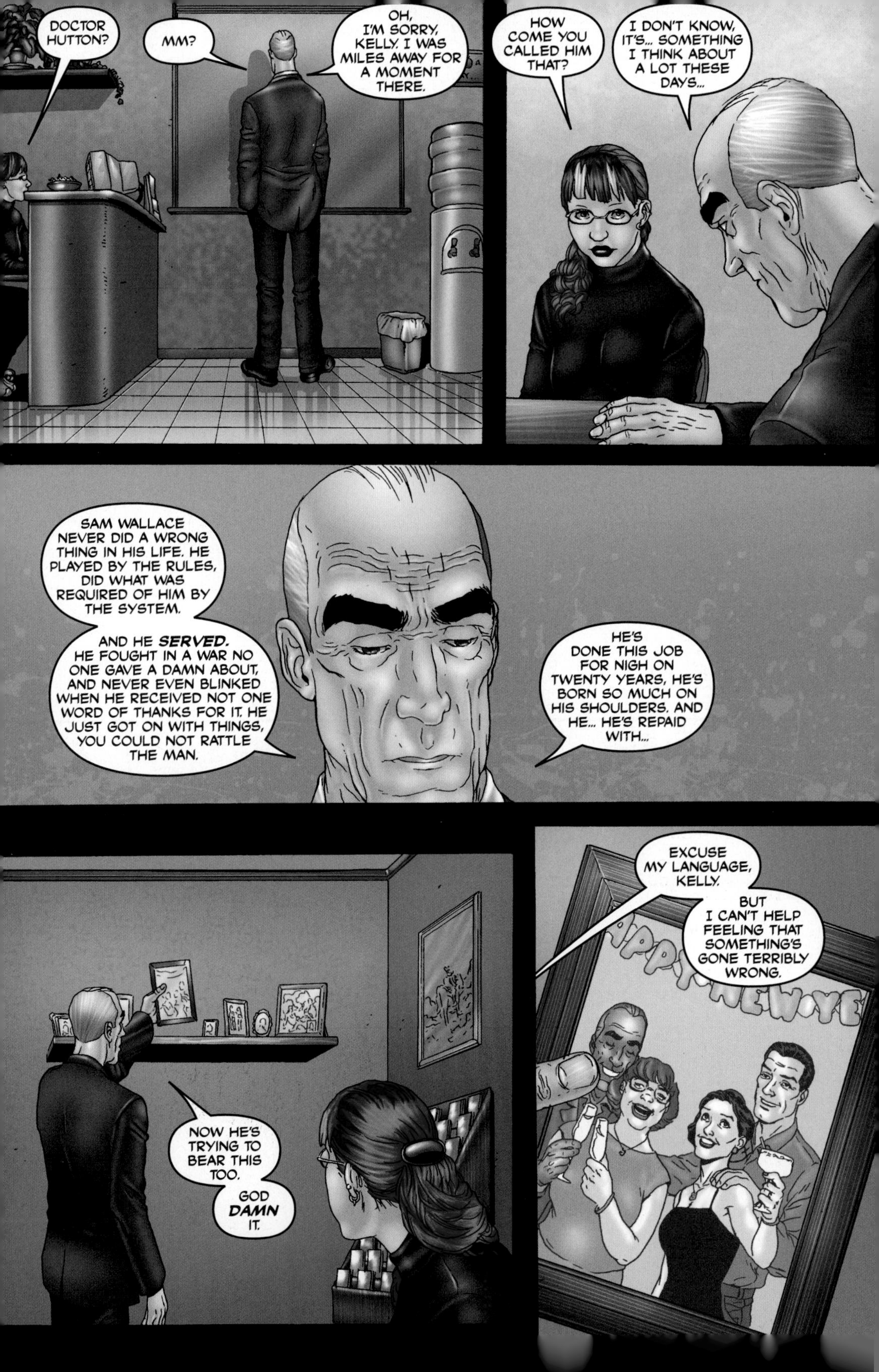

DOCTOR HUTTON?
MM?
OH, I'M SORRY, KELLY. I WAS MILES AWAY FOR A MOMENT THERE.
HOW COME YOU CALLED HIM THAT?
I DON'T KNOW, IT'S... SOMETHING I THINK ABOUT A LOT THESE DAYS...
SAM WALLACE NEVER DID A WRONG THING IN HIS LIFE. HE PLAYED BY THE RULES, DID WHAT WAS REQUIRED OF HIM BY THE SYSTEM.
AND HE *SERVED.* HE FOUGHT IN A WAR NO ONE GAVE A DAMN ABOUT, AND NEVER EVEN BLINKED WHEN HE RECEIVED NOT ONE WORD OF THANKS FOR IT. HE JUST GOT ON WITH THINGS, YOU COULD NOT RATTLE THE MAN.
HE'S DONE THIS JOB FOR NIGH ON TWENTY YEARS, HE'S BORN SO MUCH ON HIS SHOULDERS. AND HE... HE'S REPAID WITH...
NOW HE'S TRYING TO BEAR THIS TOO.
GOD *DAMN* IT.
EXCUSE MY LANGUAGE, KELLY.
BUT I CAN'T HELP FEELING THAT SOMETHING'S GONE TERRIBLY WRONG.

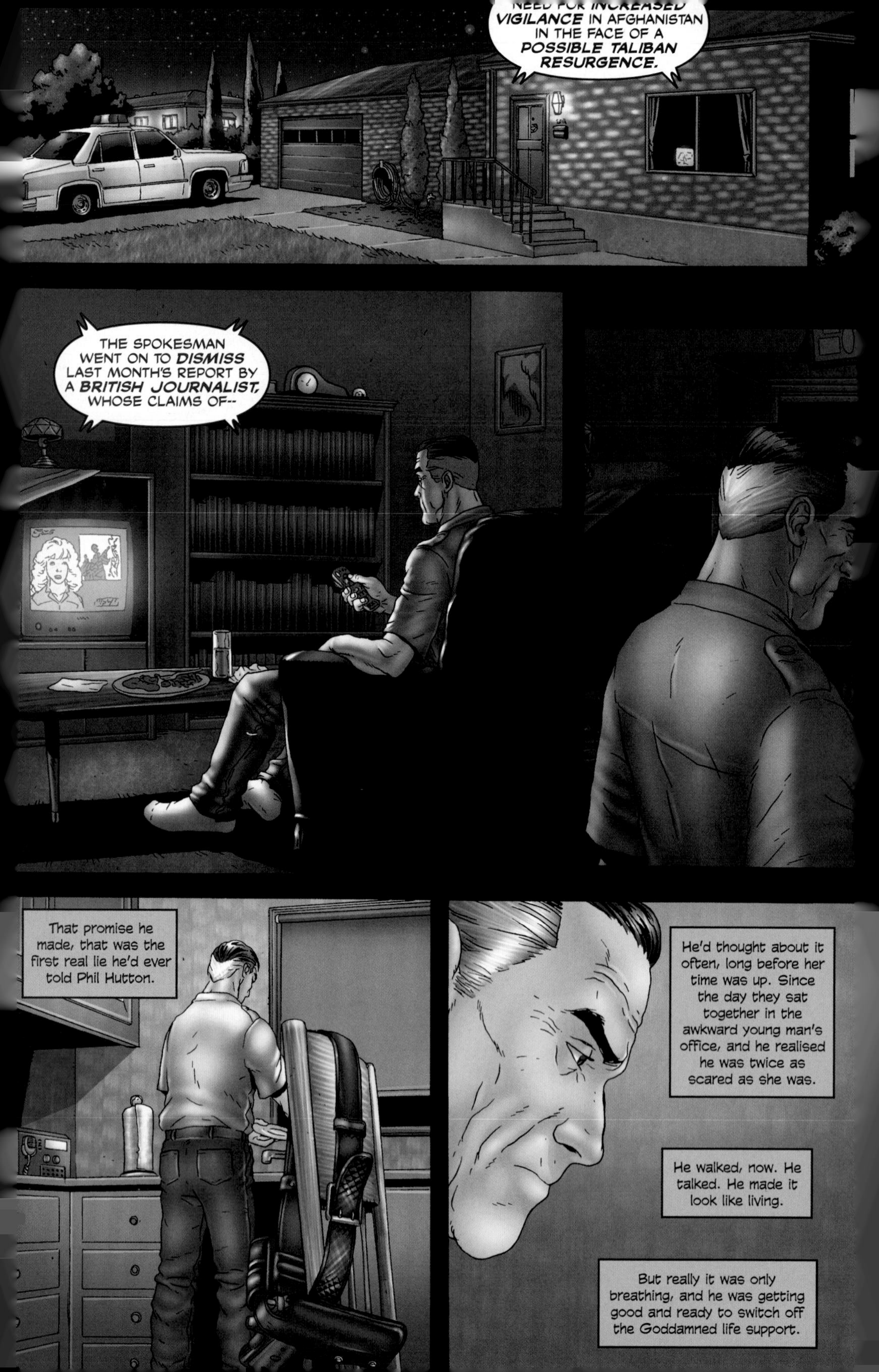
NEED FOR INCREASED VIGILANCE IN AFGHANISTAN IN THE FACE OF A POSSIBLE TALIBAN RESURGENCE.
THE SPOKESMAN WENT ON TO DISMISS LAST MONTH'S REPORT BY A BRITISH JOURNALIST, WHOSE CLAIMS OF--
That promise he made, that was the first real lie he'd ever told Phil Hutton.
He'd thought about it often, long before her time was up. Since the day they sat together in the awkward young man's office, and he realised he was twice as scared as she was.
He walked, now. He talked. He made it look like living.
But really it was only breathing, and he was getting good and ready to switch off the Goddamned life support.

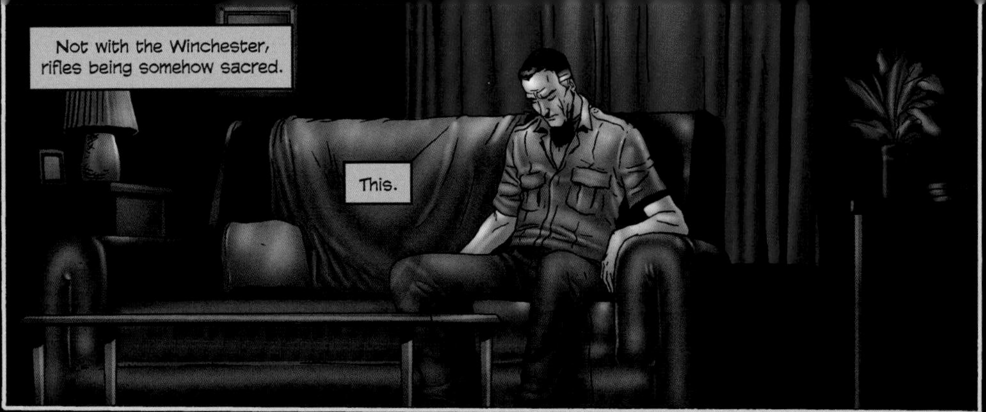
Not with the Winchester, rifles being somehow sacred.
This.

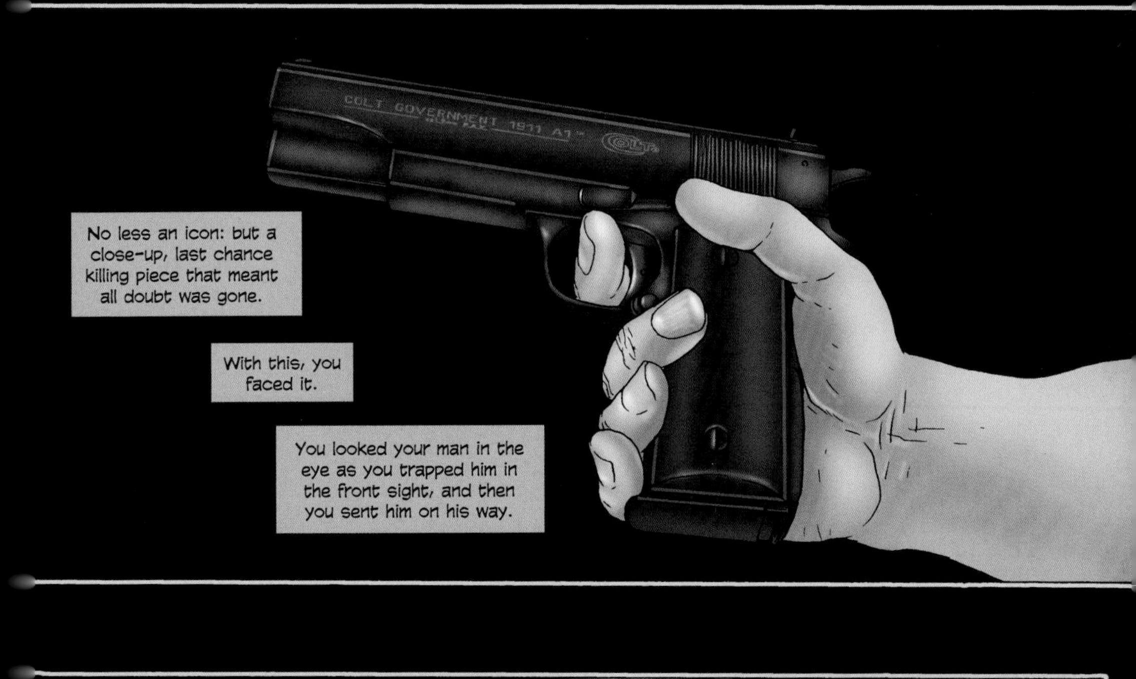
COLT GOVERNMENT 1911 A1
No less an icon: but a close-up, last chance killing piece that meant all doubt was gone.
With this, you faced it.
You looked your man in the eye as you trapped him in the front sight, and then you sent him on his way.

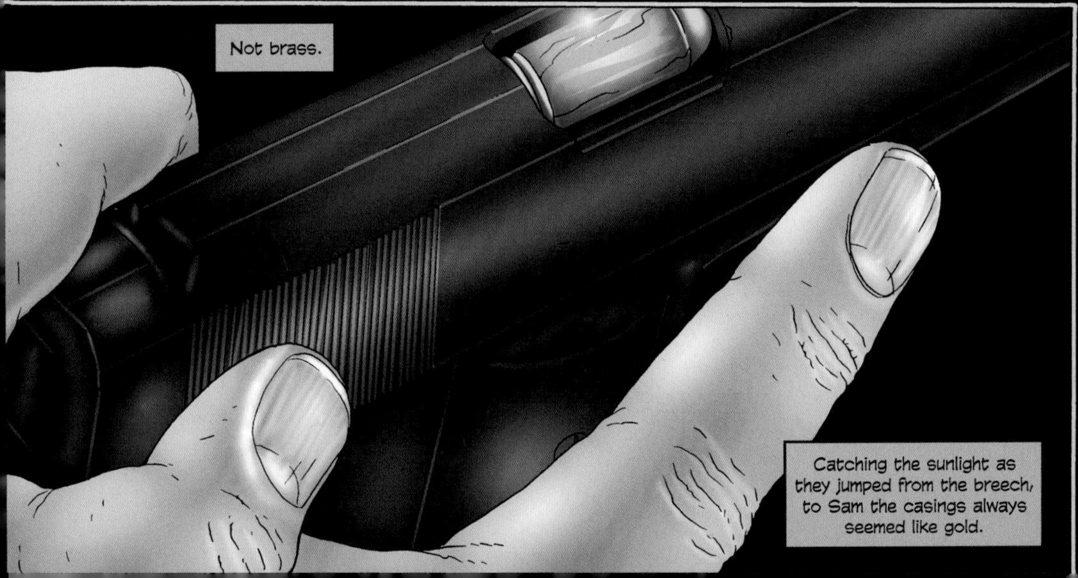
Not brass.
Catching the sunlight as they jumped from the breech, to Sam the casings always seemed like gold.

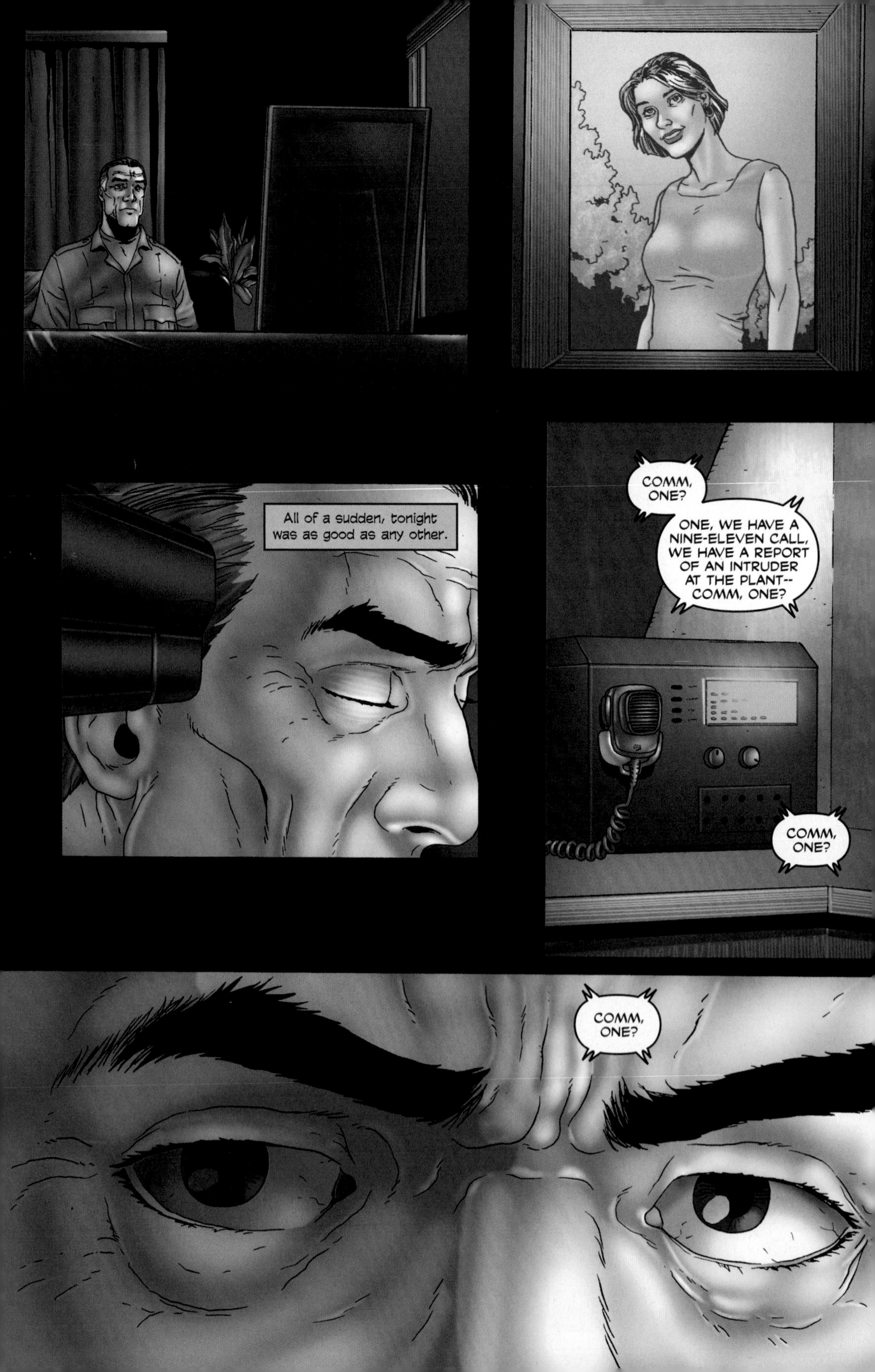
All of a sudden, tonight was as good as any other.
COMM, ONE?
ONE, WE HAVE A NINE-ELEVEN CALL, WE HAVE A REPORT OF AN INTRUDER AT THE PLANT-- COMM, ONE?
COMM, ONE?
COMM, ONE?

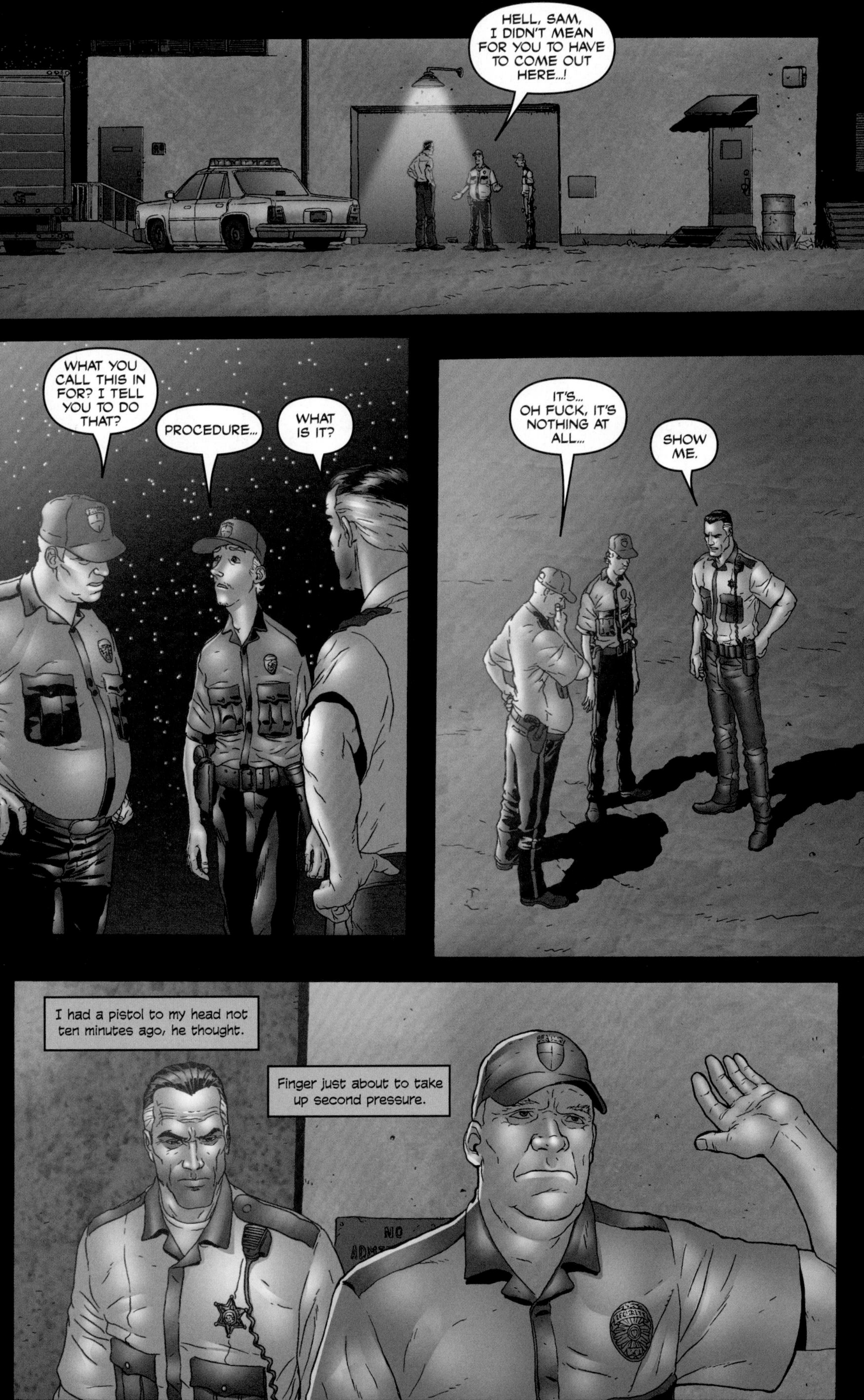
HELL, SAM, I DIDN'T MEAN FOR YOU TO HAVE TO COME OUT HERE...!
WHAT YOU CALL THIS IN FOR? I TELL YOU TO DO THAT?
PROCEDURE...
WHAT IS IT?
IT'S... OH FUCK, IT'S NOTHING AT ALL...
SHOW ME.
I had a pistol to my head not ten minutes ago, he thought.
Finger just about to take up second pressure.
NO

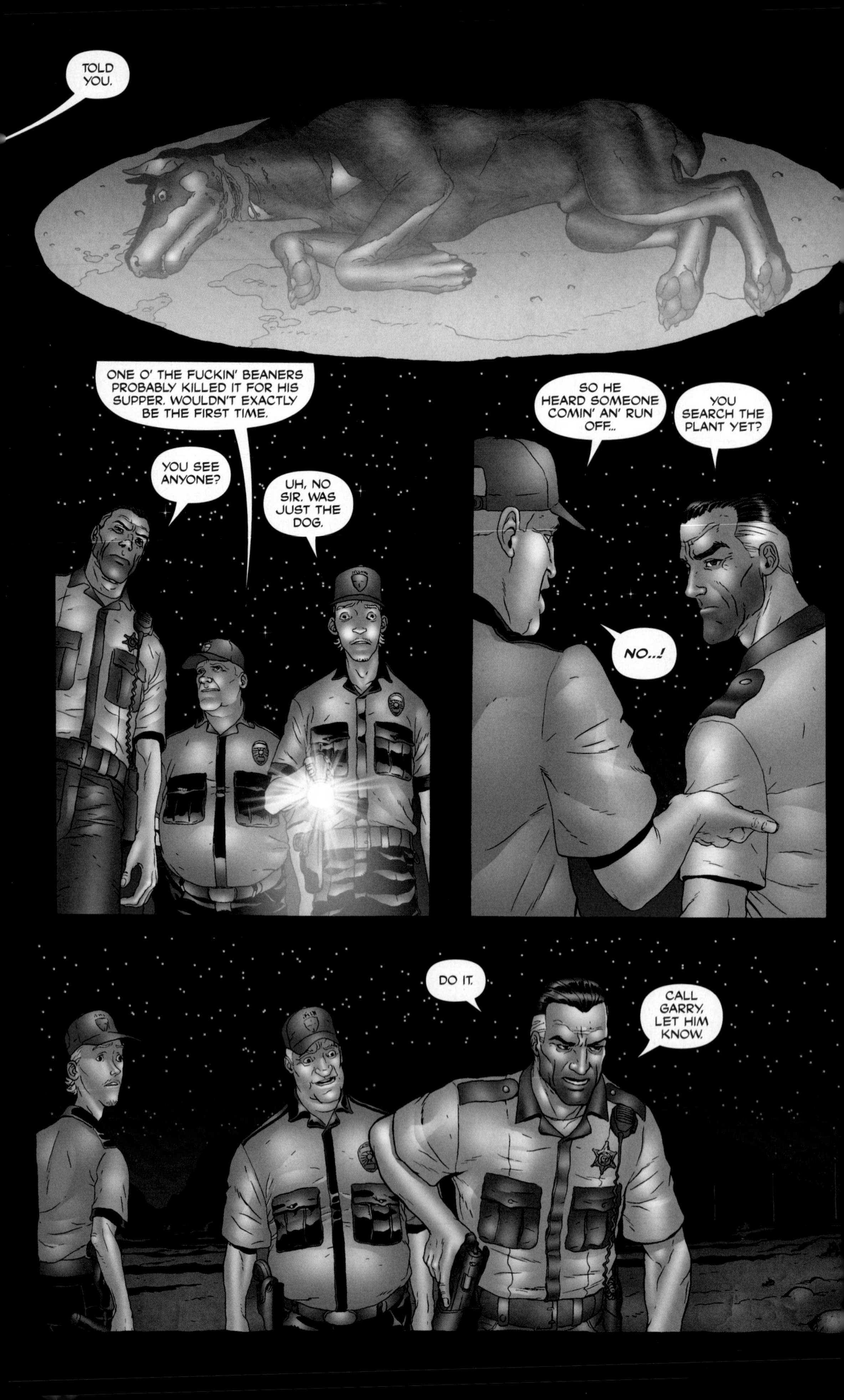
TOLD YOU.
ONE O' THE FUCKIN' BEANERS PROBABLY KILLED IT FOR HIS SUPPER. WOULDN'T EXACTLY BE THE FIRST TIME.
YOU SEE ANYONE?
UH, NO SIR. WAS JUST THE DOG.
SO HE HEARD SOMEONE COMIN' AN' RUN OFF...
YOU SEARCH THE PLANT YET?
NO...!
DO IT.
CALL GARRY, LET HIM KNOW.

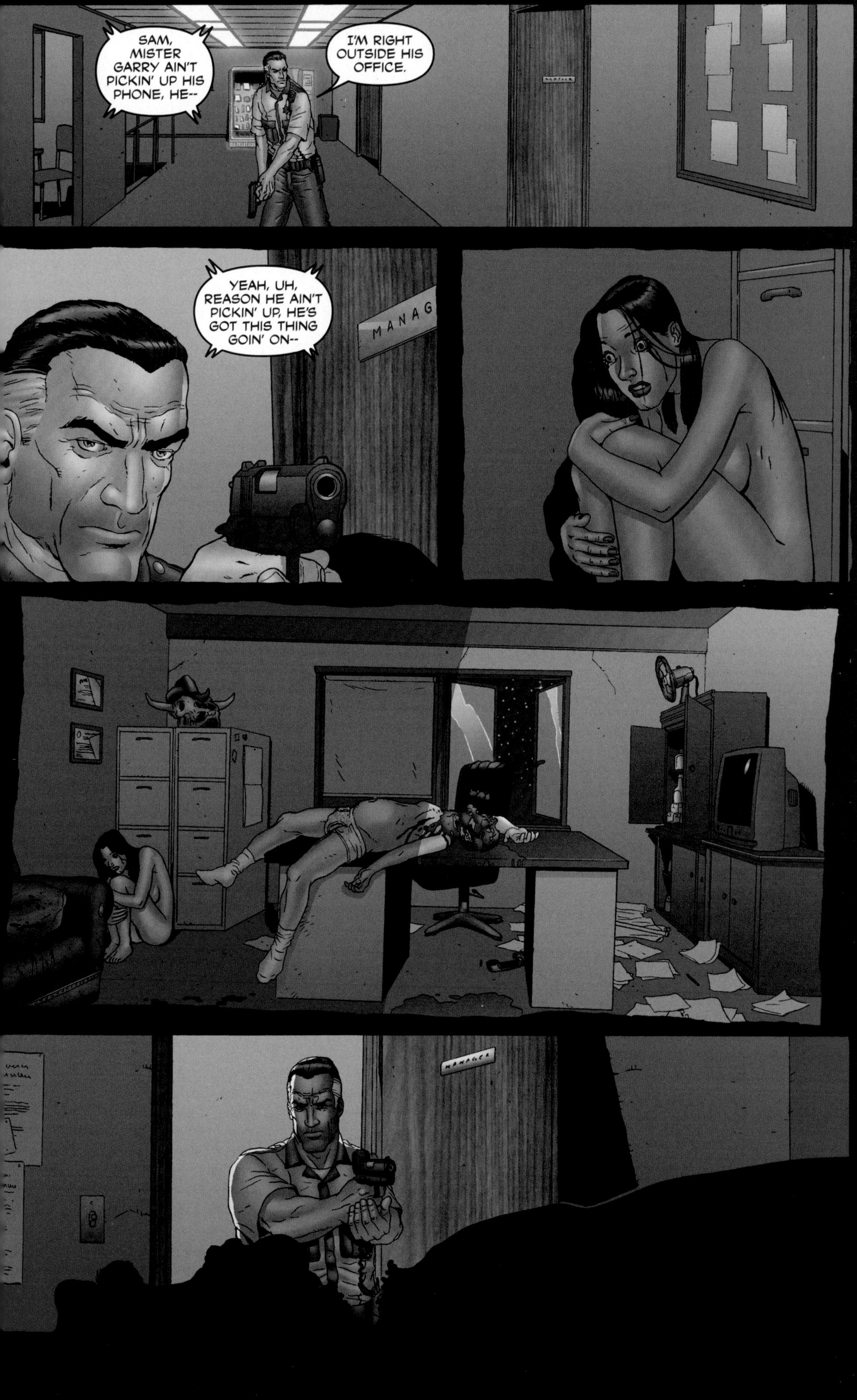
SAM, MISTER GARRY AIN'T PICKIN' UP HIS PHONE, HE--
I'M RIGHT OUTSIDE HIS OFFICE.
YEAH, UH, REASON HE AIN'T PICKIN' UP, HE'S GOT THIS THING GOIN' ON--
MANAG
MANAGER

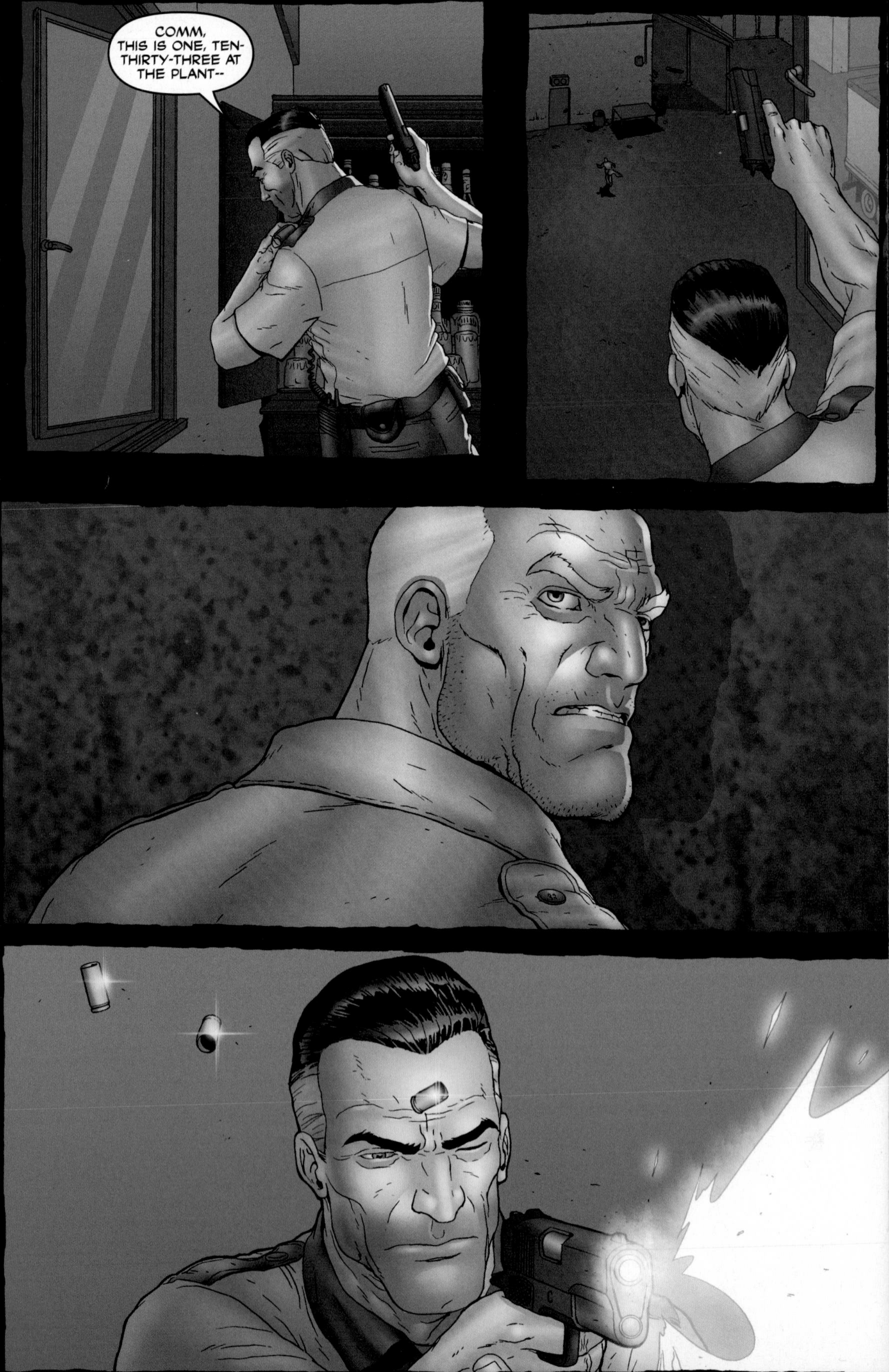
COMM, THIS IS ONE, TEN-THIRTY-THREE AT THE PLANT--

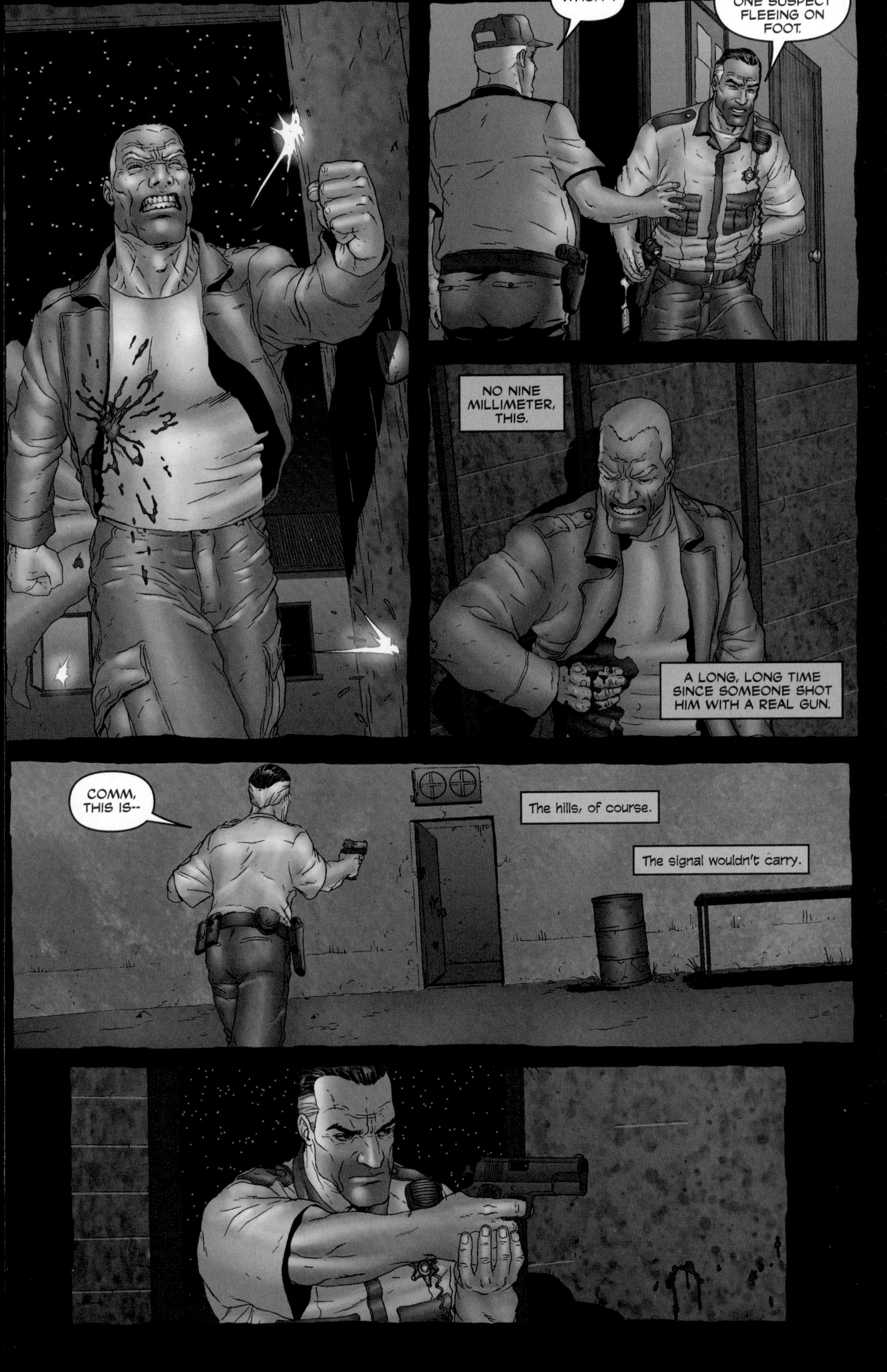

ONE SUSPECT FLEEING ON FOOT.
NO NINE MILLIMETER, THIS.
A LONG, LONG TIME SINCE SOMEONE SHOT HIM WITH A REAL GUN.
COMM, THIS IS--
The hills, of course.
The signal wouldn't carry.

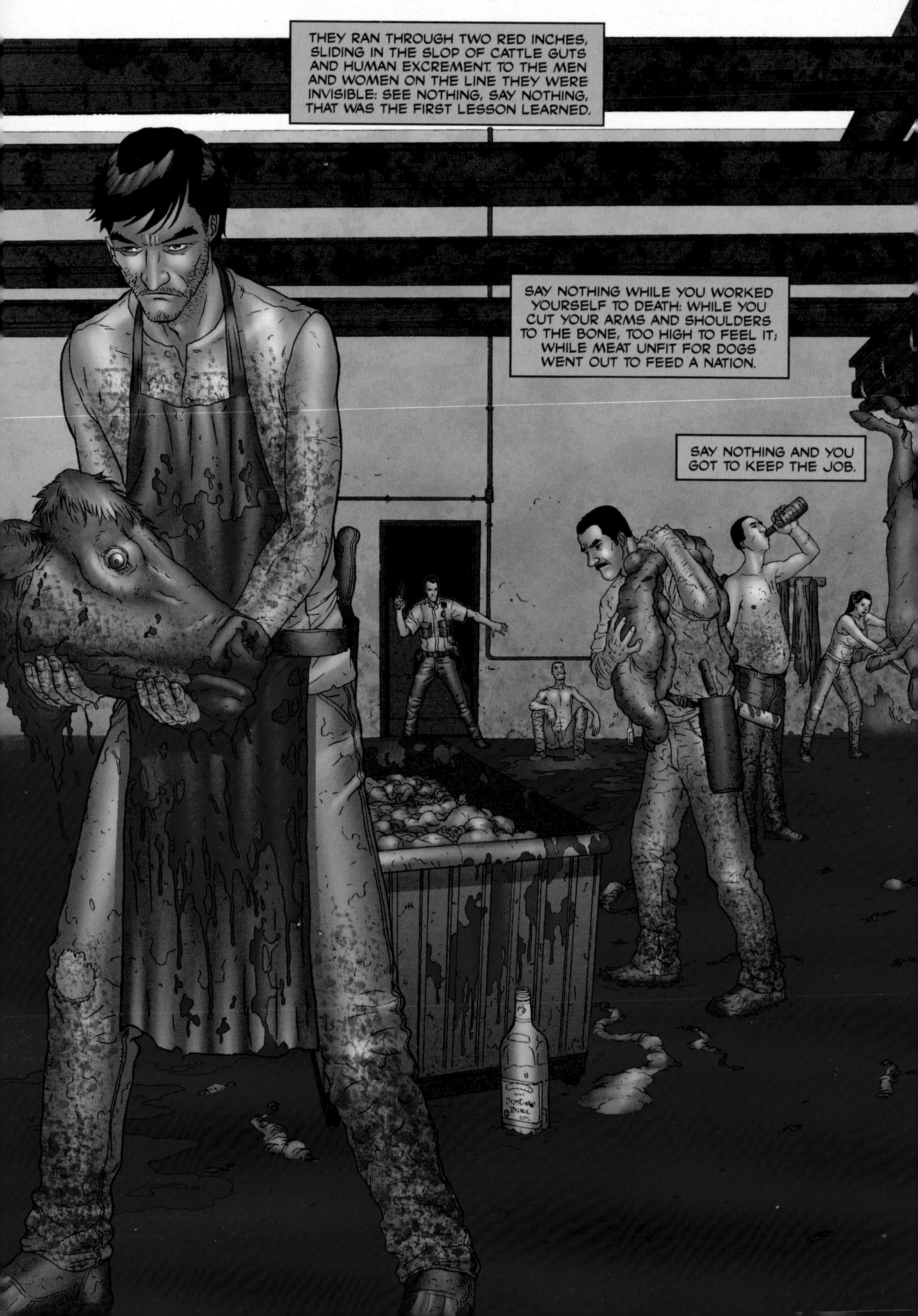
THEY RAN THROUGH TWO RED INCHES, SLIDING IN THE SLOP OF CATTLE GUTS AND HUMAN EXCREMENT. TO THE MEN AND WOMEN ON THE LINE THEY WERE INVISIBLE: SEE NOTHING, SAY NOTHING, THAT WAS THE FIRST LESSON LEARNED.
SAY NOTHING WHILE YOU WORKED YOURSELF TO DEATH: WHILE YOU CUT YOUR ARMS AND SHOULDERS TO THE BONE, TOO HIGH TO FEEL IT; WHILE MEAT UNFIT FOR DOGS WENT OUT TO FEED A NATION.
SAY NOTHING AND YOU GOT TO KEEP THE JOB.

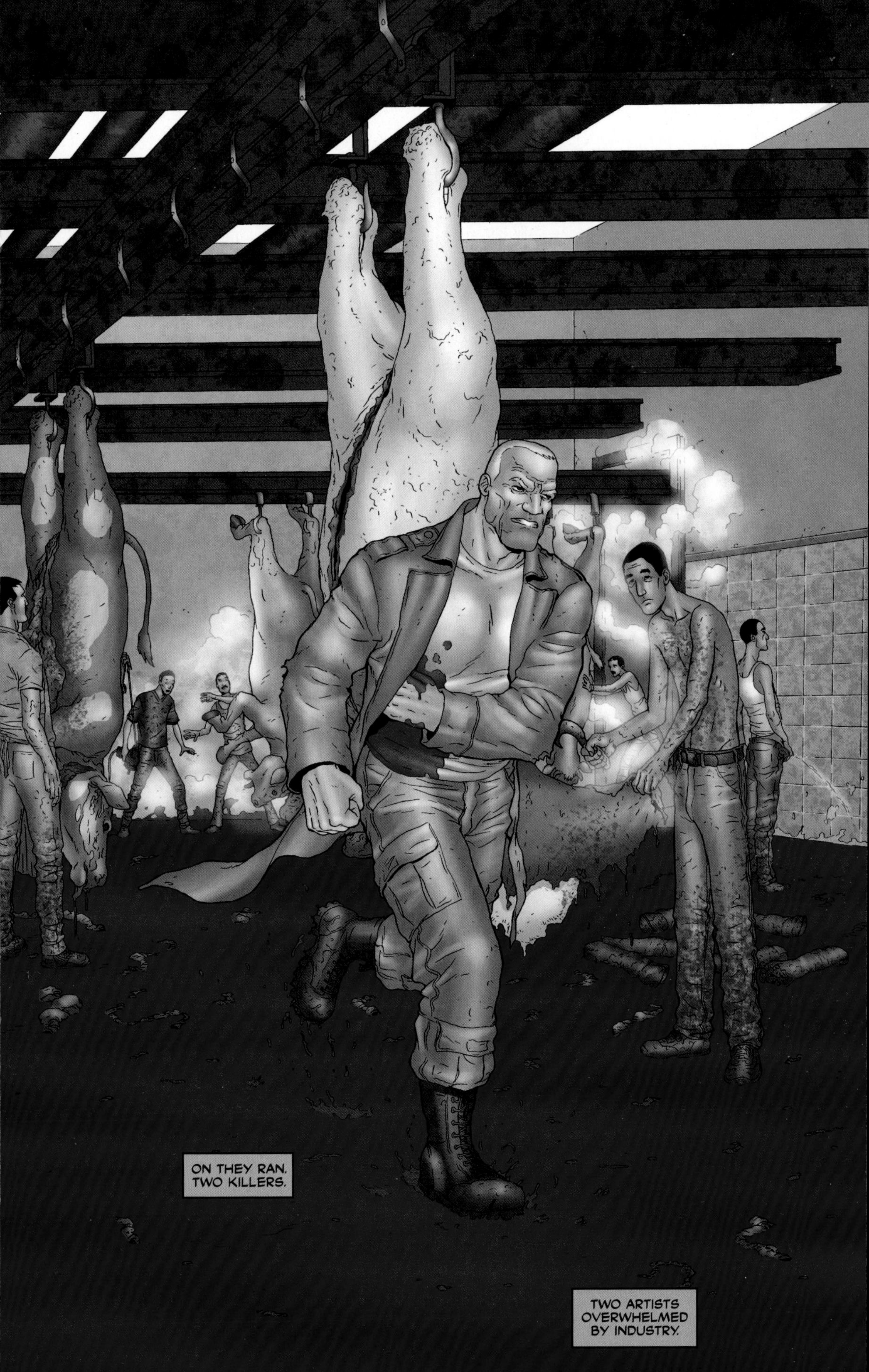
ON THEY RAN. TWO KILLERS.
TWO ARTISTS OVERWHELMED BY INDUSTRY.

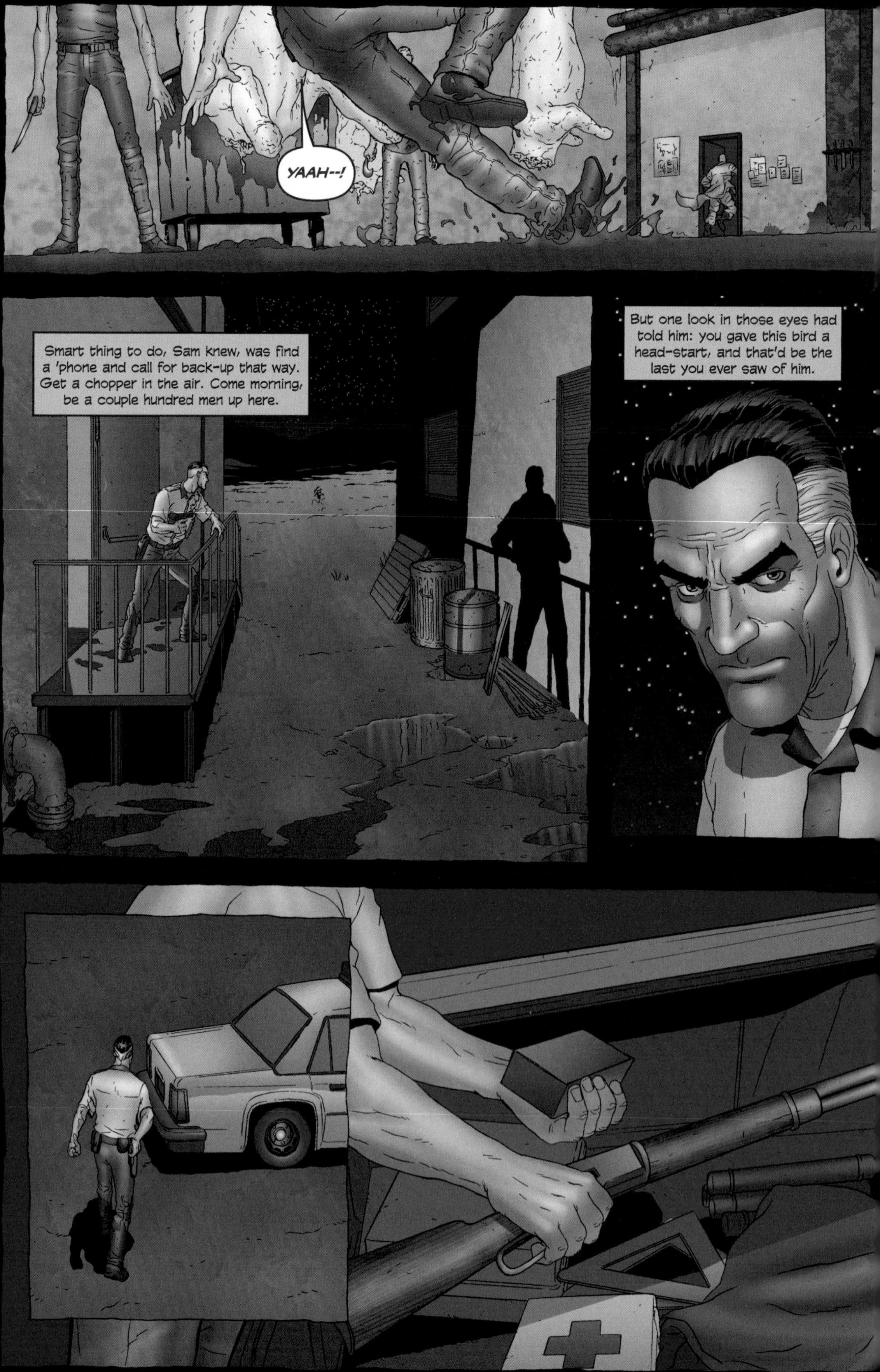
YAAH--!
Smart thing to do, Sam knew, was find a 'phone and call for back-up that way. Get a chopper in the air. Come morning, be a couple hundred men up here.
But one look in those eyes had told him: you gave this bird a head-start, and that'd be the last you ever saw of him.

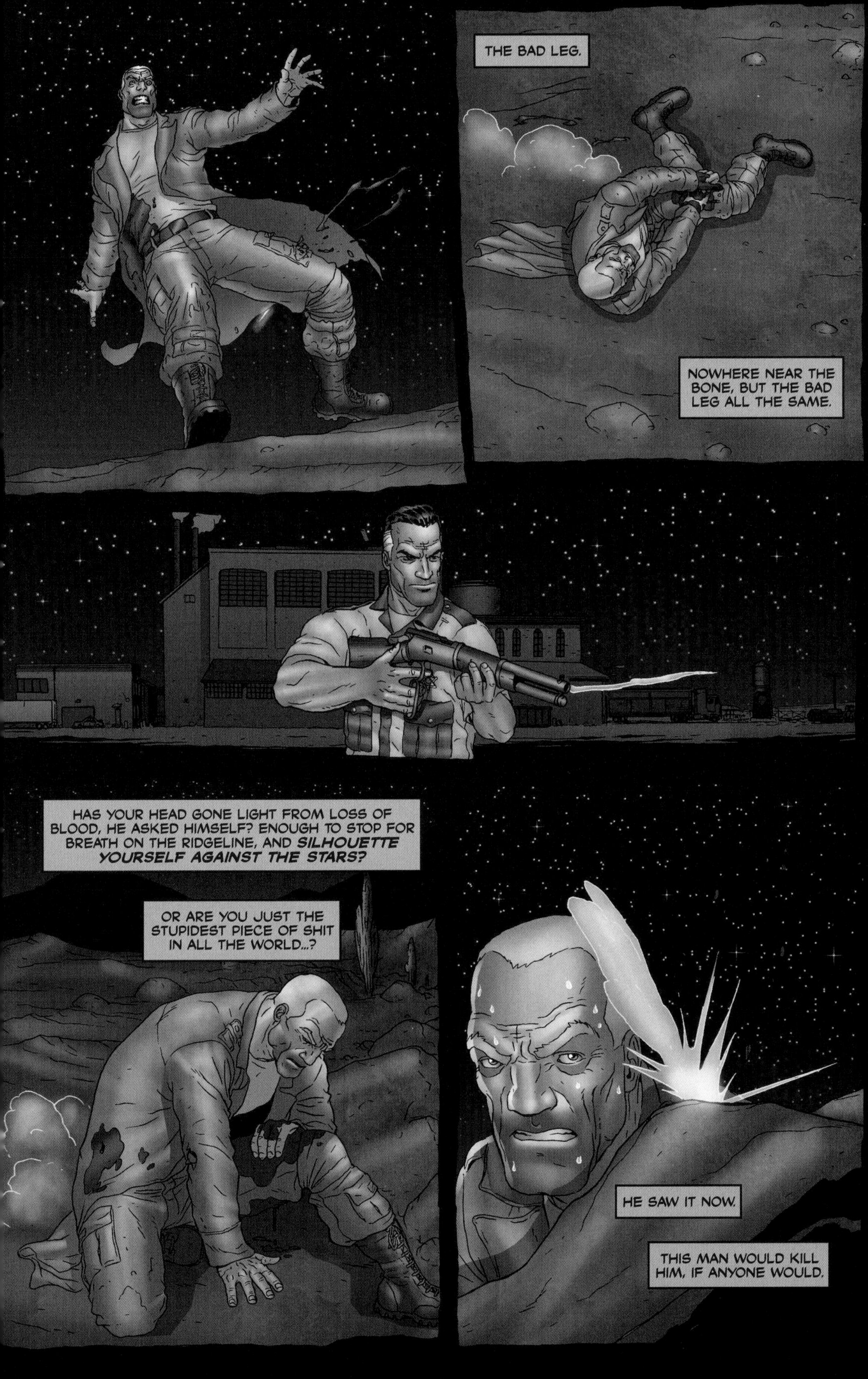
THE BAD LEG.
NOWHERE NEAR THE BONE, BUT THE BAD LEG ALL THE SAME.
HAS YOUR HEAD GONE LIGHT FROM LOSS OF BLOOD, HE ASKED HIMSELF? ENOUGH TO STOP FOR BREATH ON THE RIDGELINE, AND *SILHOUETTE YOURSELF AGAINST THE STARS?*
OR ARE YOU JUST THE STUPIDEST PIECE OF SHIT IN ALL THE WORLD...?
HE SAW IT NOW.
THIS MAN WOULD KILL HIM, IF ANYONE WOULD.

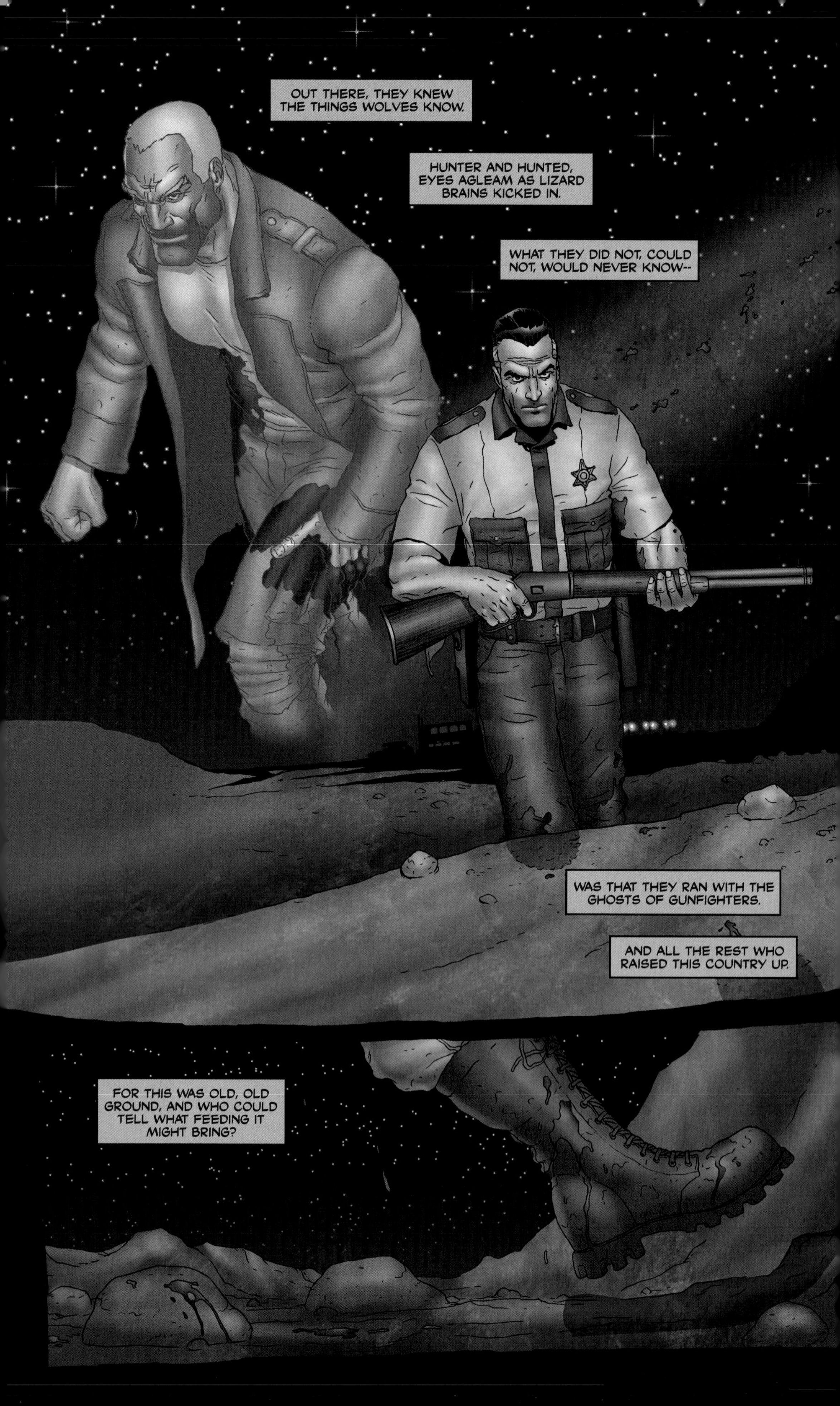
OUT THERE, THEY KNEW THE THINGS WOLVES KNOW.
HUNTER AND HUNTED, EYES AGLEAM AS LIZARD BRAINS KICKED IN.
WHAT THEY DID NOT, COULD NOT, WOULD NEVER KNOW--
WAS THAT THEY RAN WITH THE GHOSTS OF GUNFIGHTERS.
AND ALL THE REST WHO RAISED THIS COUNTRY UP.
FOR THIS WAS OLD, OLD GROUND, AND WHO COULD TELL WHAT FEEDING IT MIGHT BRING?

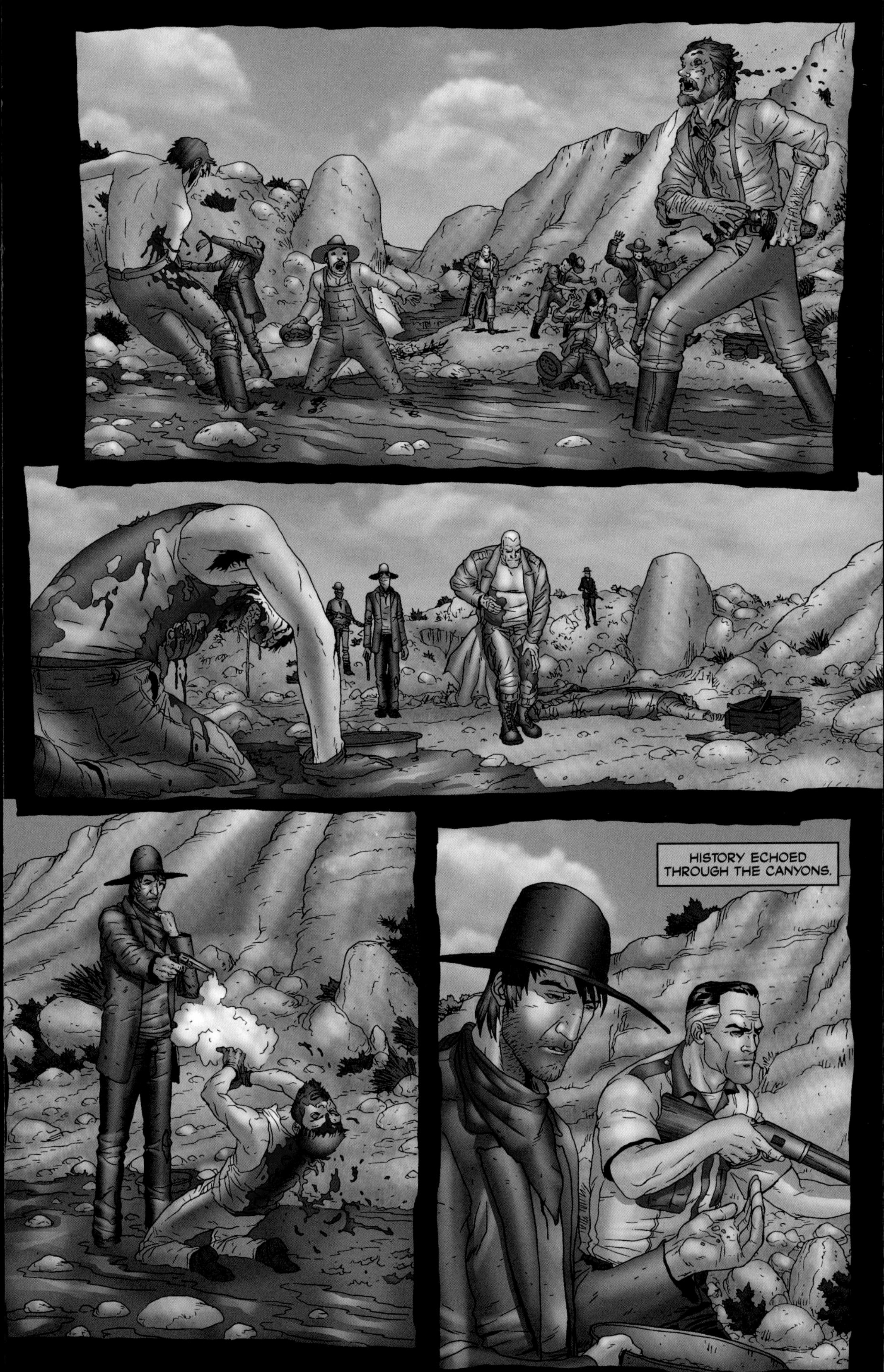
HISTORY ECHOED
THROUGH THE CANYONS.

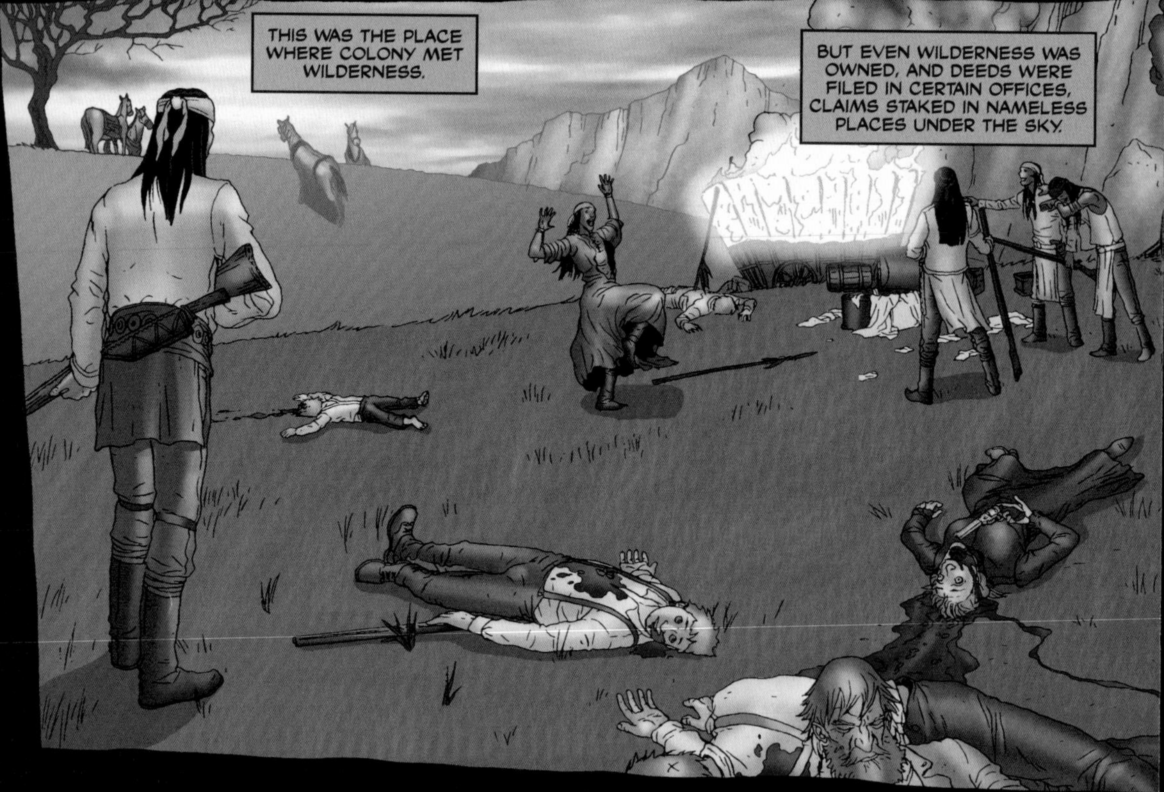
THIS WAS THE PLACE WHERE COLONY MET WILDERNESS.
BUT EVEN WILDERNESS WAS OWNED, AND DEEDS WERE FILED IN CERTAIN OFFICES, CLAIMS STAKED IN NAMELESS PLACES UNDER THE SKY.

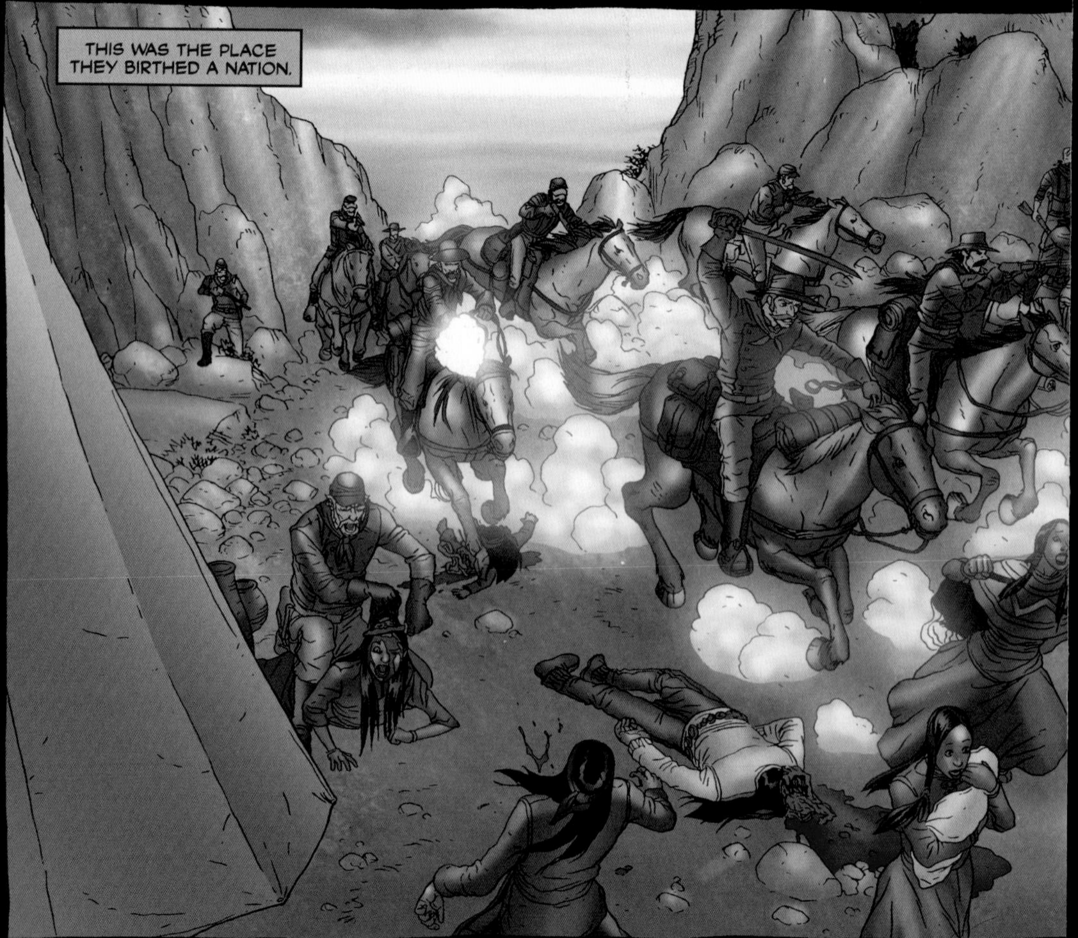
THIS WAS THE PLACE THEY BIRTHED A NATION.

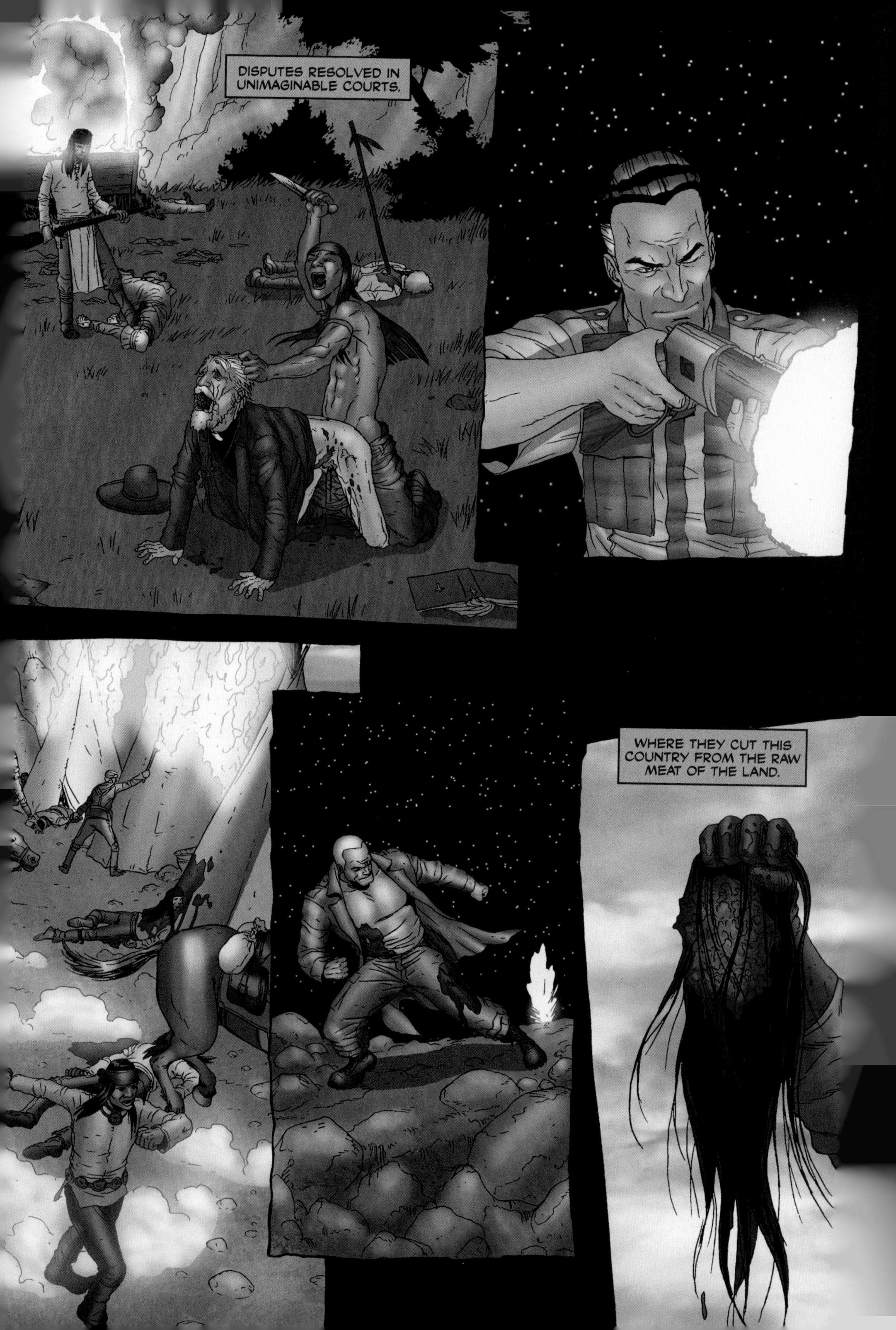
DISPUTES RESOLVED IN UNIMAGINABLE COURTS.
WHERE THEY CUT THIS COUNTRY FROM THE RAW MEAT OF THE LAND.

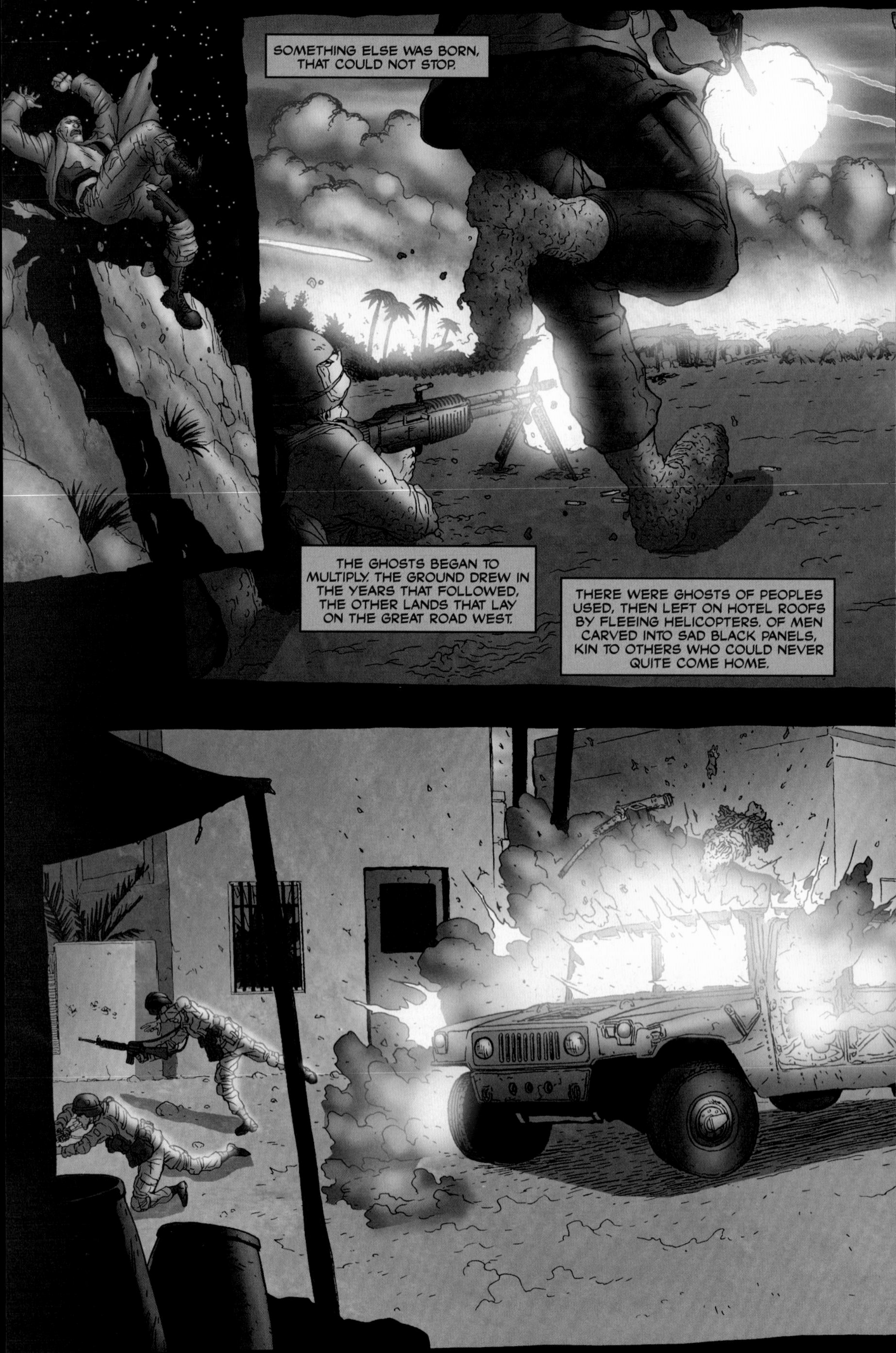
SOMETHING ELSE WAS BORN, THAT COULD NOT STOP.
THE GHOSTS BEGAN TO MULTIPLY. THE GROUND DREW IN THE YEARS THAT FOLLOWED, THE OTHER LANDS THAT LAY ON THE GREAT ROAD WEST.
THERE WERE GHOSTS OF PEOPLES USED, THEN LEFT ON HOTEL ROOFS BY FLEEING HELICOPTERS. OF MEN CARVED INTO SAD BLACK PANELS, KIN TO OTHERS WHO COULD NEVER QUITE COME HOME.

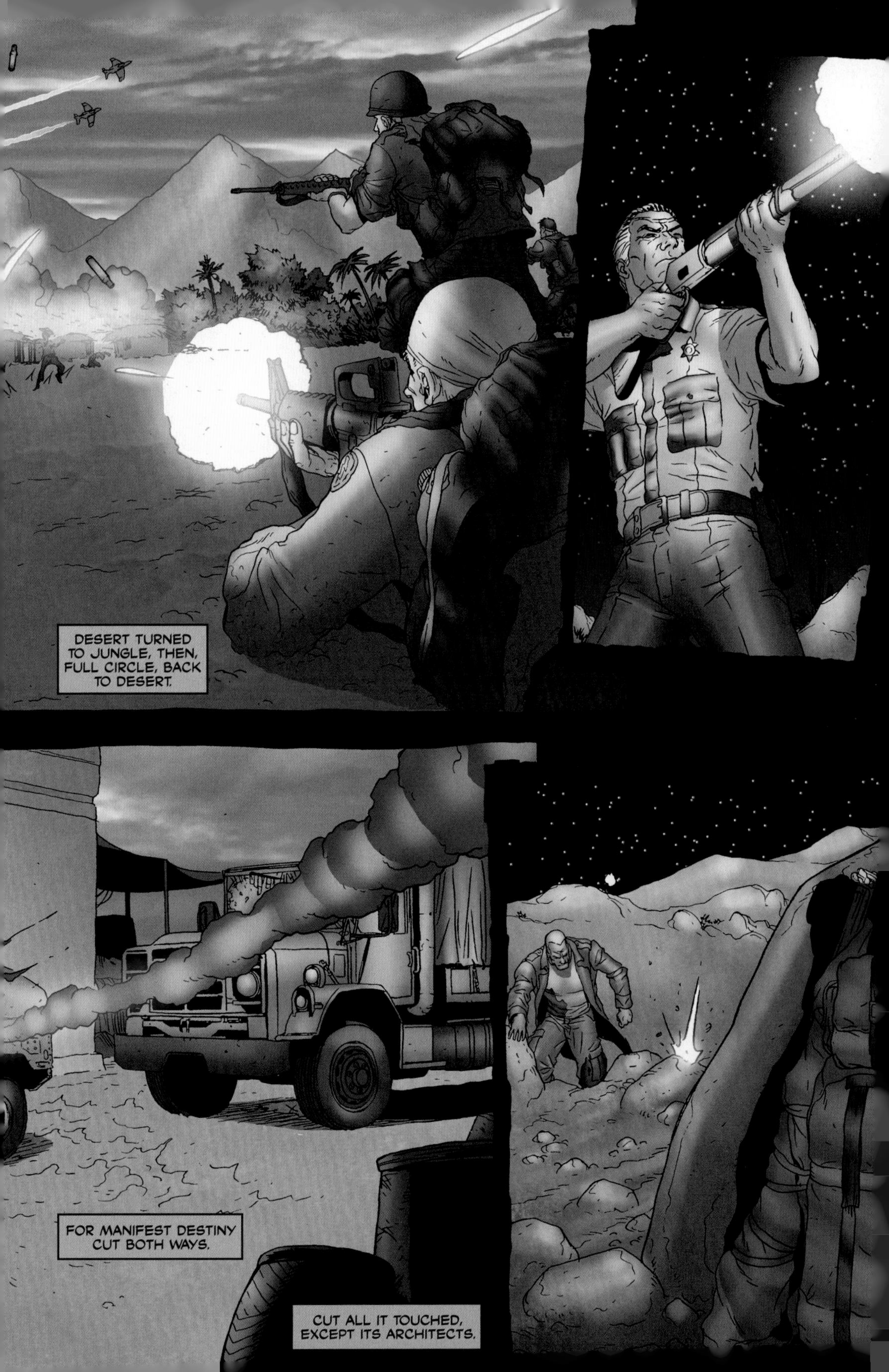
DESERT TURNED TO JUNGLE, THEN, FULL CIRCLE, BACK TO DESERT.
FOR MANIFEST DESTINY CUT BOTH WAYS.
CUT ALL IT TOUCHED, EXCEPT ITS ARCHITECTS.

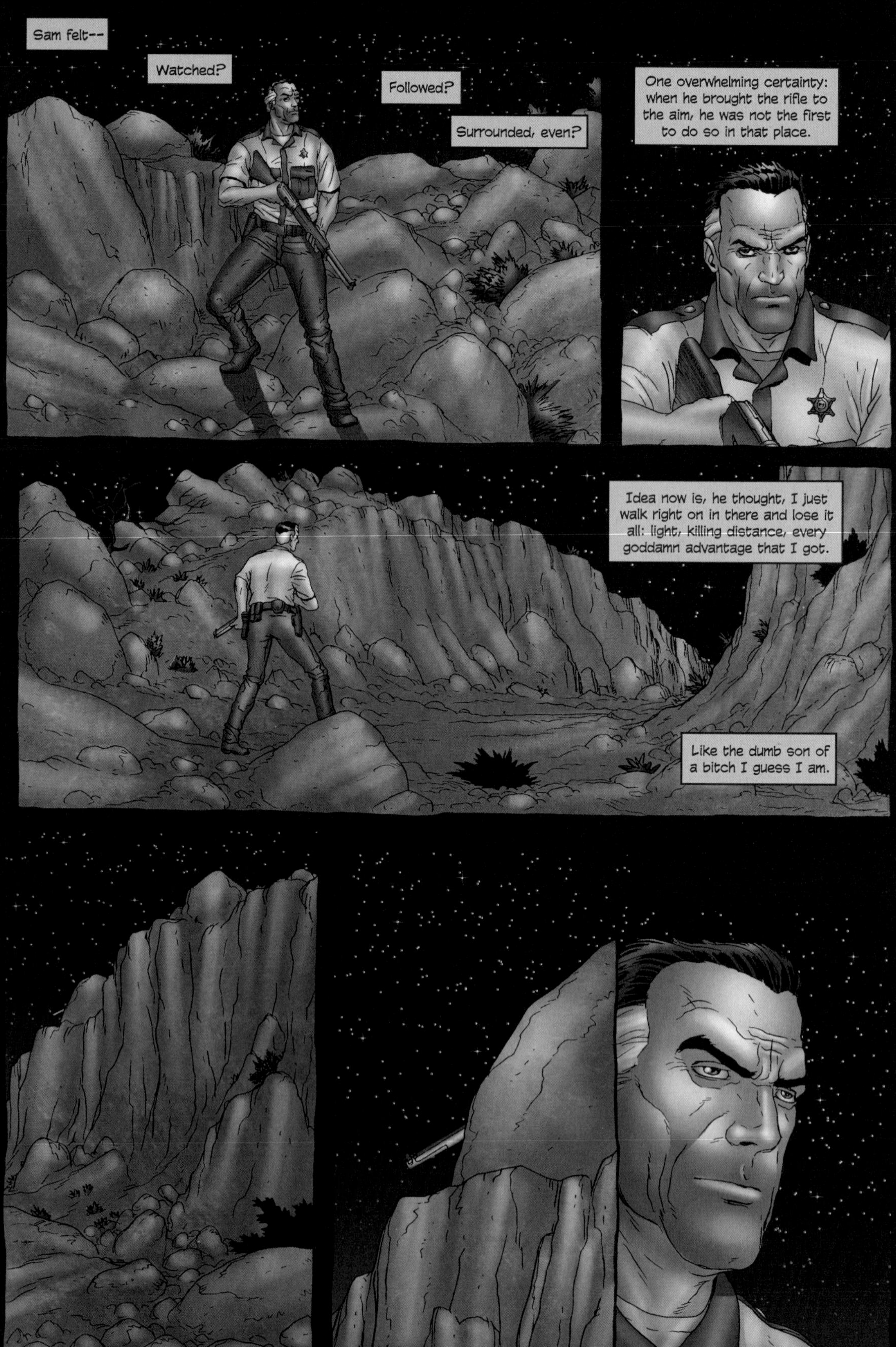
Sam felt--
Watched?
Followed?
Surrounded, even?
One overwhelming certainty: when he brought the rifle to the aim, he was not the first to do so in that place.
Idea now is, he thought, I just walk right on in there and lose it all: light, killing distance, every goddamn advantage that I got.
Like the dumb son of a bitch I guess I am.

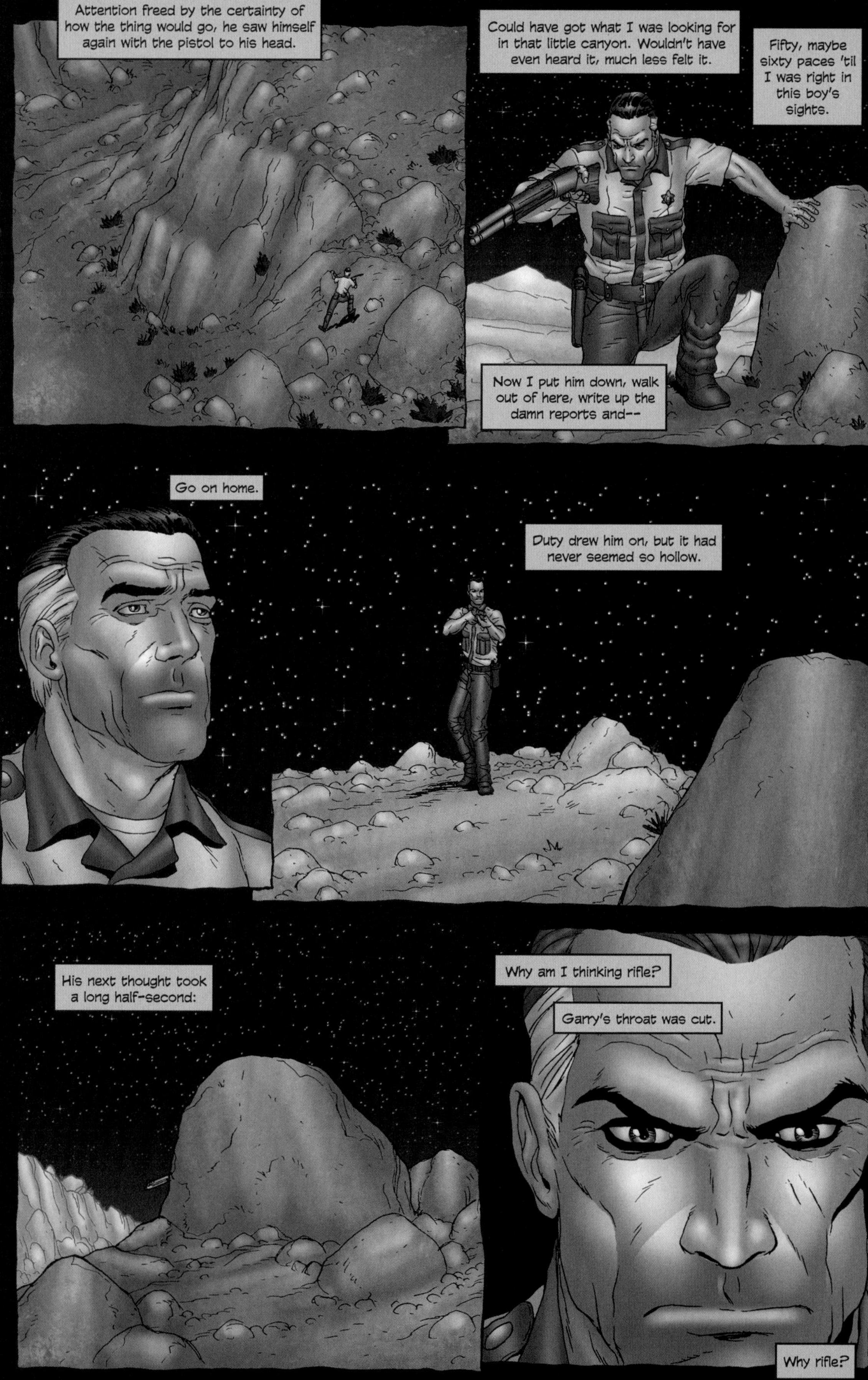
Attention freed by the certainty of how the thing would go, he saw himself again with the pistol to his head.
Could have got what I was looking for in that little canyon. Wouldn't have even heard it, much less felt it.
Fifty, maybe sixty paces 'til I was right in this boy's sights.
Now I put him down, walk out of here, write up the damn reports and--
Go on home.
Duty drew him on, but it had never seemed so hollow.
His next thought took a long half-second:
Why am I thinking rifle?
Garry's throat was cut.
Why rifle?

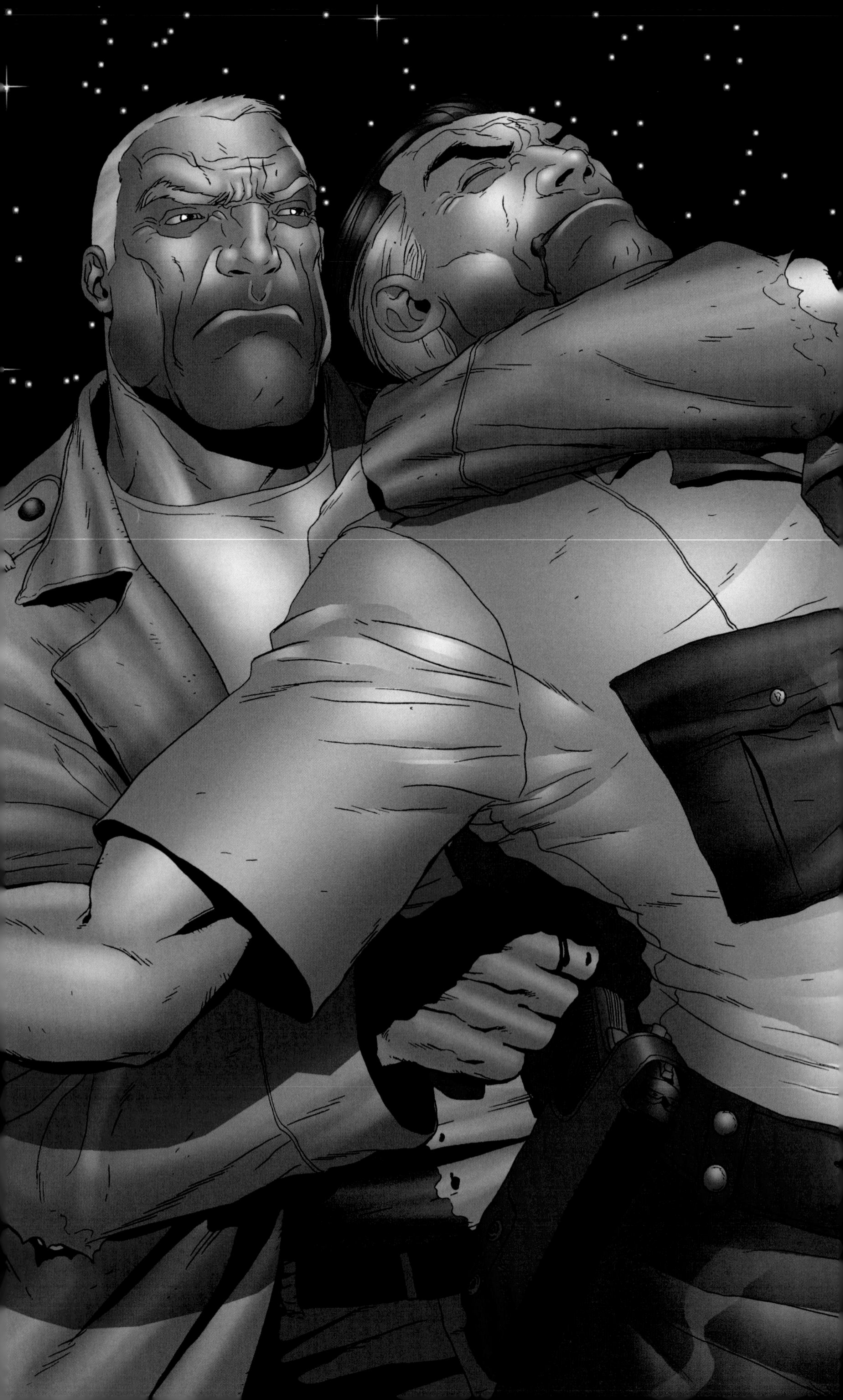

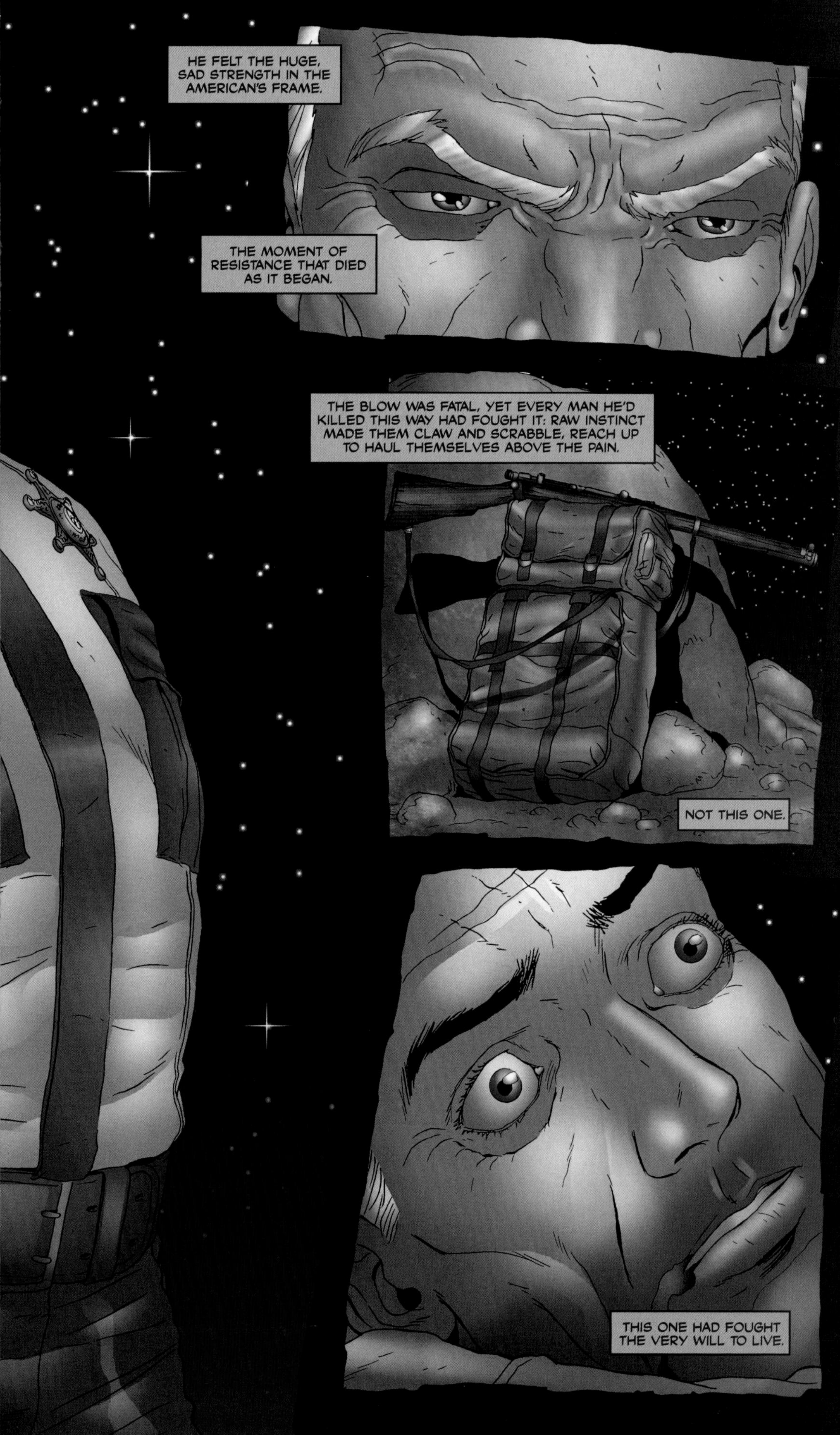
HE FELT THE HUGE, SAD STRENGTH IN THE AMERICAN'S FRAME.
THE MOMENT OF RESISTANCE THAT DIED AS IT BEGAN.
THE BLOW WAS FATAL, YET EVERY MAN HE'D KILLED THIS WAY HAD FOUGHT IT: RAW INSTINCT MADE THEM CLAW AND SCRABBLE, REACH UP TO HAUL THEMSELVES ABOVE THE PAIN.
NOT THIS ONE.
THIS ONE HAD FOUGHT THE VERY WILL TO LIVE.

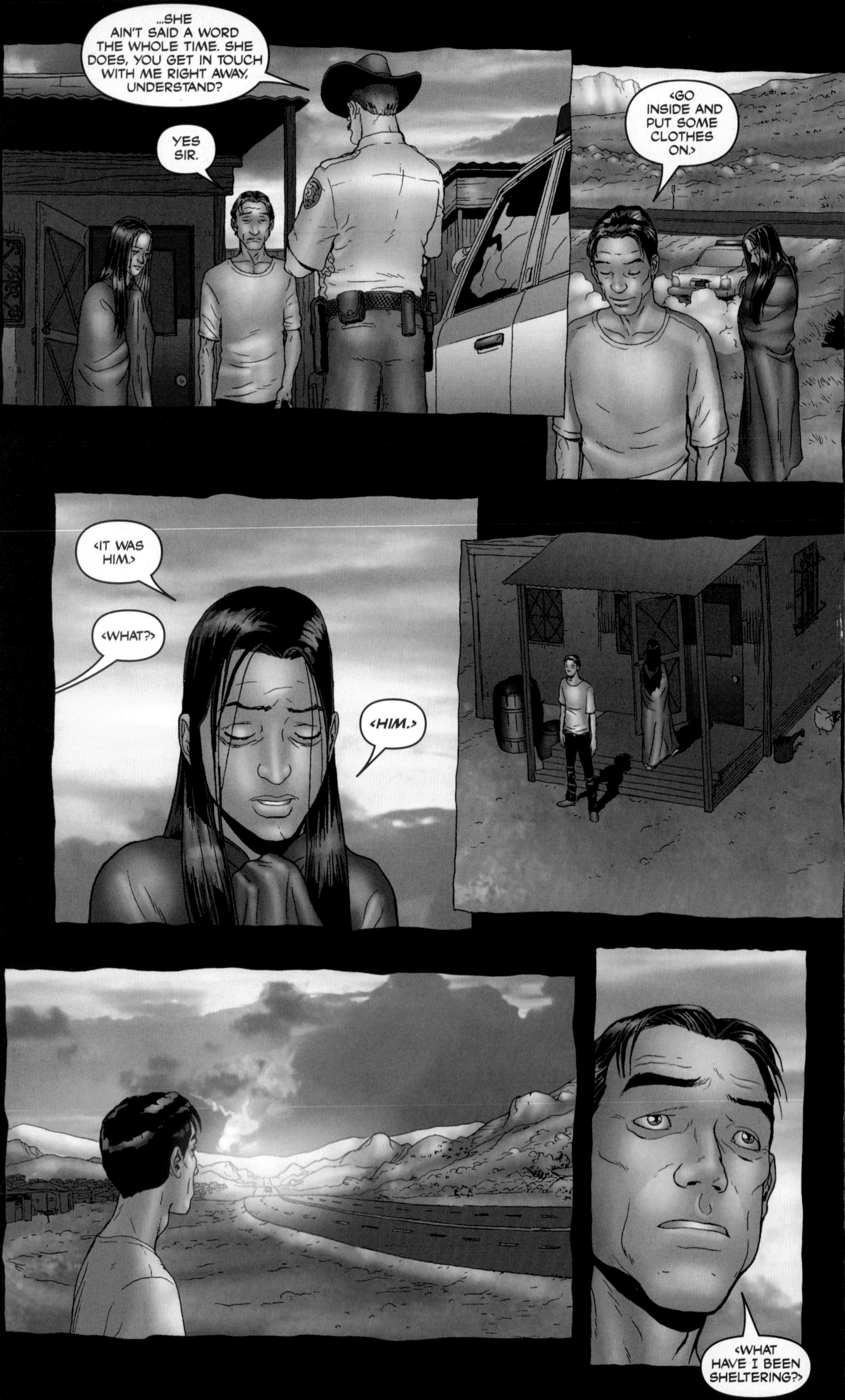
...SHE AIN'T SAID A WORD THE WHOLE TIME. SHE DOES, YOU GET IN TOUCH WITH ME RIGHT AWAY, UNDERSTAND?
YES SIR.
<GO INSIDE AND PUT SOME CLOTHES ON.>
<IT WAS HIM.>
<WHAT?>
<HIM.>
<WHAT HAVE I BEEN SHELTERING?>

NEITHER WOUND WOULD BLEED OUT.

NEITHER WOULD KILL HIM.

FIRST CHANCE HE GOT, HE'D HIT A DRUGSTORE AFTER CLOSING TIME. FIND SUTURES, PAINKILLERS, ANTIBIOTICS.

ENOUGH TO LAST HIM 'TIL THE THING WAS DONE.

HIS LUCK ASTOUNDED HIM.

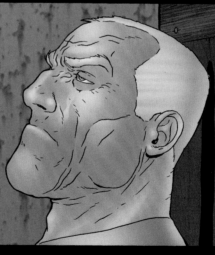

HE'D STASHED THE RIFLE AFTER NIGHTFALL, NOT PREPARED TO RISK IT ON THE JOB. A STEADY, CAUTIOUS EXIT, A ZIG-ZAG ROUTE TO PICK IT UP, THEN GO.

HE HADN'T IMAGINED FOR A SECOND THAT HE'D NEED IT.

AND NOW WHEN HE DREAMED, IT WAS NEITHER OF HIS FATHER NOR HIS DEAD--

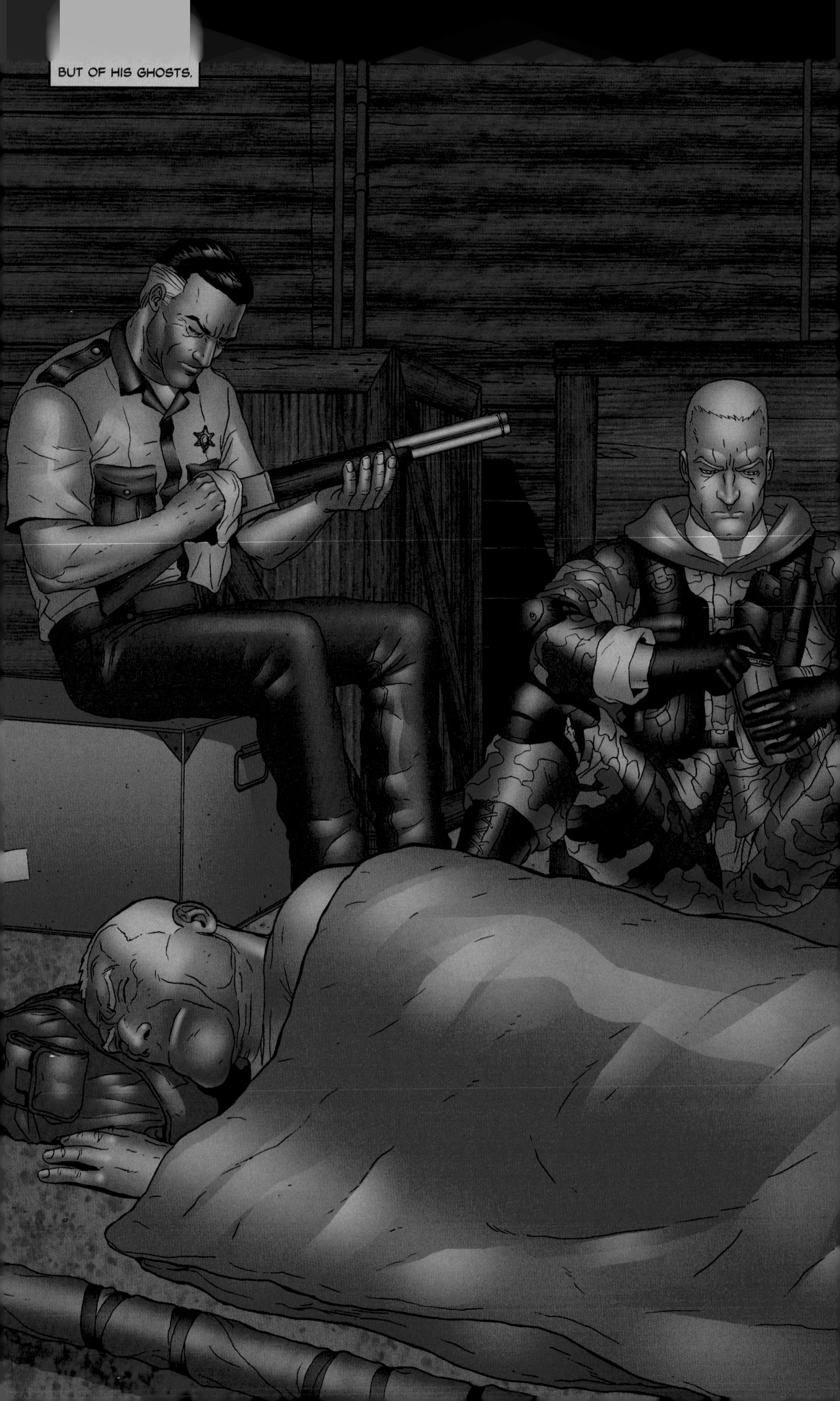
BUT OF HIS GHOSTS.

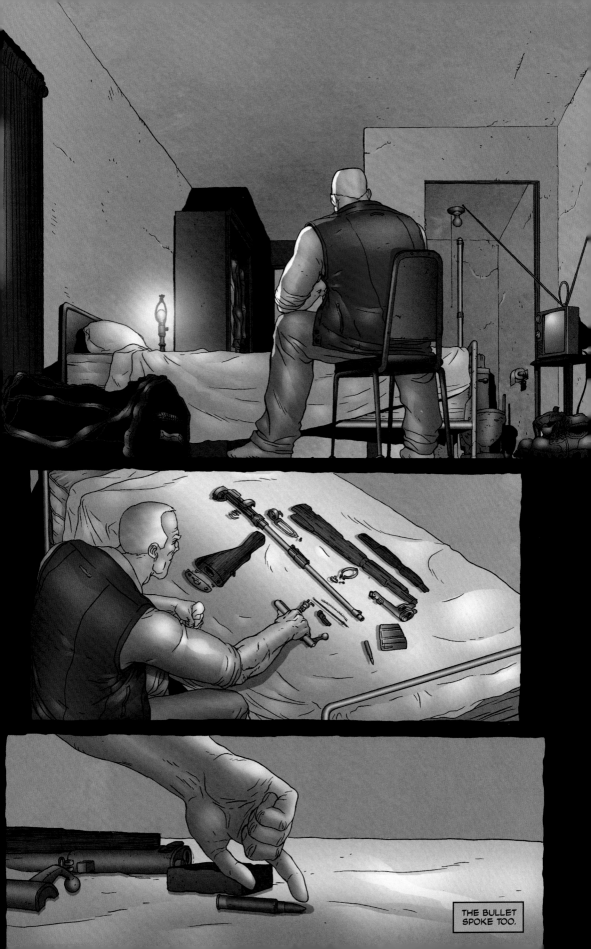

THE BULLET
SPOKE TOO.

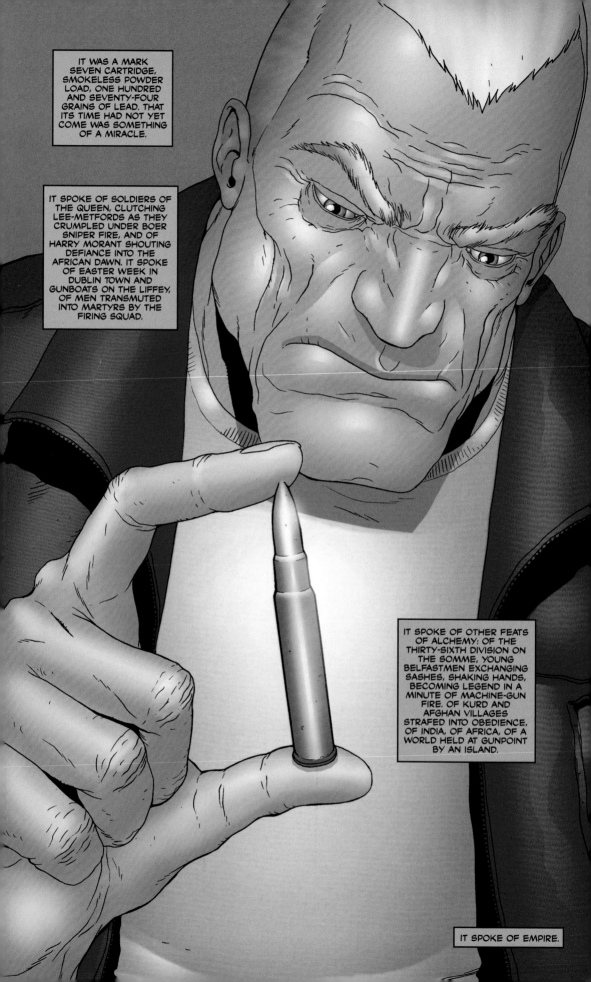

IT WAS A MARK SEVEN CARTRIDGE, SMOKELESS POWDER LOAD, ONE HUNDRED AND SEVENTY-FOUR GRAINS OF LEAD. THAT ITS TIME HAD NOT YET COME WAS SOMETHING OF A MIRACLE.

IT SPOKE OF SOLDIERS OF THE QUEEN, CLUTCHING LEE-METFORDS AS THEY CRUMPLED UNDER BOER SNIPER FIRE, AND OF HARRY MORANT SHOUTING DEFIANCE INTO THE AFRICAN DAWN. IT SPOKE OF EASTER WEEK IN DUBLIN TOWN AND GUNBOATS ON THE LIFFEY, OF MEN TRANSMUTED INTO MARTYRS BY THE FIRING SQUAD.

IT SPOKE OF OTHER FEATS OF ALCHEMY: OF THE THIRTY-SIXTH DIVISION ON THE SOMME, YOUNG BELFASTMEN EXCHANGING SASHES, SHAKING HANDS, BECOMING LEGEND IN A MINUTE OF MACHINE-GUN FIRE. OF KURD AND AFGHAN VILLAGES STRAFED INTO OBEDIENCE, OF INDIA, OF AFRICA, OF A WORLD HELD AT GUNPOINT BY AN ISLAND.

IT SPOKE OF EMPIRE.

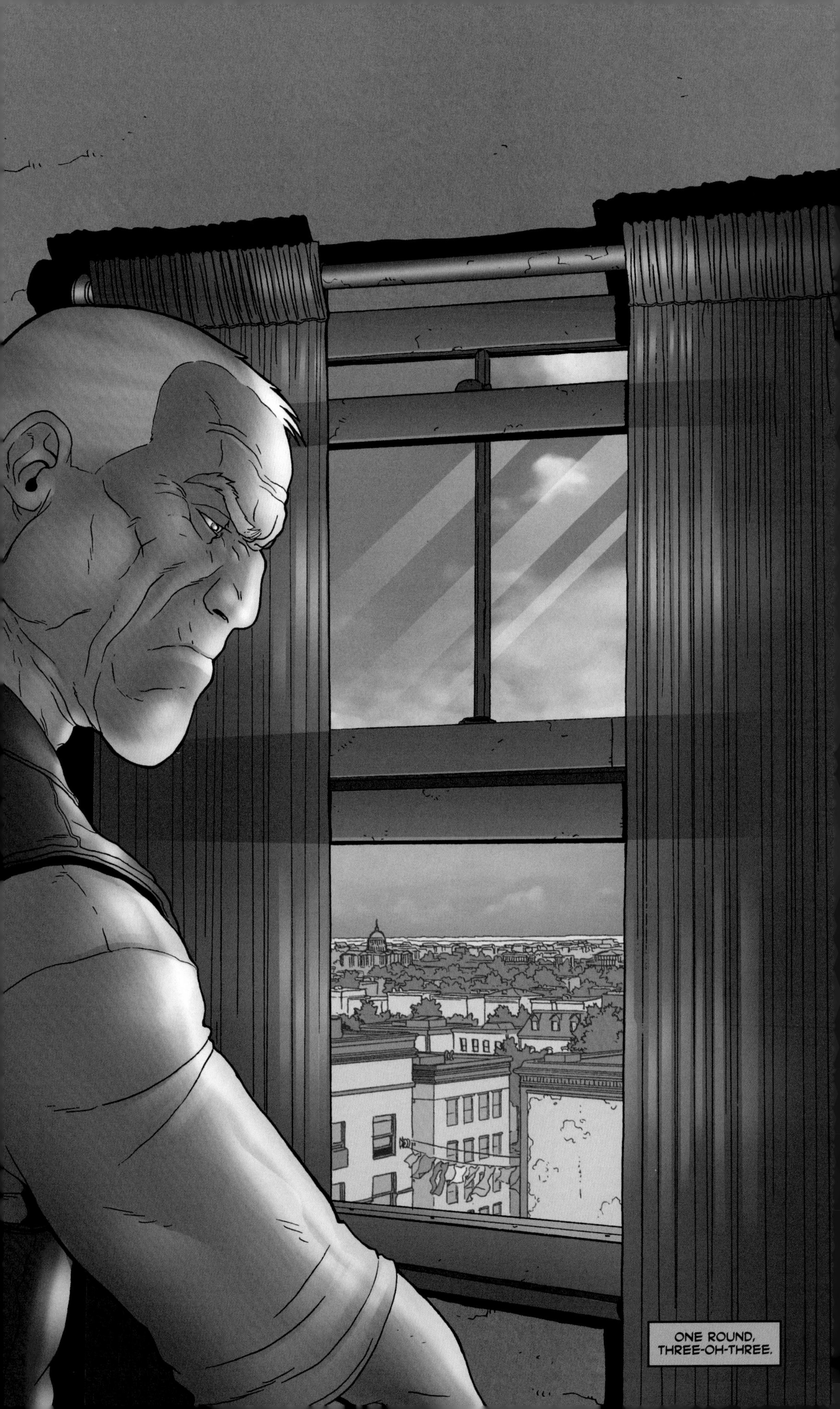
ONE ROUND, THREE-OH-THREE.

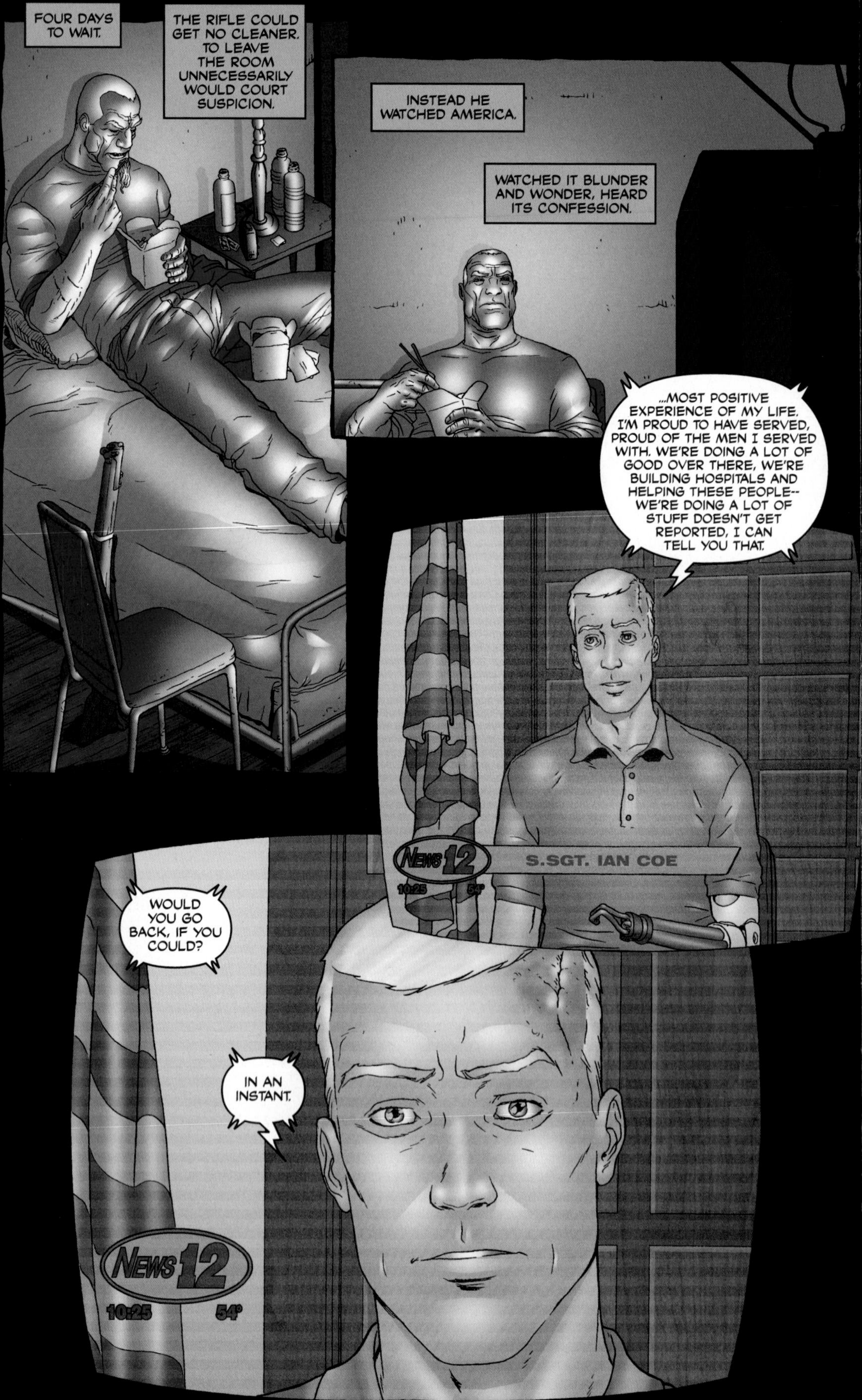
FOUR DAYS TO WAIT.
THE RIFLE COULD GET NO CLEANER. TO LEAVE THE ROOM UNNECESSARILY WOULD COURT SUSPICION.
INSTEAD HE WATCHED AMERICA.
WATCHED IT BLUNDER AND WONDER, HEARD ITS CONFESSION.
...MOST POSITIVE EXPERIENCE OF MY LIFE. I'M PROUD TO HAVE SERVED, PROUD OF THE MEN I SERVED WITH. WE'RE DOING A LOT OF GOOD OVER THERE, WE'RE BUILDING HOSPITALS AND HELPING THESE PEOPLE-- WE'RE DOING A LOT OF STUFF DOESN'T GET REPORTED, I CAN TELL YOU THAT.
NEWS 12
S.SGT. IAN COE
10:25 54°
WOULD YOU GO BACK, IF YOU COULD?
IN AN INSTANT.
NEWS 12
10:25 54°

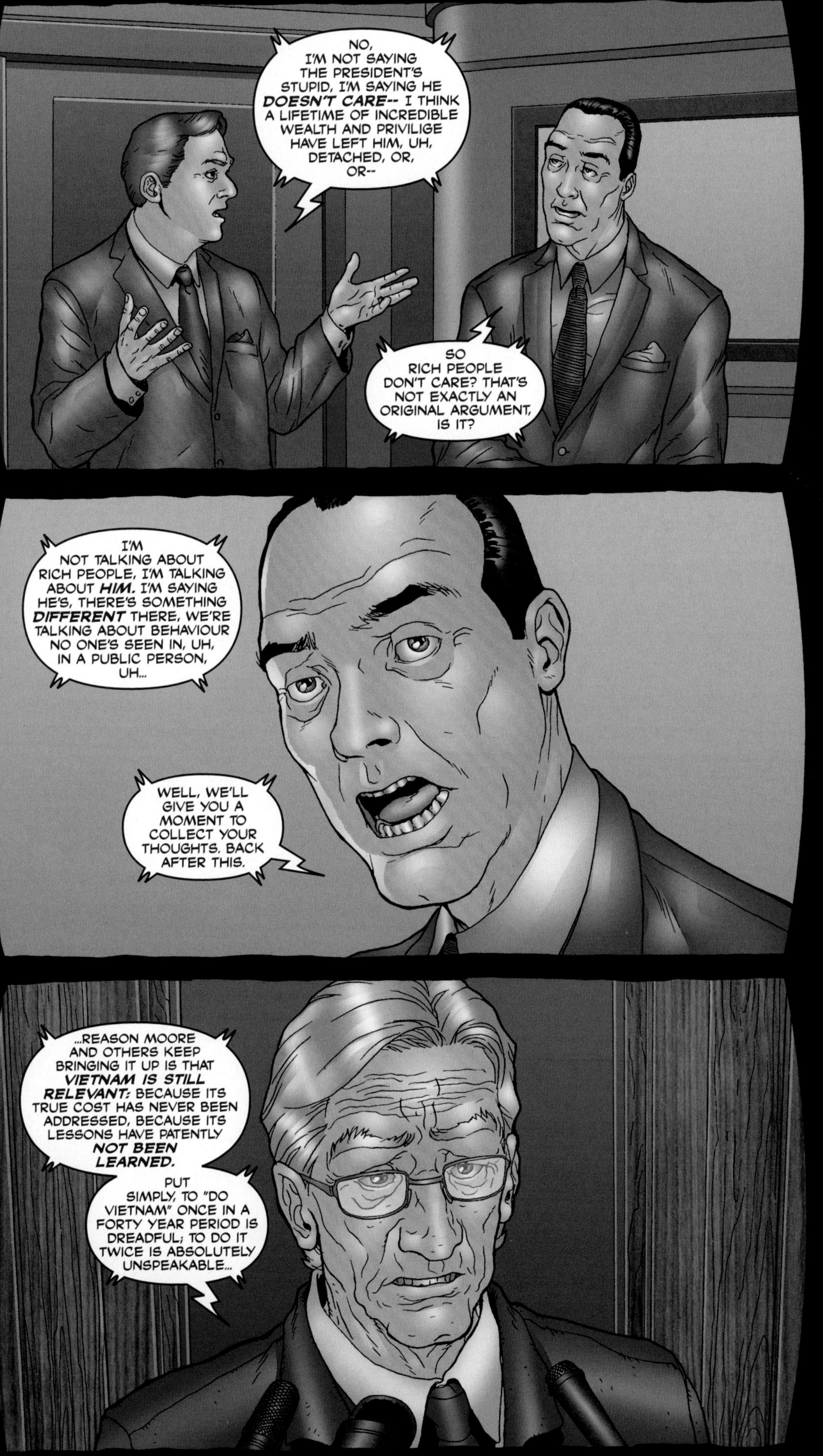
NO, I'M NOT SAYING THE PRESIDENT'S STUPID, I'M SAYING HE DOESN'T CARE-- I THINK A LIFETIME OF INCREDIBLE WEALTH AND PRIVILIGE HAVE LEFT HIM, UH, DETACHED, OR, OR--
SO RICH PEOPLE DON'T CARE? THAT'S NOT EXACTLY AN ORIGINAL ARGUMENT, IS IT?
I'M NOT TALKING ABOUT RICH PEOPLE, I'M TALKING ABOUT HIM. I'M SAYING HE'S, THERE'S SOMETHING DIFFERENT THERE, WE'RE TALKING ABOUT BEHAVIOUR NO ONE'S SEEN IN, UH, IN A PUBLIC PERSON, UH...
WELL, WE'LL GIVE YOU A MOMENT TO COLLECT YOUR THOUGHTS. BACK AFTER THIS.
...REASON MOORE AND OTHERS KEEP BRINGING IT UP IS THAT VIETNAM IS STILL RELEVANT: BECAUSE ITS TRUE COST HAS NEVER BEEN ADDRESSED, BECAUSE ITS LESSONS HAVE PATENTLY NOT BEEN LEARNED.
PUT SIMPLY, TO "DO VIETNAM" ONCE IN A FORTY YEAR PERIOD IS DREADFUL; TO DO IT TWICE IS ABSOLUTELY UNSPEAKABLE...

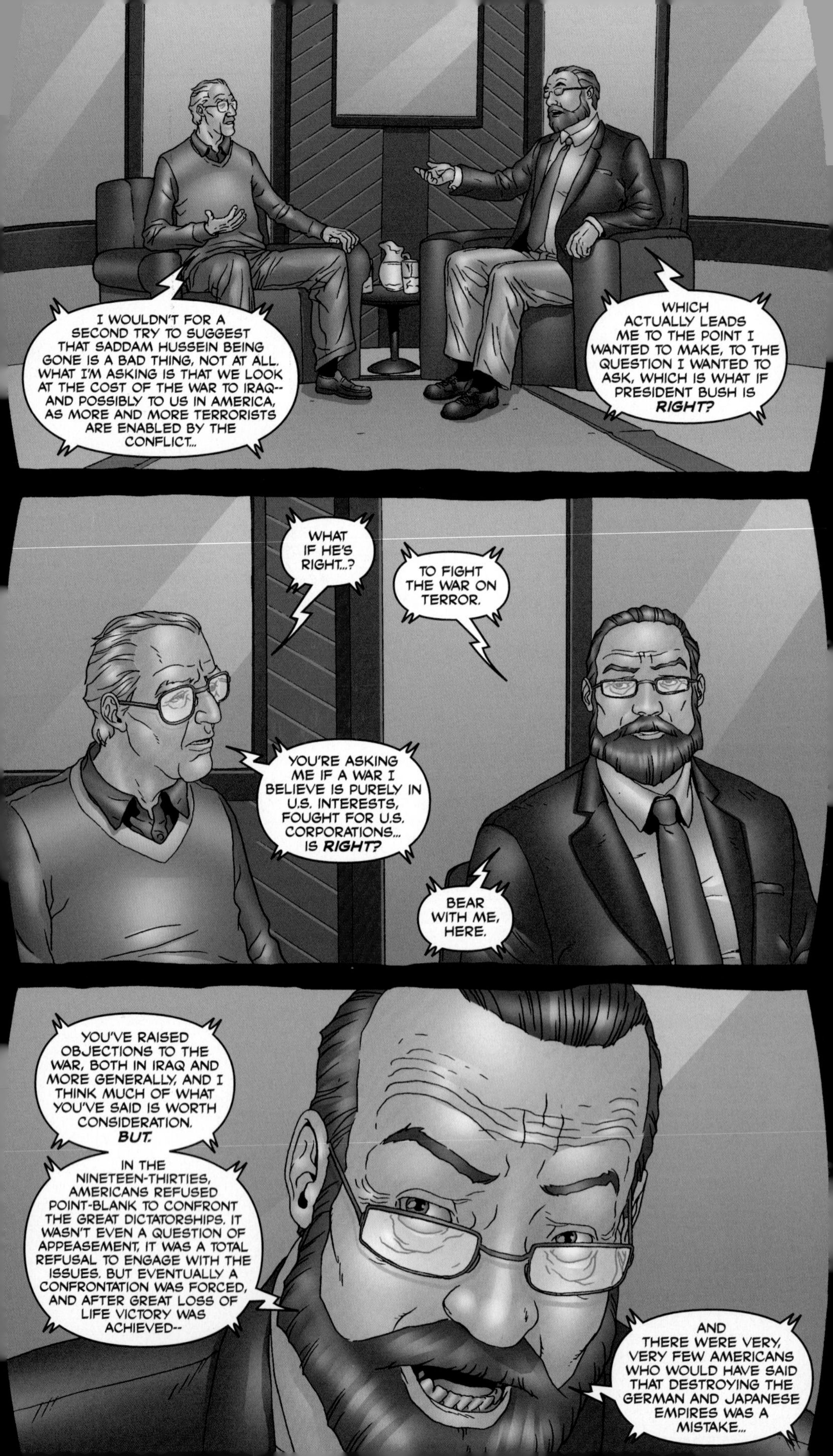
I WOULDN'T FOR A SECOND TRY TO SUGGEST THAT SADDAM HUSSEIN BEING GONE IS A BAD THING, NOT AT ALL. WHAT I'M ASKING IS THAT WE LOOK AT THE COST OF THE WAR TO IRAQ-- AND POSSIBLY TO US IN AMERICA, AS MORE AND MORE TERRORISTS ARE ENABLED BY THE CONFLICT...
WHICH ACTUALLY LEADS ME TO THE POINT I WANTED TO MAKE, TO THE QUESTION I WANTED TO ASK, WHICH IS WHAT IF PRESIDENT BUSH IS *RIGHT?*
WHAT IF HE'S RIGHT...?
TO FIGHT THE WAR ON TERROR.
YOU'RE ASKING ME IF A WAR I BELIEVE IS PURELY IN U.S. INTERESTS, FOUGHT FOR U.S. CORPORATIONS... IS *RIGHT?*
BEAR WITH ME, HERE.
YOU'VE RAISED OBJECTIONS TO THE WAR, BOTH IN IRAQ AND MORE GENERALLY, AND I THINK MUCH OF WHAT YOU'VE SAID IS WORTH CONSIDERATION. *BUT.*
IN THE NINETEEN-THIRTIES, AMERICANS REFUSED POINT-BLANK TO CONFRONT THE GREAT DICTATORSHIPS. IT WASN'T EVEN A QUESTION OF APPEASEMENT, IT WAS A TOTAL REFUSAL TO ENGAGE WITH THE ISSUES. BUT EVENTUALLY A CONFRONTATION WAS FORCED, AND AFTER GREAT LOSS OF LIFE VICTORY WAS ACHIEVED--
AND THERE WERE VERY, VERY FEW AMERICANS WHO WOULD HAVE SAID THAT DESTROYING THE GERMAN AND JAPANESE EMPIRES WAS A MISTAKE...

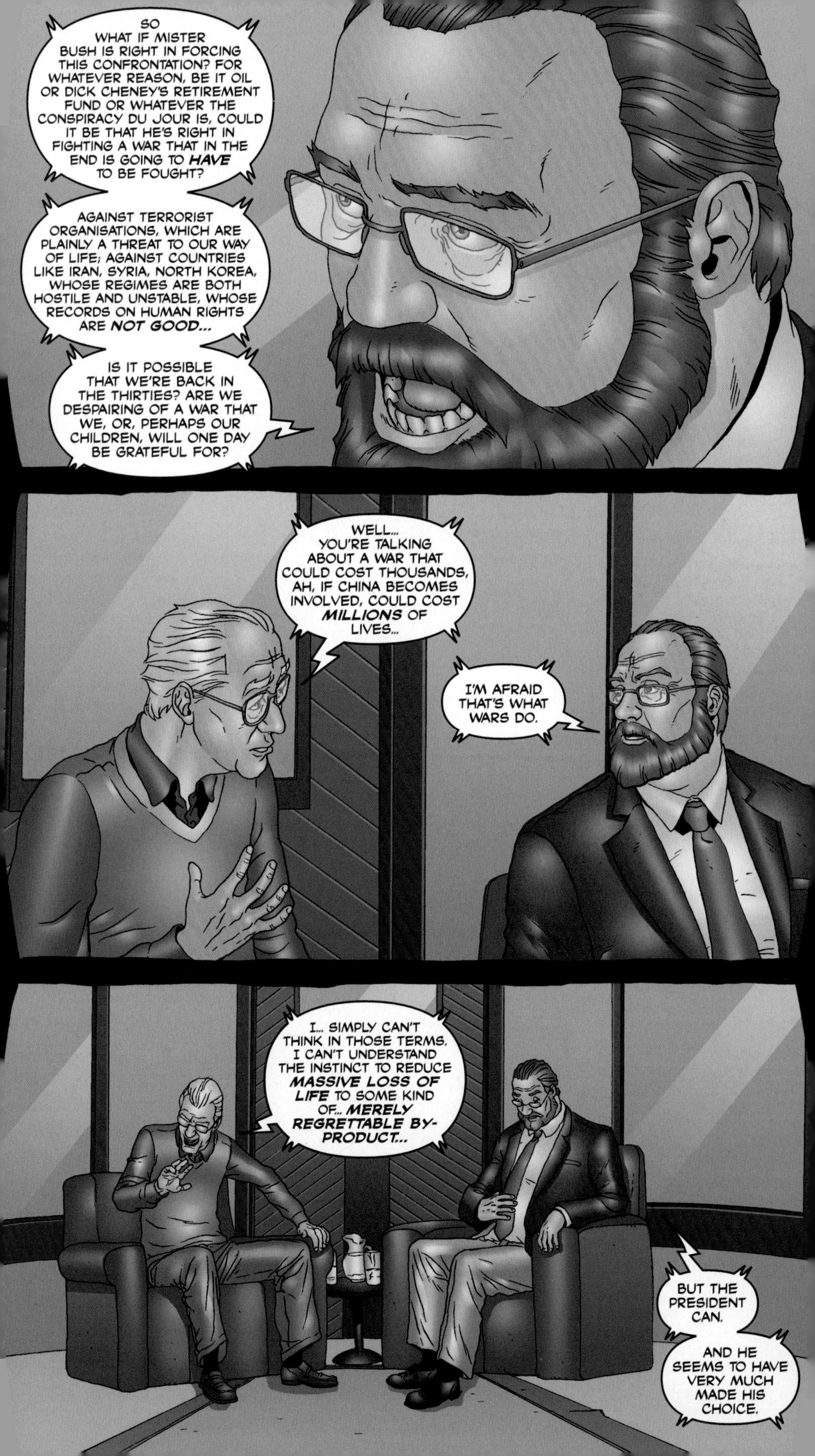

SO WHAT IF MISTER BUSH IS RIGHT IN FORCING THIS CONFRONTATION? FOR WHATEVER REASON, BE IT OIL OR DICK CHENEY'S RETIREMENT FUND OR WHATEVER THE CONSPIRACY DU JOUR IS, COULD IT BE THAT HE'S RIGHT IN FIGHTING A WAR THAT IN THE END IS GOING TO *HAVE* TO BE FOUGHT?
AGAINST TERRORIST ORGANISATIONS, WHICH ARE PLAINLY A THREAT TO OUR WAY OF LIFE; AGAINST COUNTRIES LIKE IRAN, SYRIA, NORTH KOREA, WHOSE REGIMES ARE BOTH HOSTILE AND UNSTABLE, WHOSE RECORDS ON HUMAN RIGHTS ARE *NOT GOOD...*
IS IT POSSIBLE THAT WE'RE BACK IN THE THIRTIES? ARE WE DESPAIRING OF A WAR THAT WE, OR, PERHAPS OUR CHILDREN, WILL ONE DAY BE GRATEFUL FOR?
WELL... YOU'RE TALKING ABOUT A WAR THAT COULD COST THOUSANDS, AH, IF CHINA BECOMES INVOLVED, COULD COST *MILLIONS* OF LIVES...
I'M AFRAID THAT'S WHAT WARS DO.
I... SIMPLY CAN'T THINK IN THOSE TERMS. I CAN'T UNDERSTAND THE INSTINCT TO REDUCE *MASSIVE LOSS OF LIFE* TO SOME KIND OF... *MERELY REGRETTABLE BY-PRODUCT...*
BUT THE PRESIDENT CAN.
AND HE SEEMS TO HAVE VERY MUCH MADE HIS CHOICE.

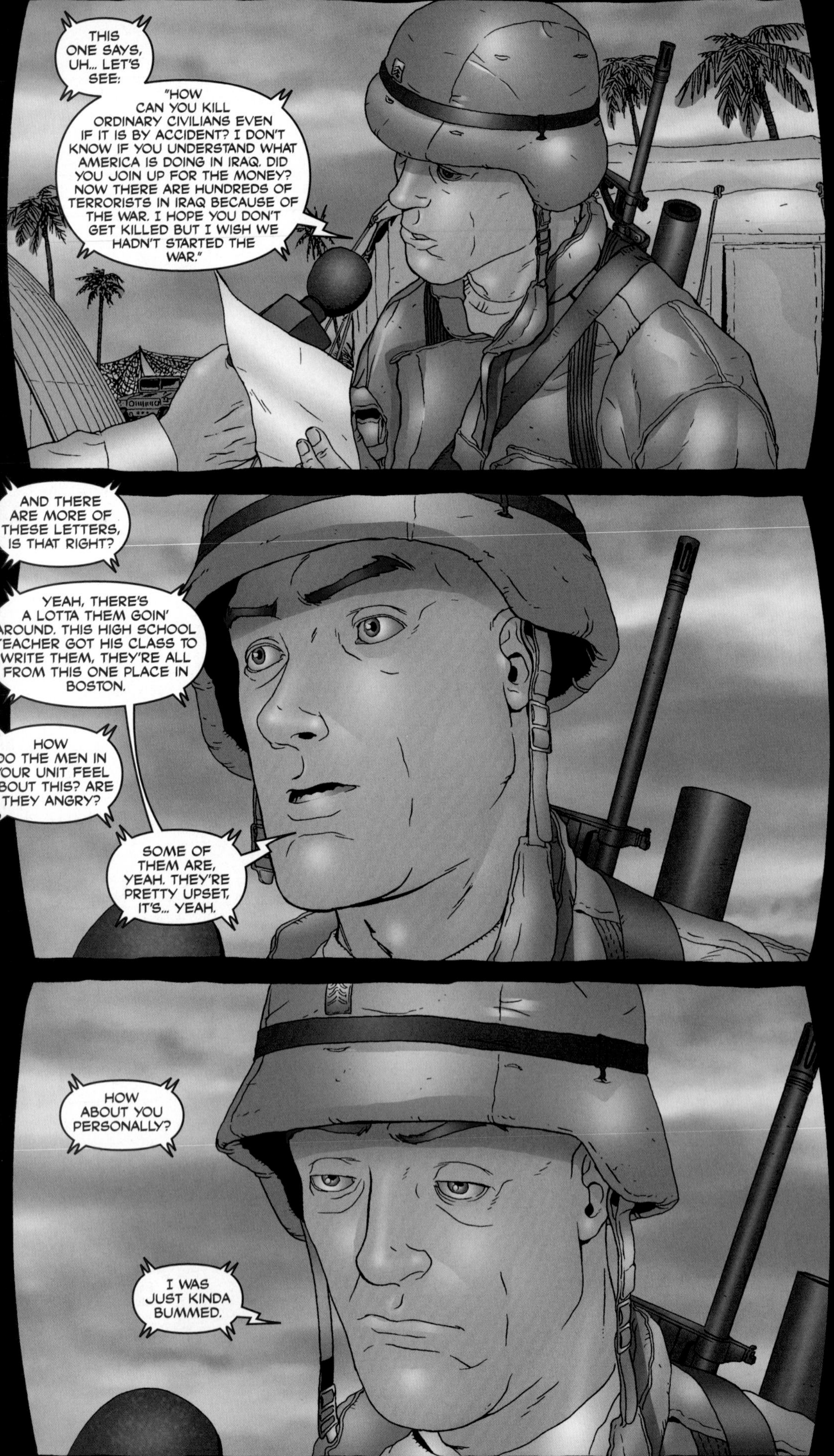

THIS ONE SAYS, UH... LET'S SEE:
"HOW CAN YOU KILL ORDINARY CIVILIANS EVEN IF IT IS BY ACCIDENT? I DON'T KNOW IF YOU UNDERSTAND WHAT AMERICA IS DOING IN IRAQ. DID YOU JOIN UP FOR THE MONEY? NOW THERE ARE HUNDREDS OF TERRORISTS IN IRAQ BECAUSE OF THE WAR. I HOPE YOU DON'T GET KILLED BUT I WISH WE HADN'T STARTED THE WAR."
AND THERE ARE MORE OF THESE LETTERS, IS THAT RIGHT?
YEAH, THERE'S A LOTTA THEM GOIN' AROUND. THIS HIGH SCHOOL TEACHER GOT HIS CLASS TO WRITE THEM, THEY'RE ALL FROM THIS ONE PLACE IN BOSTON.
HOW DO THE MEN IN YOUR UNIT FEEL ABOUT THIS? ARE THEY ANGRY?
SOME OF THEM ARE, YEAH. THEY'RE PRETTY UPSET, IT'S... YEAH.
HOW ABOUT YOU PERSONALLY?
I WAS JUST KINDA BUMMED.

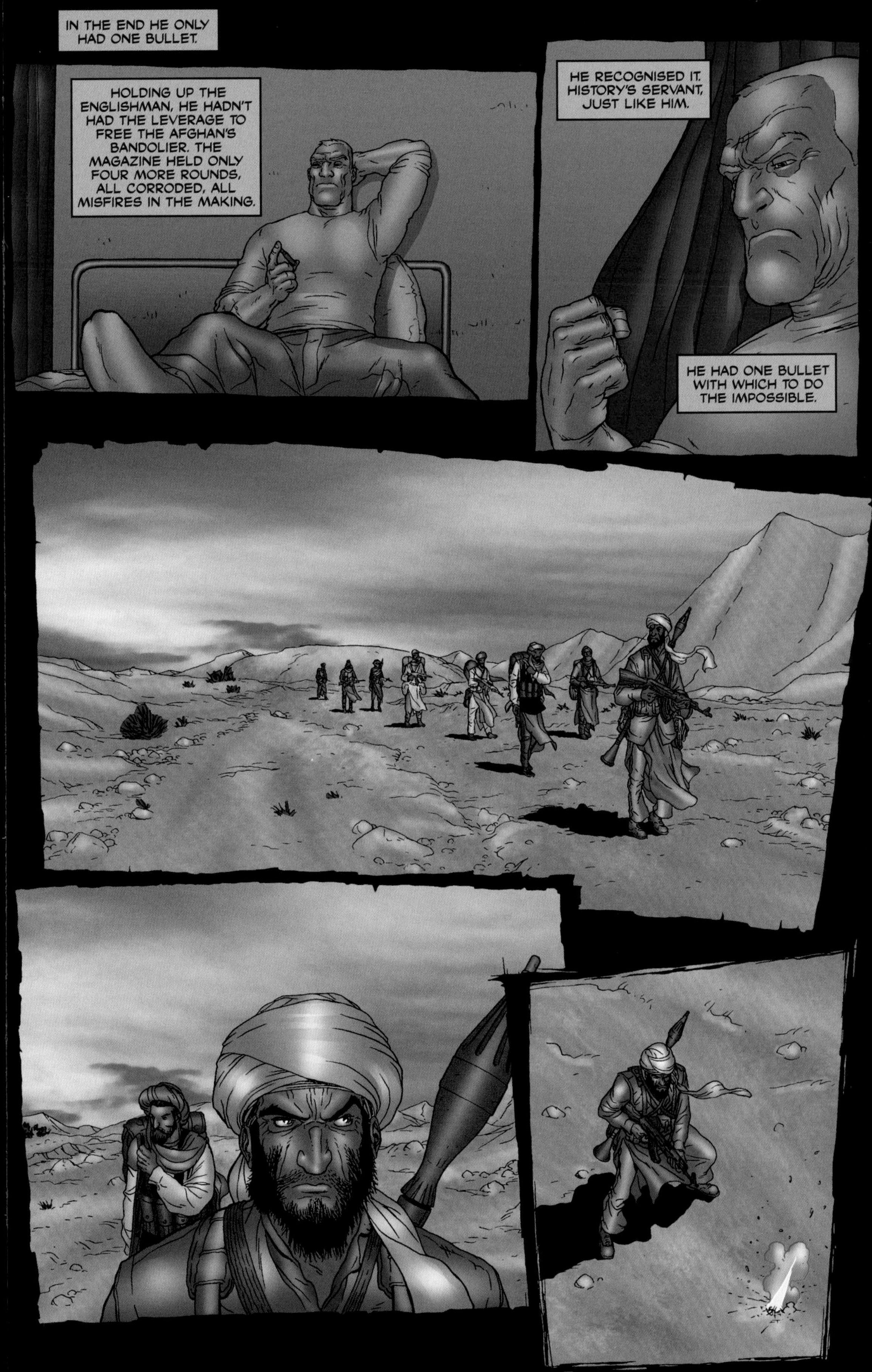
IN THE END HE ONLY HAD ONE BULLET.
HOLDING UP THE ENGLISHMAN, HE HADN'T HAD THE LEVERAGE TO FREE THE AFGHAN'S BANDOLIER. THE MAGAZINE HELD ONLY FOUR MORE ROUNDS, ALL CORRODED, ALL MISFIRES IN THE MAKING.
HE RECOGNISED IT. HISTORY'S SERVANT, JUST LIKE HIM.
HE HAD ONE BULLET WITH WHICH TO DO THE IMPOSSIBLE.

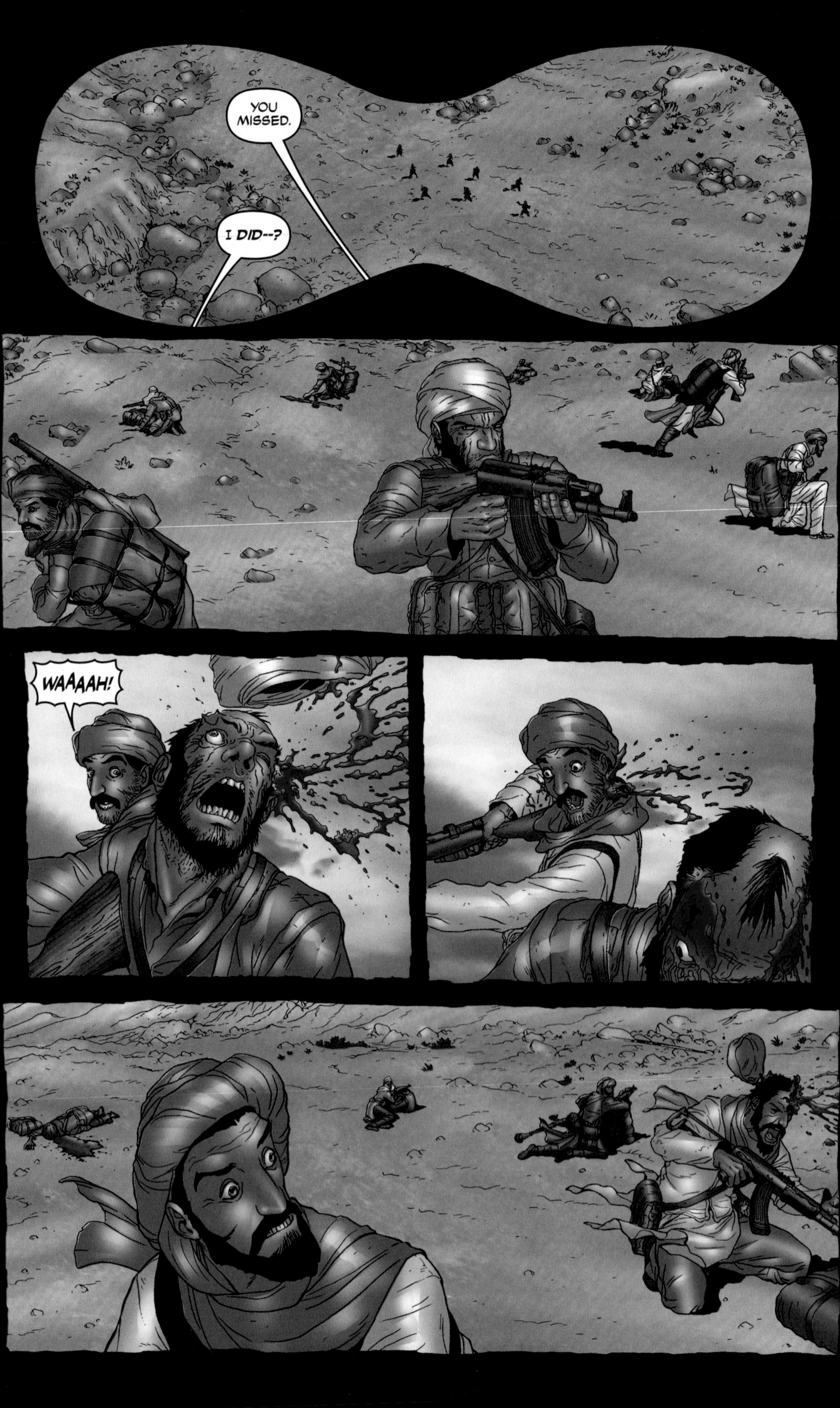
YOU MISSED.
I DID--?
WAAAAH!

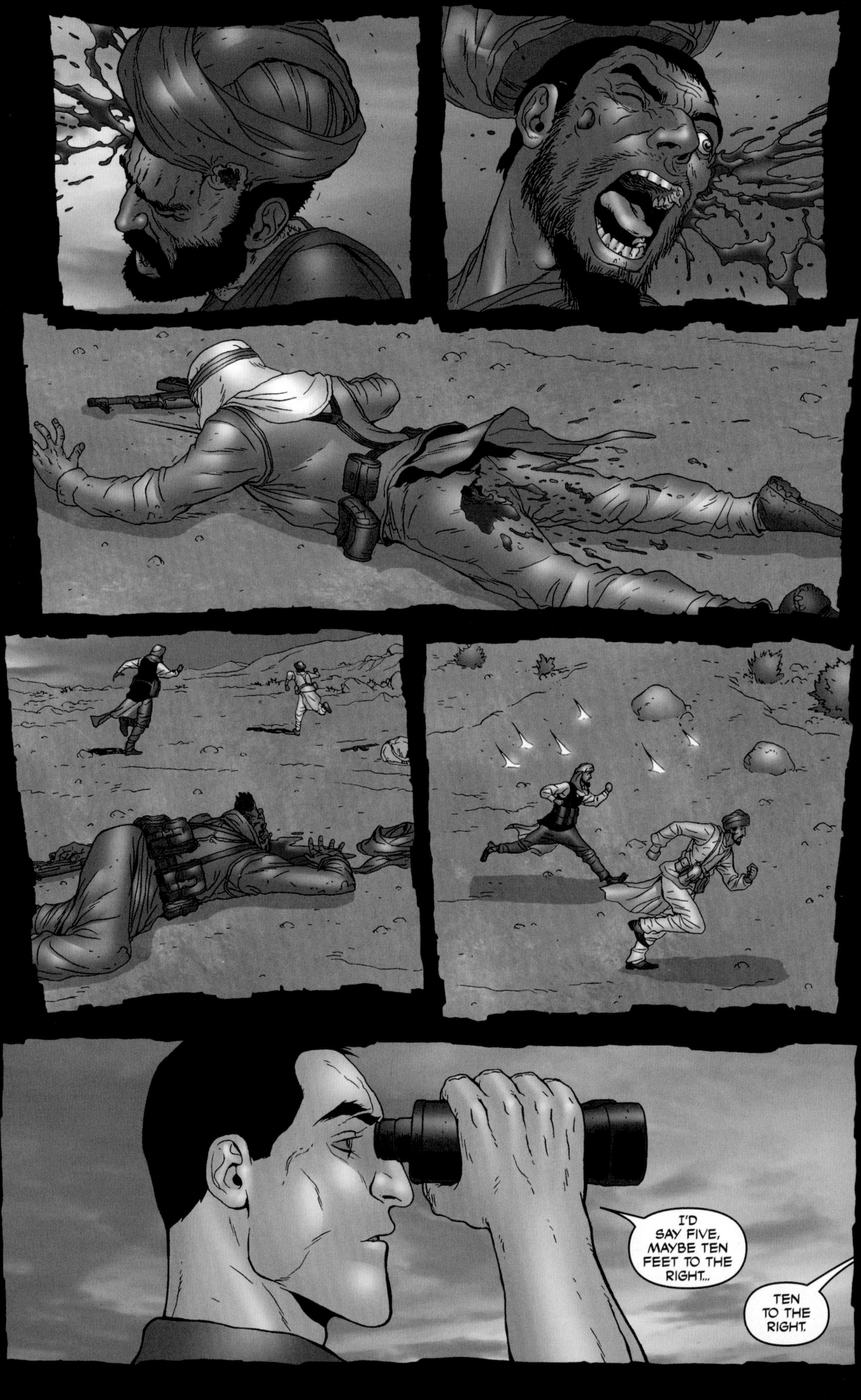
I'D SAY FIVE, MAYBE TEN FEET TO THE RIGHT...
TEN TO THE RIGHT.

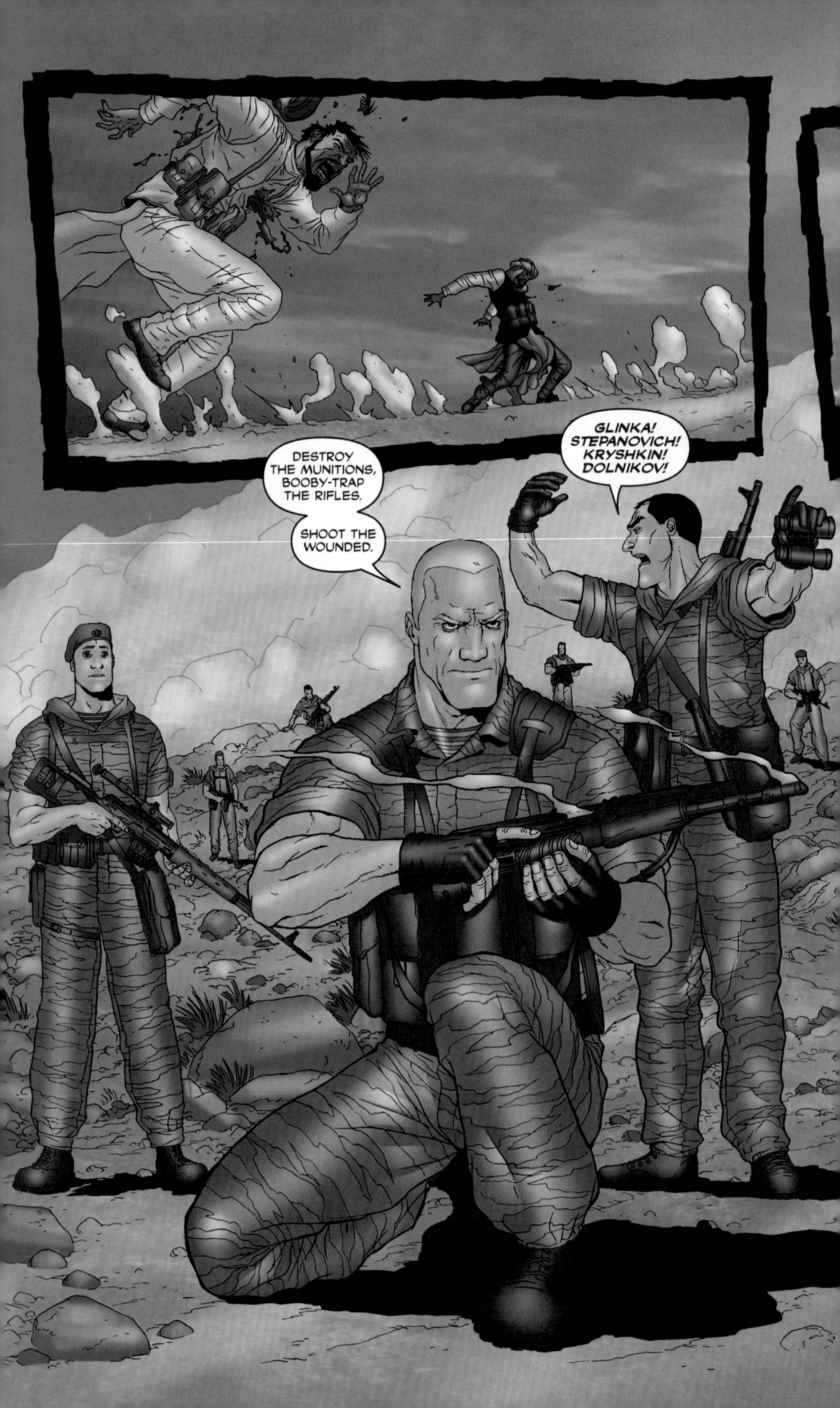
DESTROY THE MUNITIONS, BOOBY-TRAP THE RIFLES.
SHOOT THE WOUNDED.
GLINKA! STEPANOVICH! KRYSHKIN! DOLNIKOV!

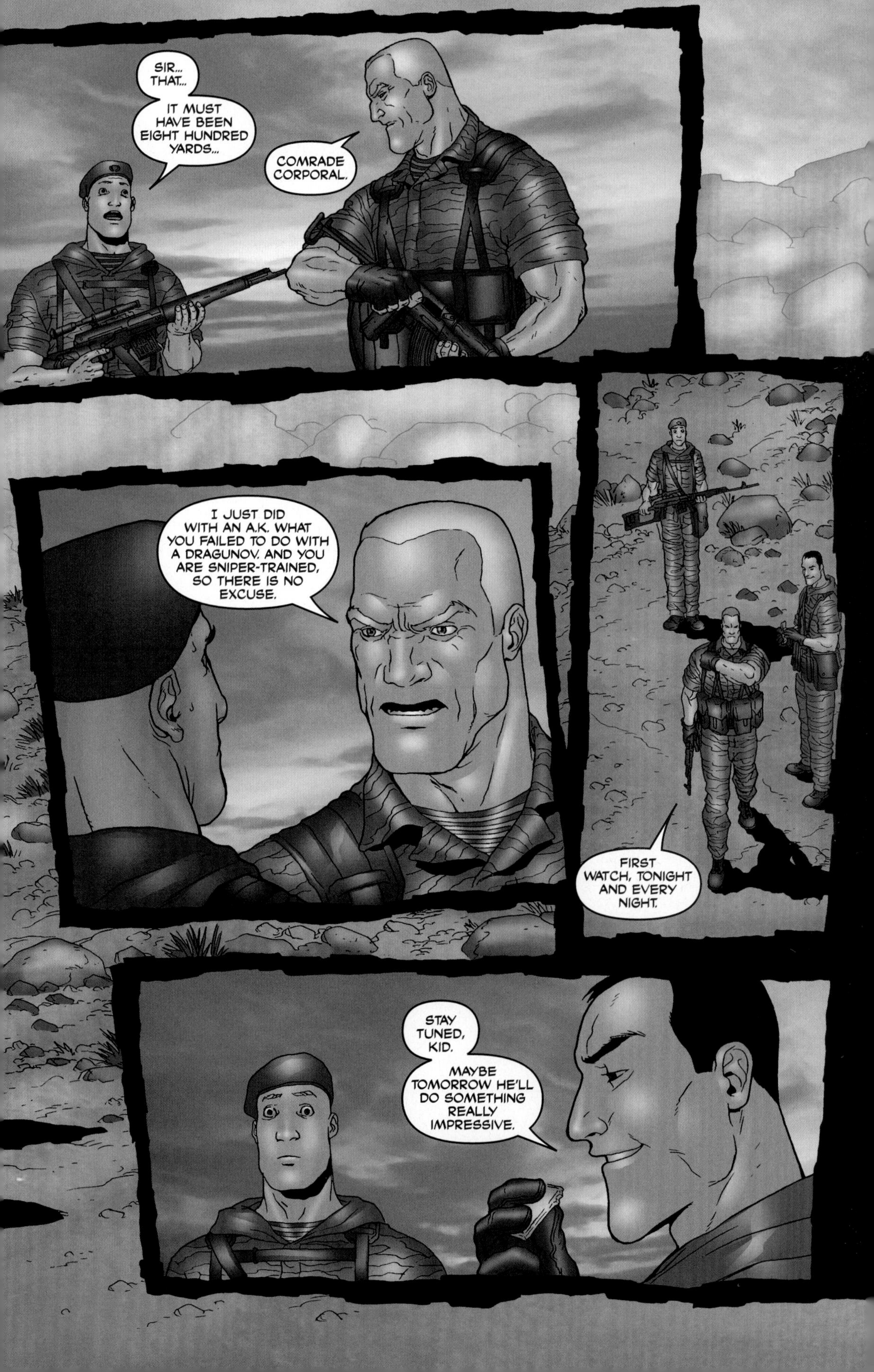

SIR... THAT...
IT MUST HAVE BEEN EIGHT HUNDRED YARDS...
COMRADE CORPORAL.
I JUST DID WITH AN A.K. WHAT YOU FAILED TO DO WITH A DRAGUNOV. AND YOU ARE SNIPER-TRAINED, SO THERE IS NO EXCUSE.
FIRST WATCH, TONIGHT AND EVERY NIGHT.
STAY TUNED, KID.
MAYBE TOMORROW HE'LL DO SOMETHING REALLY IMPRESSIVE.

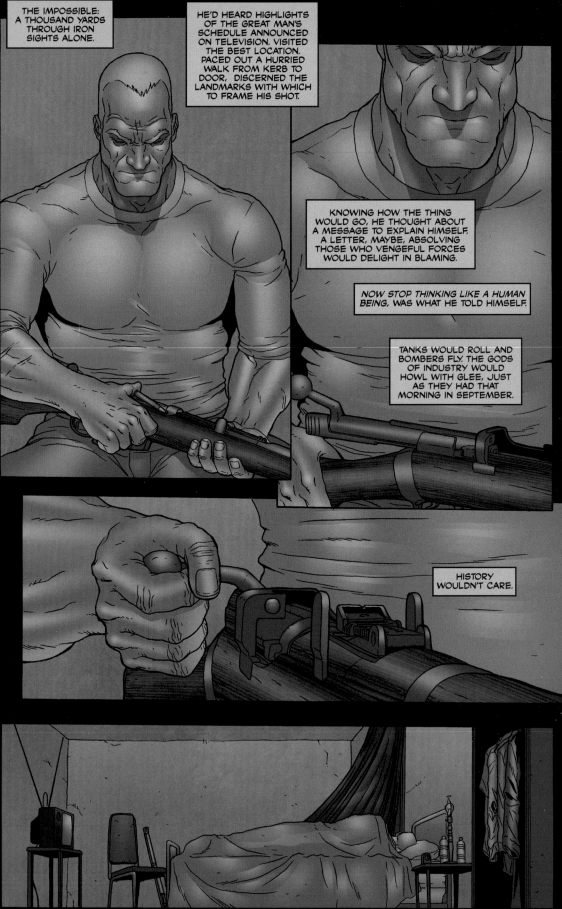

THE IMPOSSIBLE: A THOUSAND YARDS THROUGH IRON SIGHTS ALONE.

HE'D HEARD HIGHLIGHTS OF THE GREAT MAN'S SCHEDULE ANNOUNCED ON TELEVISION. VISITED THE BEST LOCATION. PACED OUT A HURRIED WALK FROM KERB TO DOOR, DISCERNED THE LANDMARKS WITH WHICH TO FRAME HIS SHOT.

KNOWING HOW THE THING WOULD GO, HE THOUGHT ABOUT A MESSAGE TO EXPLAIN HIMSELF. A LETTER, MAYBE, ABSOLVING THOSE WHO VENGEFUL FORCES WOULD DELIGHT IN BLAMING.

NOW STOP THINKING LIKE A HUMAN BEING, WAS WHAT HE TOLD HIMSELF.

TANKS WOULD ROLL AND BOMBERS FLY. THE GODS OF INDUSTRY WOULD HOWL WITH GLEE, JUST AS THEY HAD THAT MORNING IN SEPTEMBER.

HISTORY WOULDN'T CARE.

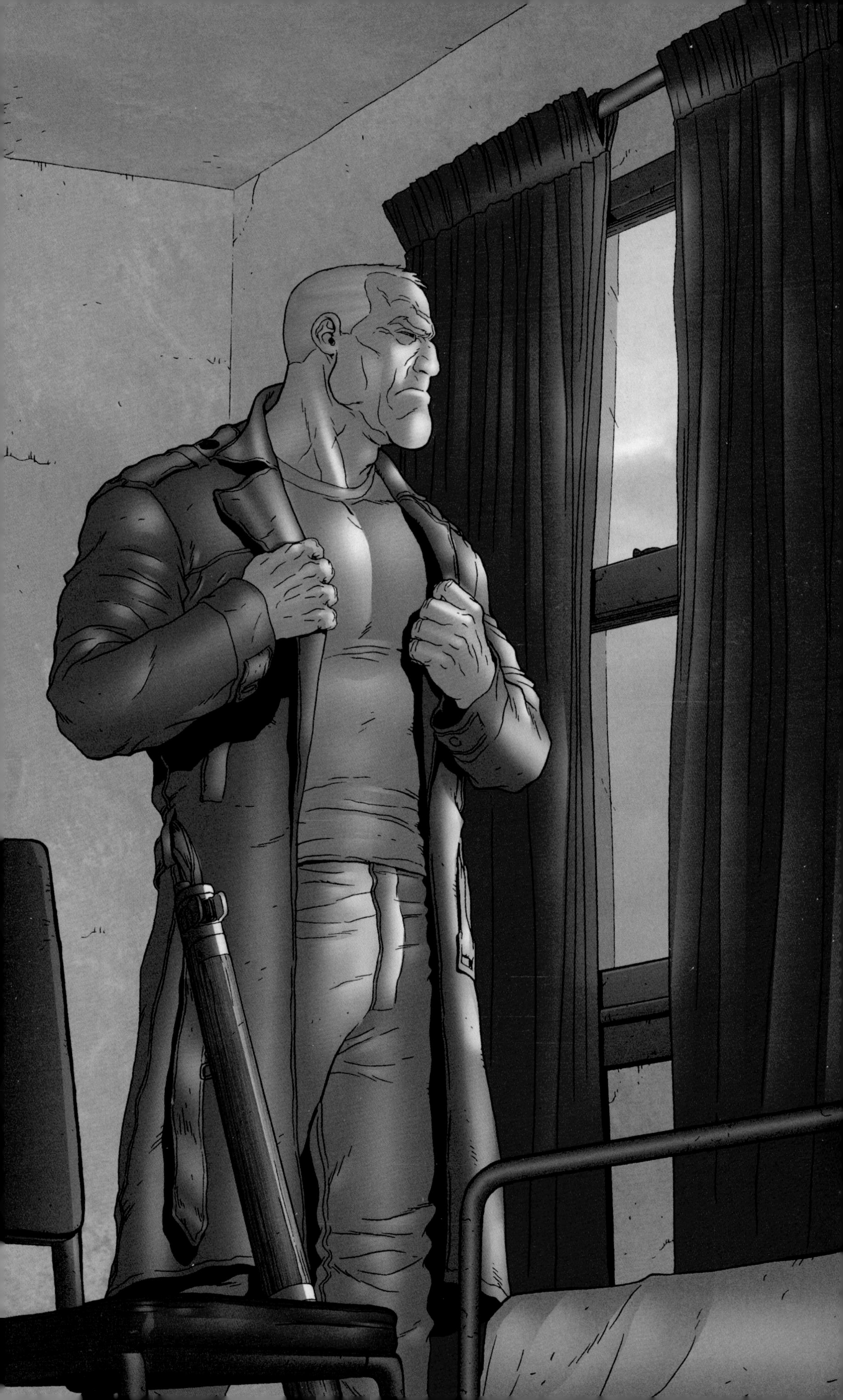

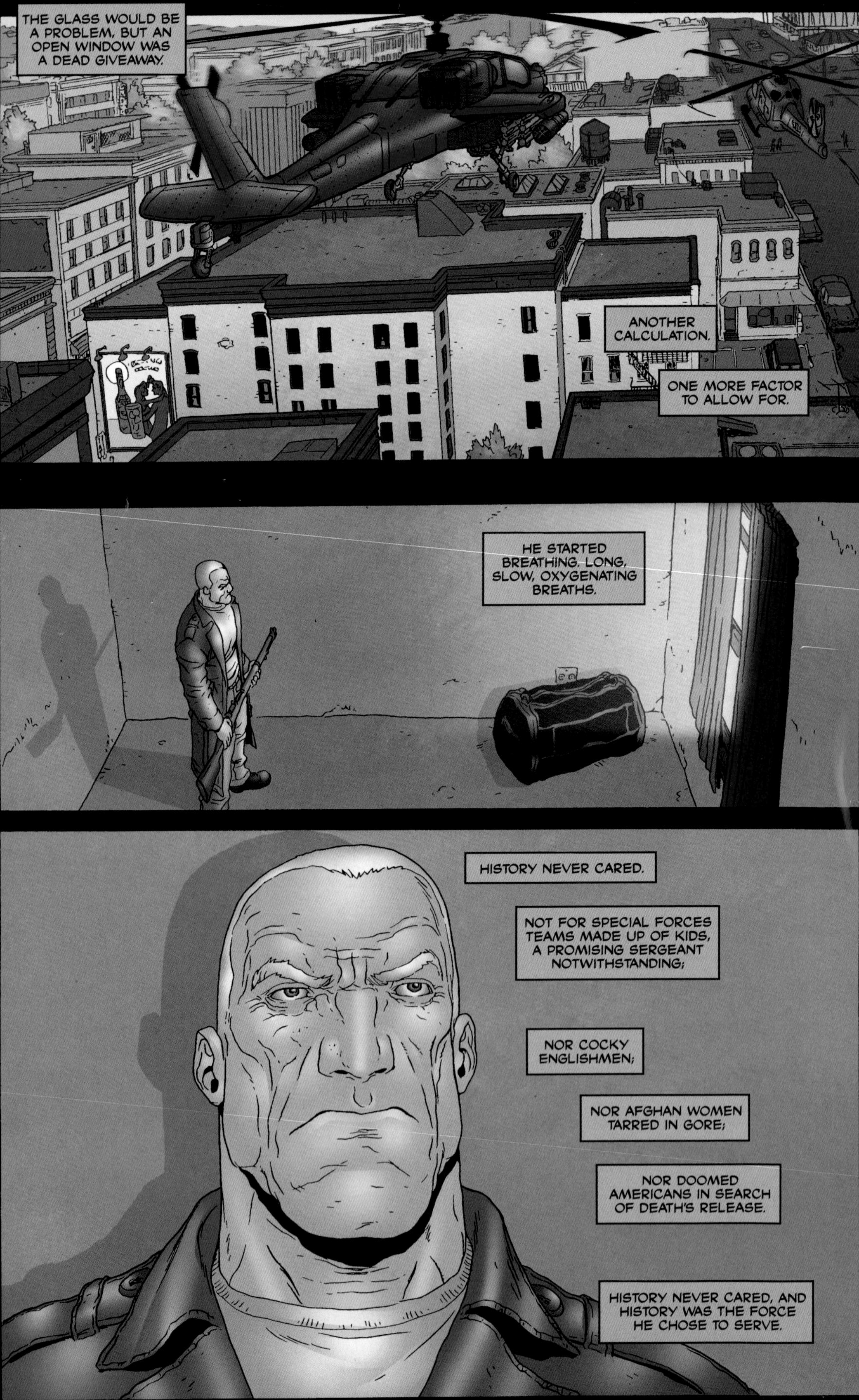
THE GLASS WOULD BE A PROBLEM, BUT AN OPEN WINDOW WAS A DEAD GIVEAWAY.
ANOTHER CALCULATION.
ONE MORE FACTOR TO ALLOW FOR.
HE STARTED BREATHING. LONG, SLOW, OXYGENATING BREATHS.
HISTORY NEVER CARED.
NOT FOR SPECIAL FORCES TEAMS MADE UP OF KIDS, A PROMISING SERGEANT NOTWITHSTANDING;
NOR COCKY ENGLISHMEN;
NOR AFGHAN WOMEN TARRED IN GORE;
NOR DOOMED AMERICANS IN SEARCH OF DEATH'S RELEASE.
HISTORY NEVER CARED, AND HISTORY WAS THE FORCE HE CHOSE TO SERVE.

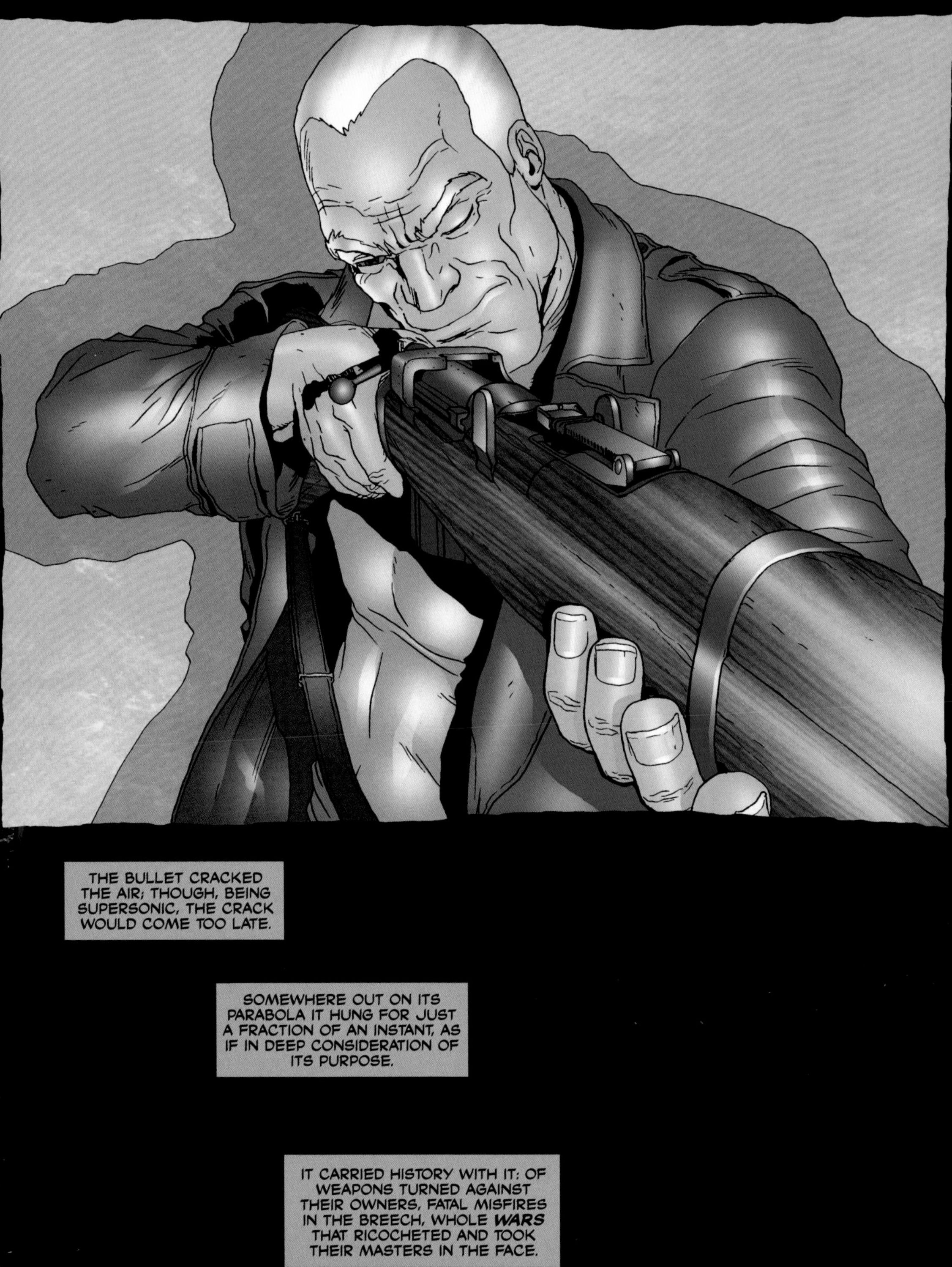
THE BULLET CRACKED THE AIR; THOUGH, BEING SUPERSONIC, THE CRACK WOULD COME TOO LATE.
SOMEWHERE OUT ON ITS PARABOLA IT HUNG FOR JUST A FRACTION OF AN INSTANT, AS IF IN DEEP CONSIDERATION OF ITS PURPOSE.
IT CARRIED HISTORY WITH IT: OF WEAPONS TURNED AGAINST THEIR OWNERS, FATAL MISFIRES IN THE BREECH, WHOLE WARS THAT RICOCHETED AND TOOK THEIR MASTERS IN THE FACE.

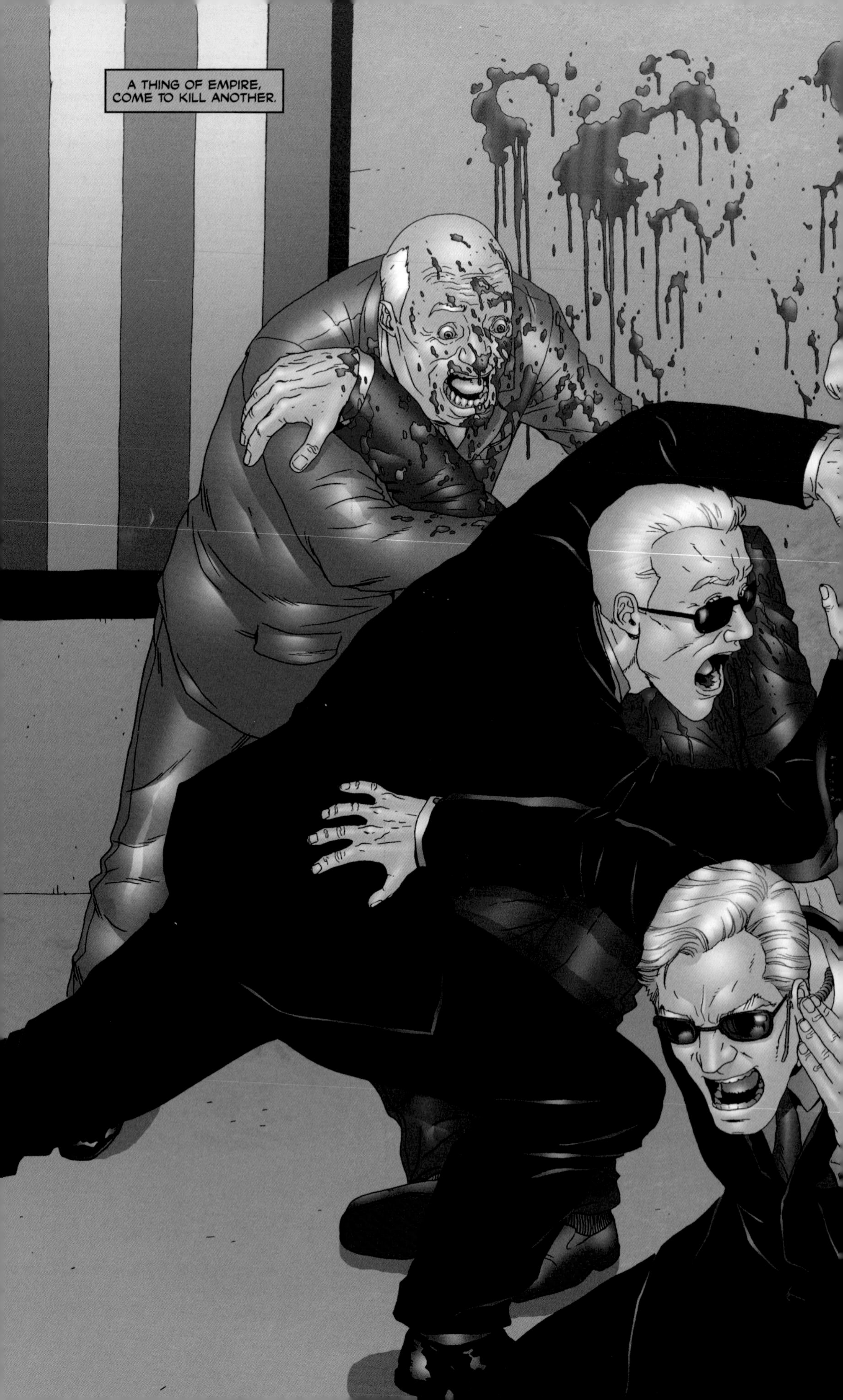
A THING OF EMPIRE, COME TO KILL ANOTHER.

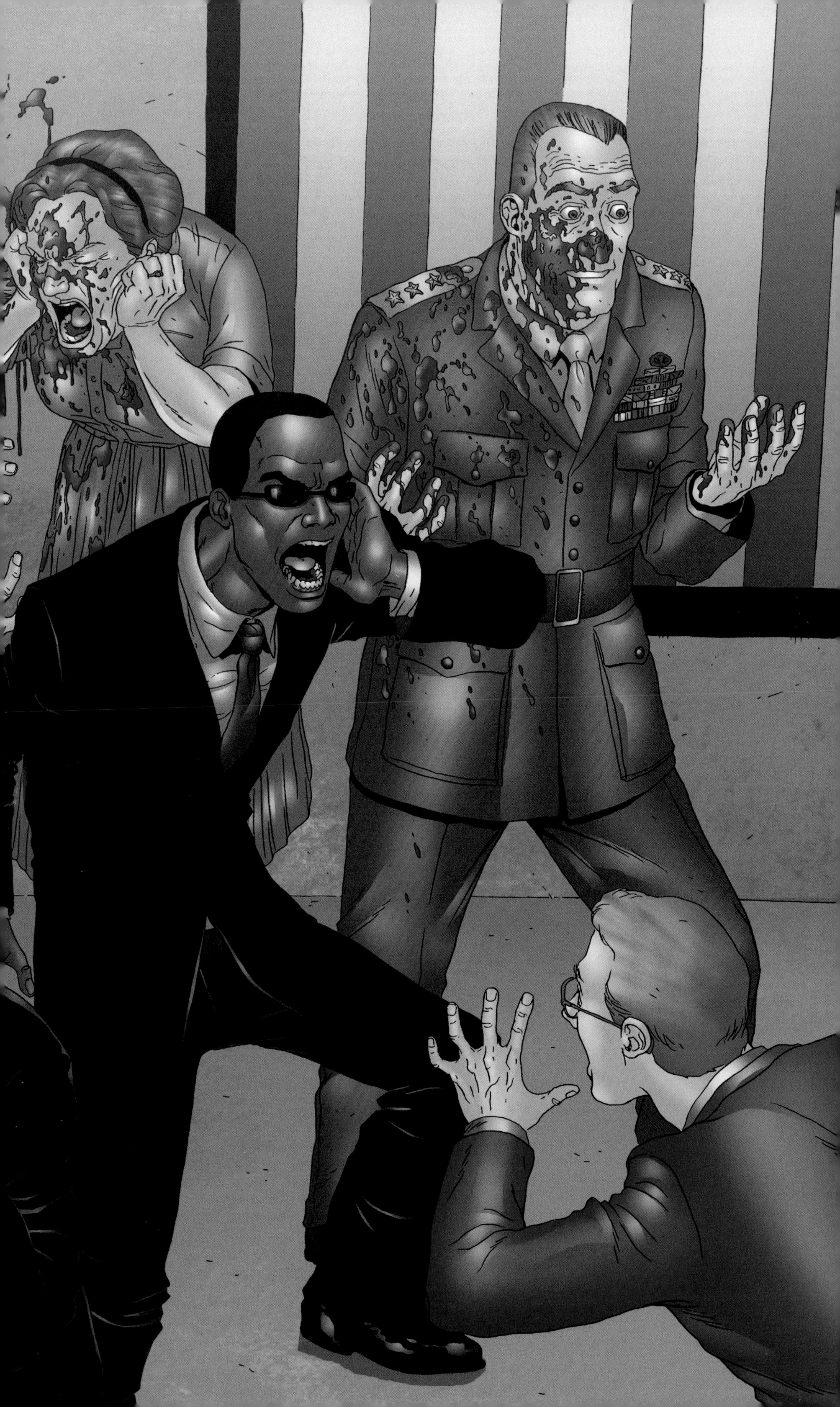

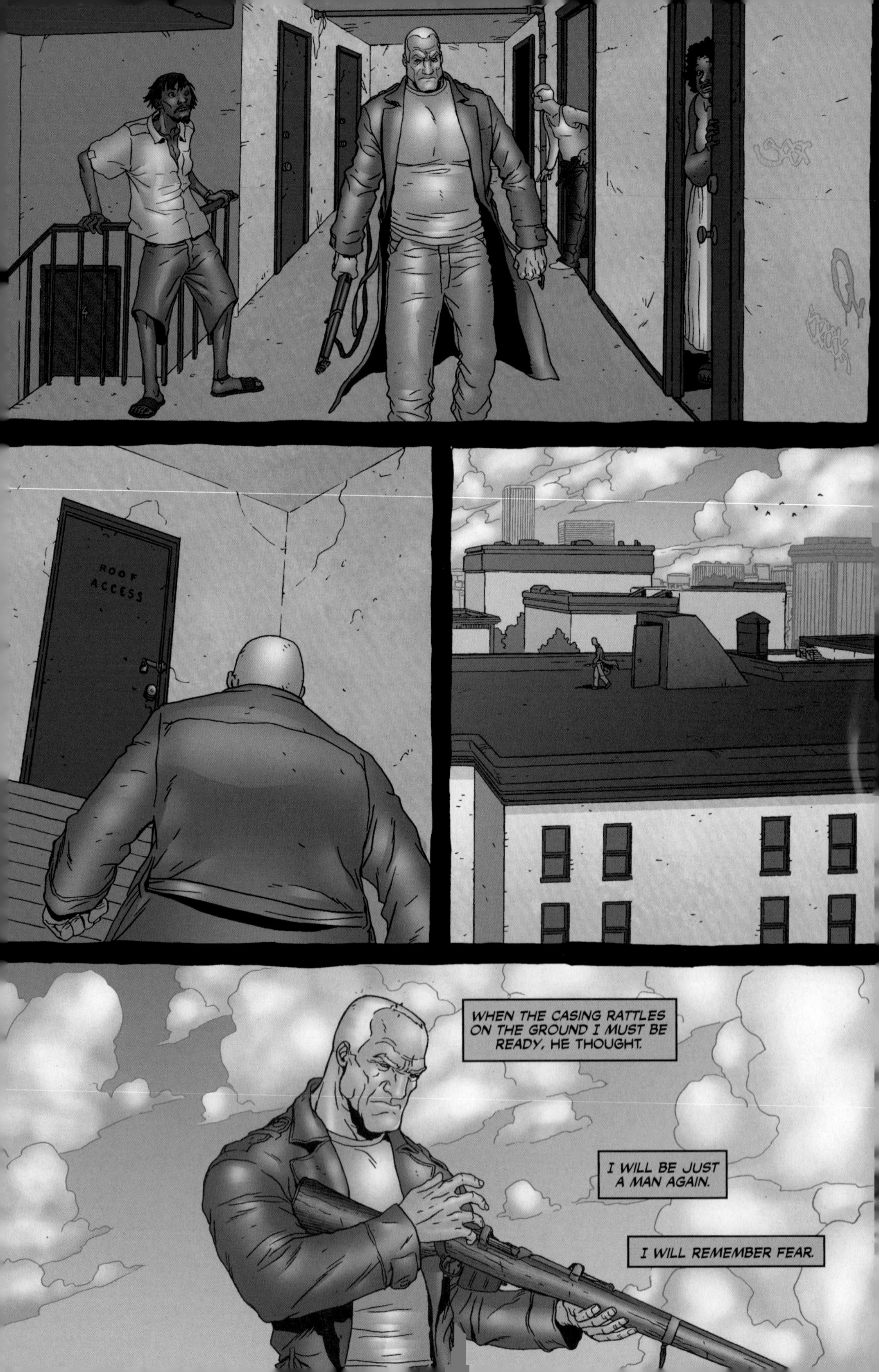
ROOF ACCESS
WHEN THE CASING RATTLES ON THE GROUND I MUST BE READY, HE THOUGHT.
I WILL BE JUST A MAN AGAIN.
I WILL REMEMBER FEAR.

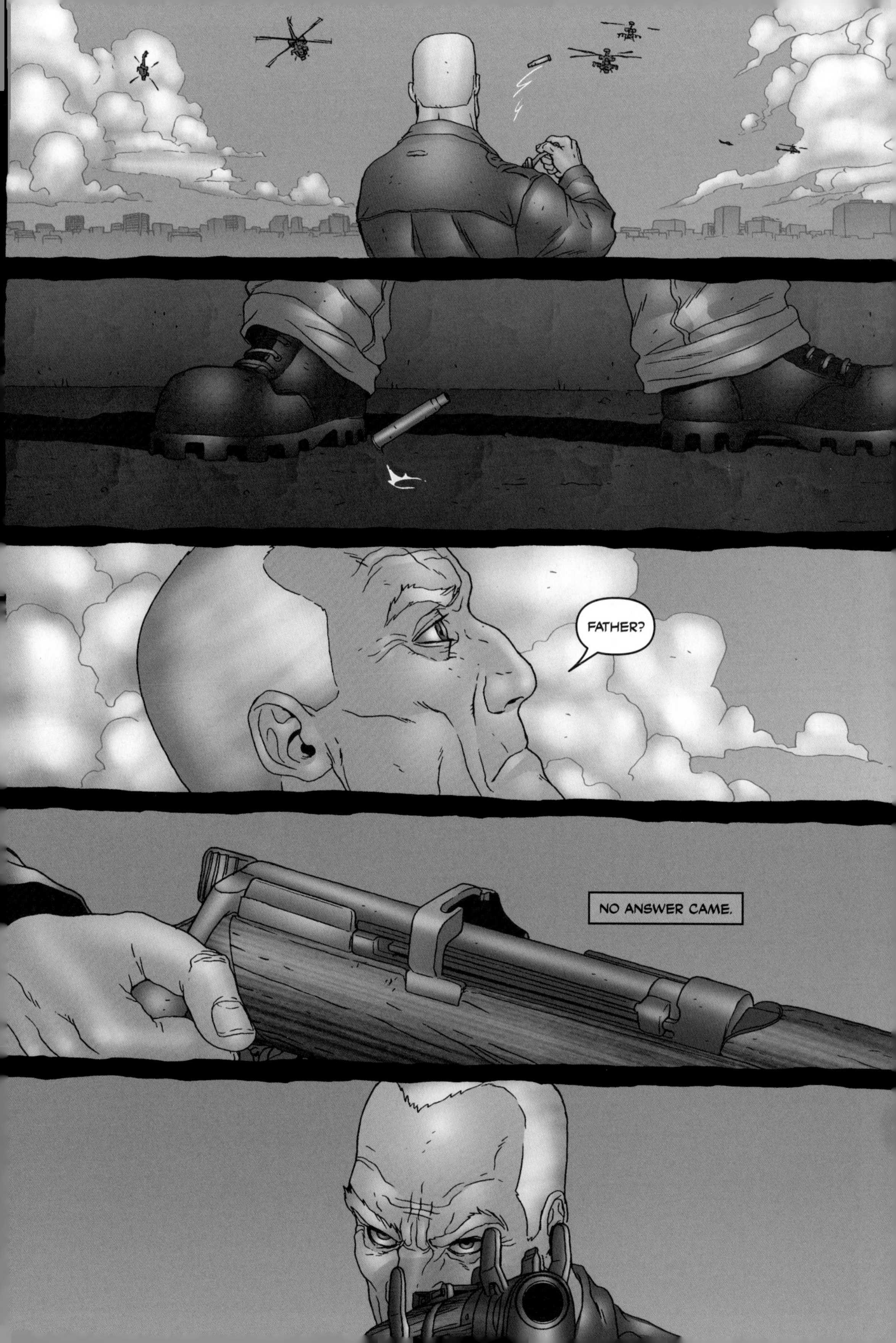
FATHER?
NO ANSWER CAME.

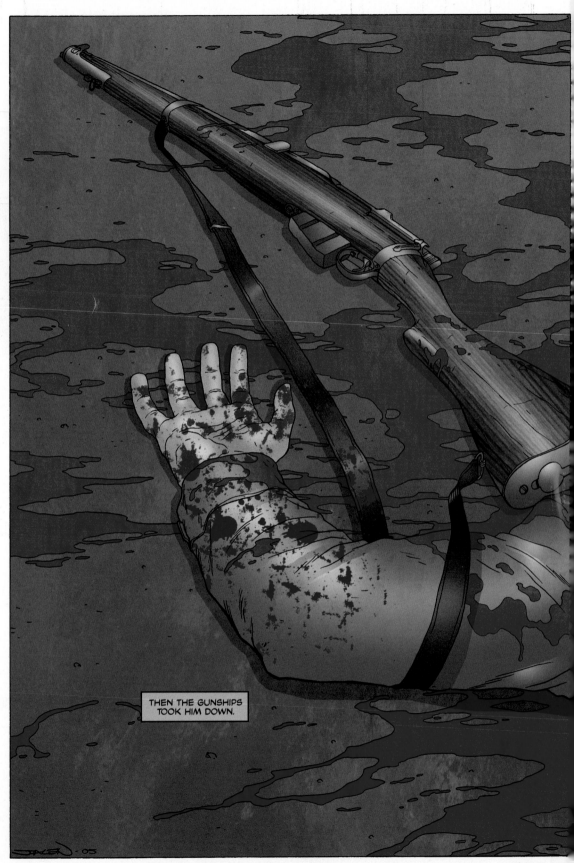

THEN THE GUNSHIPS
TOOK HIM DOWN.

THE END

303
COVER GALLERY

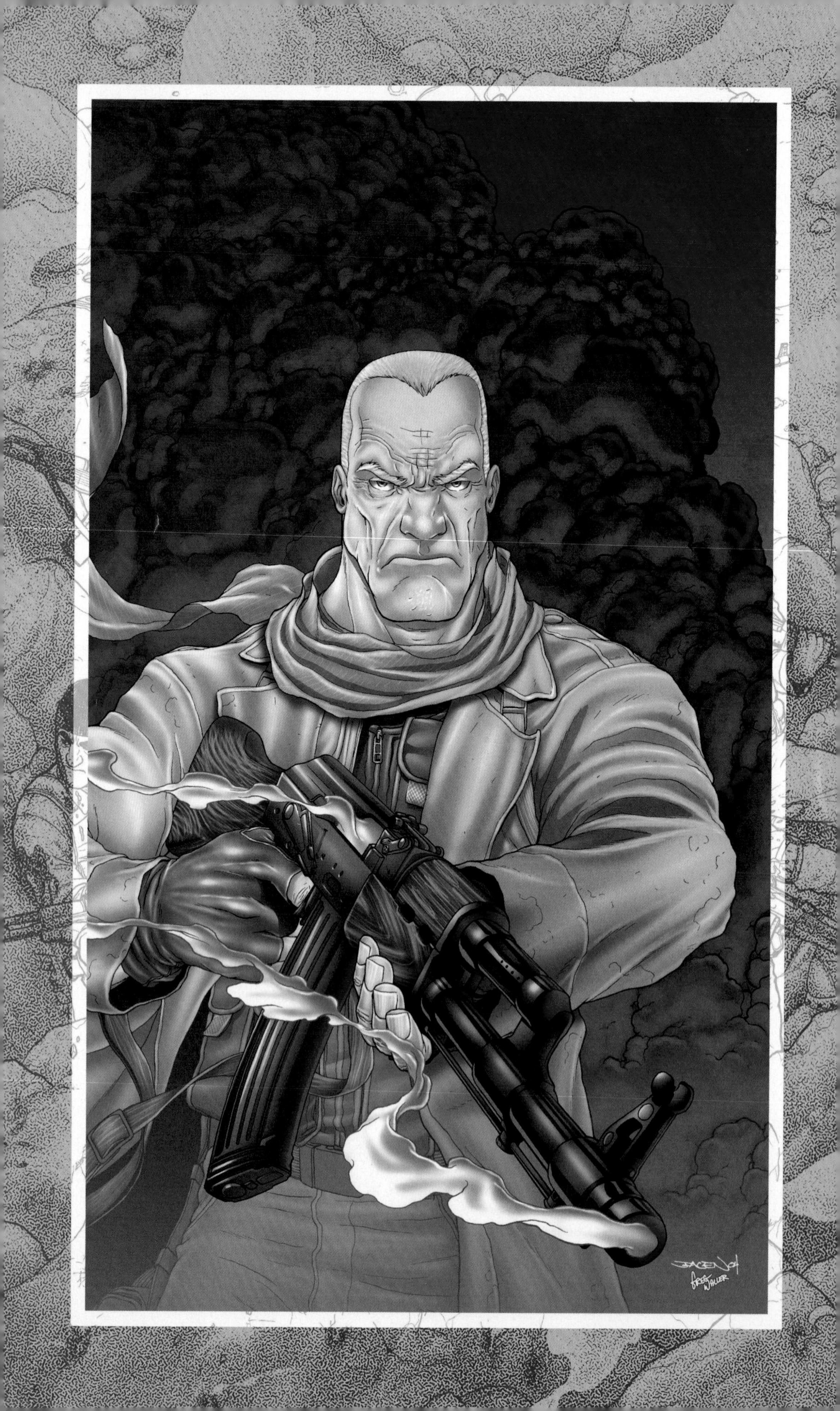

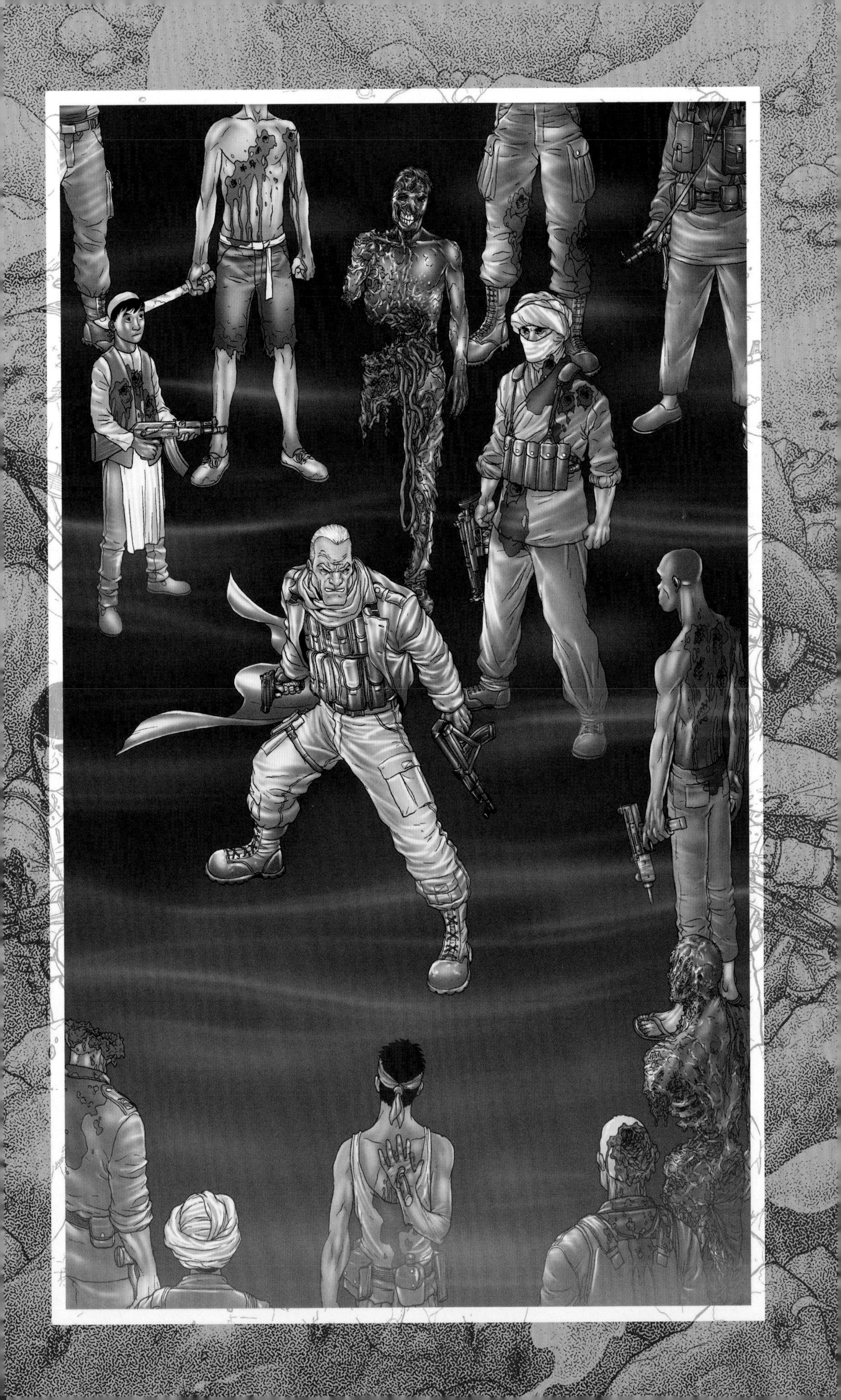

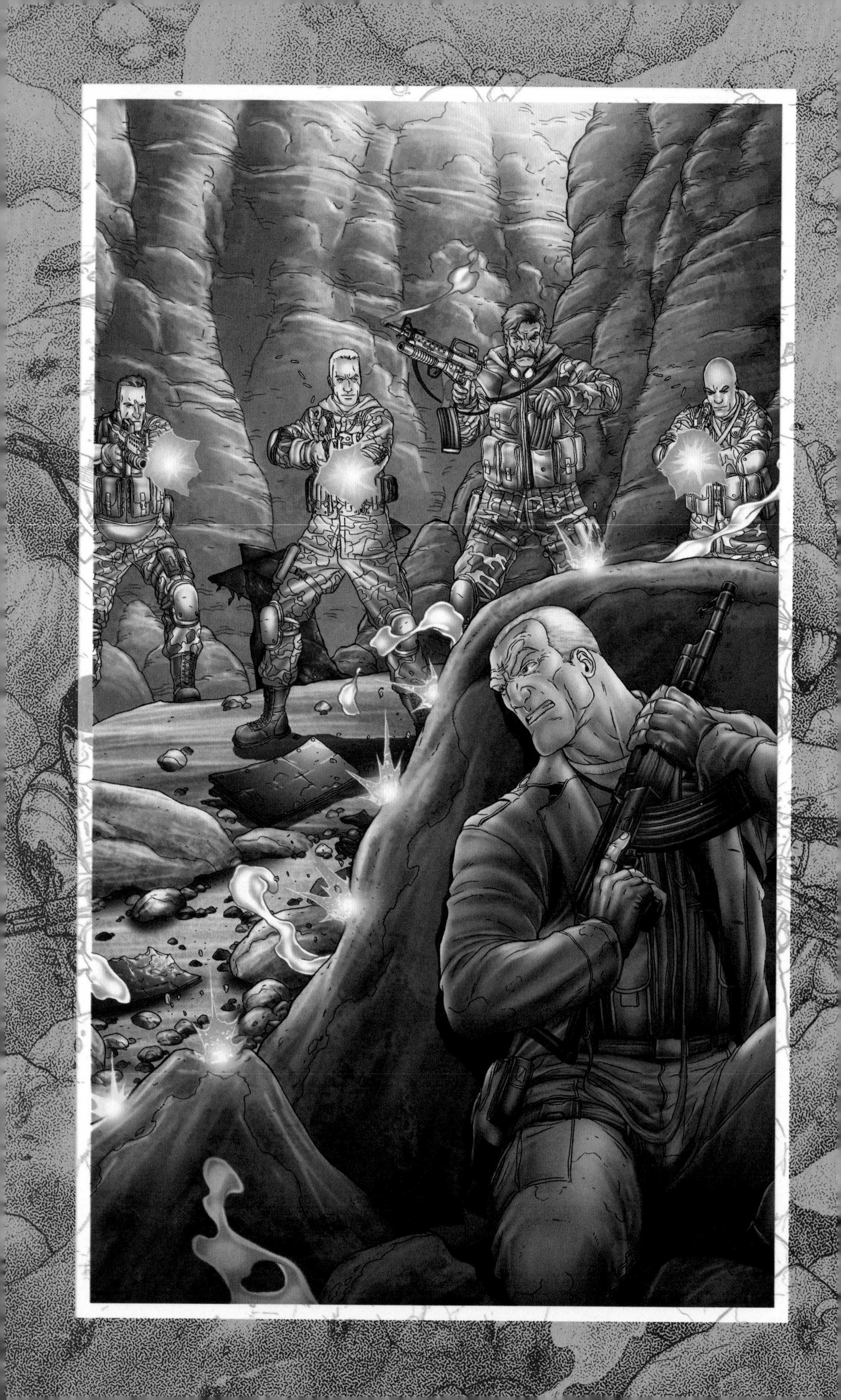

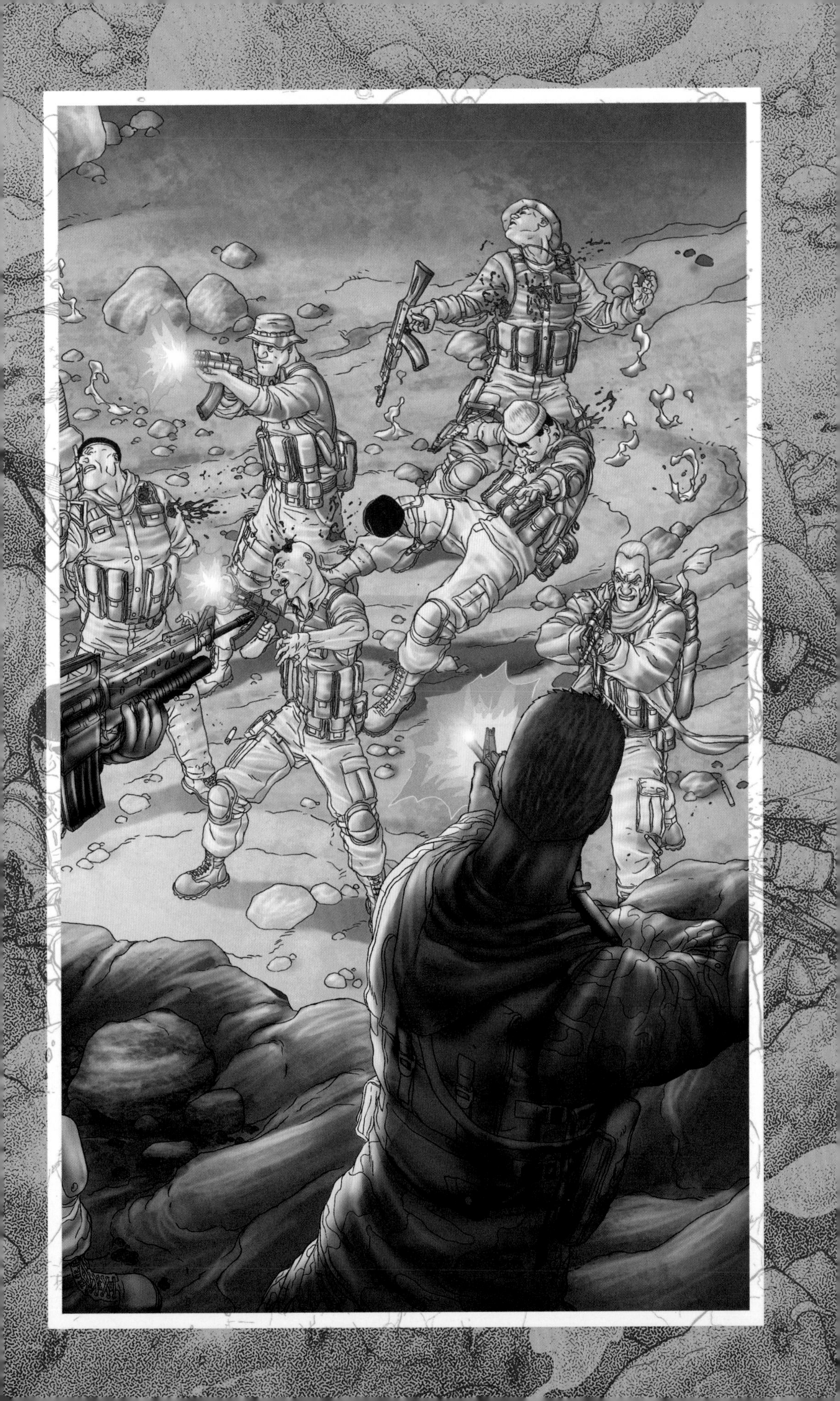

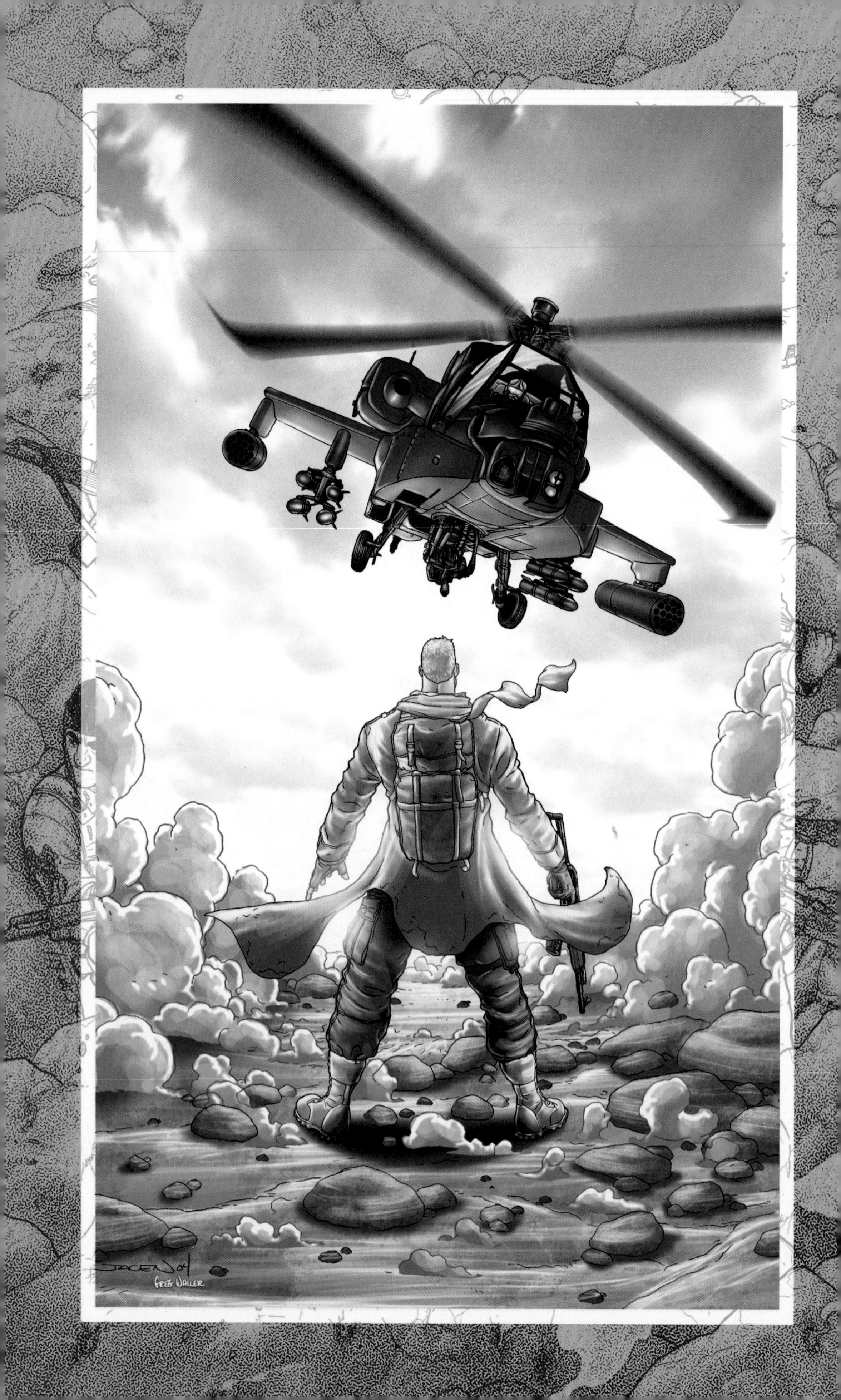

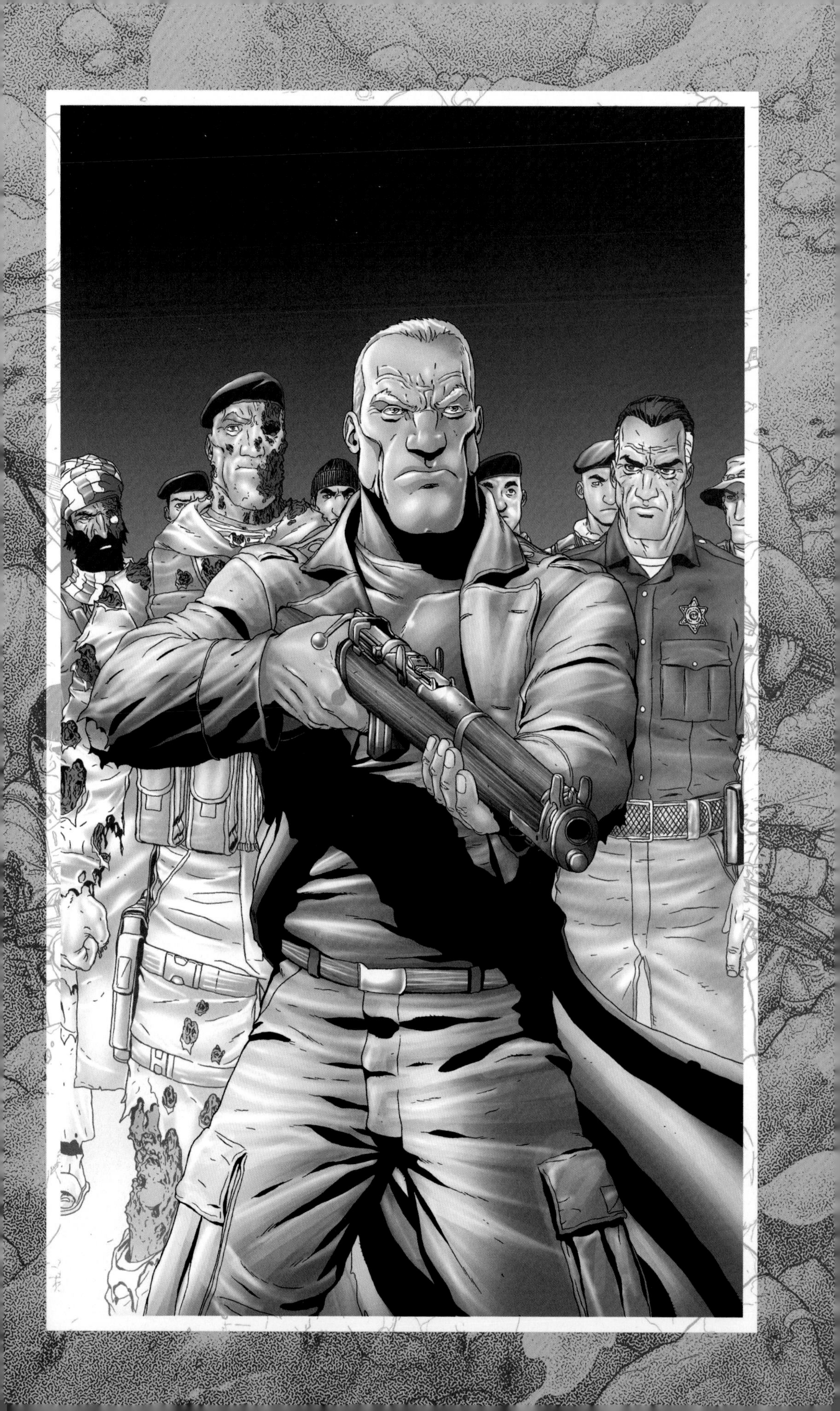

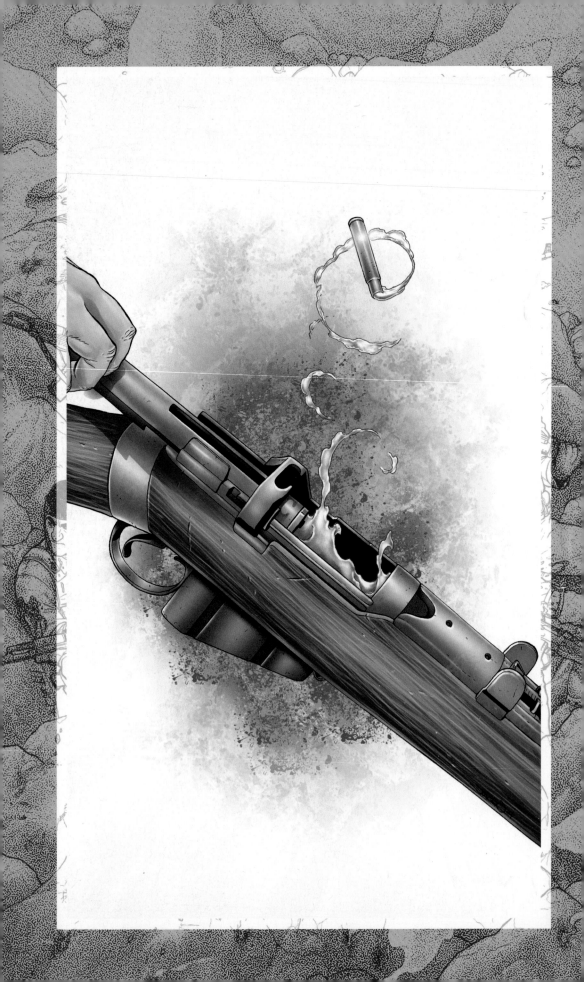